CORPORATE PORTALS

CORPORATE PORTALS

Revolutionizing Information Access to Increase Productivity and Drive the Bottom Line

Heidi Collins

AMACOM

American Management Association

New York • Atlanta • Boston • Chicago • Kansas City • San Francisco • Washington, D.C.
Brussels • Mexico City • Tokyo • Toronto

This publication is designed to provide accurate and authoritative information in regard to the subject matter covered. It is sold with the understanding that the publisher is not engaged in rendering legal, accounting, or other professional service. If legal advice or other expert assistance is required, the services of a competent professional person should be sought.

Library of Congress Cataloging-in-Publication Data

Collins, Heidi.
    Corporate portals : revolutionizing information access to increase productivity and drive the bottom line / Heidi Collins.
        p.   cm.
    Includes bibliographical references and index.
    ISBN 0-8144-0593-2
    1. Intranets (Computer networks)   I. Title.

    HD30.285.C66 2001
    658'.0546—dc21   00-045116

Printing number

10   9   8   7   6   5   4

For the glory of God alone

Contents

List of Figures

Preface

The corporate portal market has evolved into a broad industry segment. The name and definition of the solution, the breadth of the market vendors offering software products, the number and types of features offered by these software products—all are very confusing. The goal of this book is twofold:

• *To define the corporate portal solution by analyzing the features of a corporate portal.* This definition should provide enough information for you to make an initial evaluation regarding the advantages of a corporate portal solution in your organization.

• *To provide a clear and concise introduction to the types of research and analysis activities required to create a corporate portal business case.* This business case is essential in order to present a corporate portal proposal to decision makers in your organization.

WHY THIS BOOK WAS WRITTEN

When I undertook the writing of this book, there were no books that I was aware of that even attempted to capture the body of knowledge associated with corporate portal solutions. Because the corporate portal has become a major component of any business strategy, it seemed clear to me that a book needed to be written by someone who is knowledgeable about the subject and who is also aware of the complexity of planning a solution of this scope. More important is how a corporate portal solution can benefit your organization, and in this regard you need to know how to present this solution to executives and decision makers. I conceived this book as an approach to defining corporate portals as a collection of software functions and features (i.e., building blocks) that can be selected and designed to fit the specific objectives of your organization.

WHO SHOULD READ THIS BOOK?

This book will help you identify the components, functions, and features of a corporate portal solution. You should be able to evaluate each of these features and functions and weigh each aspect individually, and then, as the next step, determine the collection of features and functions that your specific organization wants to take advantage of. In this way you will be able to better understand how the complete corporate portal solution is greater than the sum of the individual components identified. This book is designed to give you insight into the activities you need to complete and the information you must collect, evaluate, and analyze in developing a corporate portal solution. Your analysis will determine whether your organization would benefit from and should pursue a corporate portal solution. The book includes information on how to organize and present a corporate portal business case to decision makers and executives in your organization. The material collected will be valuable to individuals who are evaluating intranet solutions, trying to implement knowledge management initiatives, writing proposals and business cases, and evaluating proposals and business cases, as well as anyone interested in knowing more about corporate portals or enterprise information portals.

KEY BENEFITS OF THIS BOOK

Whatever your background, this book can help you in several ways. You and your team can use it as a:

1. *Corporate Portal Reference.* This book contains broad-based information needed to understand what the definition and features of a corporate portal solution are.

2. *Guide to Corporate Portal Business Case Development.* This book contains the information needed to write an effective business case for a corporate portal project or any other information technology (IT) project in less time and with fewer headaches.

3. *Assessment Tool with Predefined Checklists.* This book contains checklists you can use to assess your project's mission, values, goals, objectives, benefits, success factors, financial requirements, infrastructure requirements, business features, and more.

4. *Guide to Other Information Sources.* This book collects several resources available on portal information and associated software functions and features. Additional reading material (i.e., books and articles) is provided in the bibliography for you to gain further knowledge on topics that may require additional investigation.

Acknowledgments

Thanks first to my husband Jeff and our son C. James Collins for their belief and support in my ability. They helped me decide to start and complete the *Corporate Portals* project. It is their understanding and encouragement that have inspired me personally to write this book.

The work of several individuals at InfoImage has significantly influenced this book, and they should be acknowledged: Randy Eckel, David Oderberg, and Diana Sykes. The work of these three individuals and the contribution of many other associates deserve recognition. Their efforts to collect hard facts from real-world experiences and projects directly affect the future direction of the design and implementation of corporate portal solutions. It is the work of these individuals that will eventually shape and define the corporate portal market.

I would also like to acknowledge several people I had initial conversations with while the book was in the early stages of development. Bjorn Aannestad, David Annis, and Cindy Bailen influenced the tone and direction of the book while the contents were still being researched. The perception of these unique people was used to determine the scope of the material to be covered and how to effectively frame and organize the information that was selected.

Extra thanks go to Chance Houston for his talent as a graphic artist. The illustrations he provided make all the aspects of a corporate portal come to life. A special thank you to Melissa Fraser for creating the www.heidicollins.com website. Their work embodies the phrase "a picture is worth a thousand words."

One of the most interesting aspects of writing this book has been learning about the publishing industry and processes. A special thank-you to my literary agent Jeff Herman and The Jeff Herman Agency, LLC. Jeff makes a very difficult job look incredibly simple.

My final acknowledgment is to the hardworking individuals at AMACOM for their contribution to the *Corporate Portals* project. This group of individuals includes Jacqueline Flynn, Neil Levine, and Mike Sivilli.

Heidi Collins
Phoenix, Arizona
November 1, 2000

CORPORATE PORTALS

1

Welcome to Corporate Portals

The industry is flooded with portal articles, opinions, ideas, and suggested software solutions to select from. It is difficult to determine what the definition of a portal is, what kinds of portal solutions are available, and whether your organization would benefit from a business-to-employee or business-to-business portal application. If your organization needs to share information among employees, locate information that is difficult to find, push information to users, or create a central location to navigate through data that employees can benefit from, then a portal can help. A portal solution is a facilitator to knowledge that helps employees make decisions.

There are several issues and perspectives to consider when looking at how your organization can leverage knowledge for the purpose of making better, faster, consistent, and more informed decisions. The perspectives are operational and strategic. Operational issues are the ones faced by employees responsible for completing transactional, day-to-day, and well-established tasks. Employees responsible for operational issues in your organization are constantly looking for ways to improve or simplify existing processes or tasks. Strategic issues are the ones faced by employees responsible for ensuring that the overall mission of your organization is met or exceeded. Employees responsible for making strategic decisions in your organization are tracking financial and other information that accurately measures how well your organization is performing. This group of employees is always looking for the appropriate objectives that can be combined with qualitative measures to respond accurately to your customers. The information presented to strategic decision makers is used to monitor and analyze the performance of your organization so that, when necessary, appropriate modifications can be made for your organization to remain effective in the marketplace. The primary objective for a portal software solution, then, is to create a working environment that users can easily navigate in order to find the information they specifically need to quickly perform their operational or strategic functions and make decisions.

Any knowledge mining, filtering, and management strategy that you establish must focus primarily on the mission of your organization and the operational or strategic requirements of your employees. One information technology (IT) strategy to strongly consider is an enterprise or corporate portal solution. The portal solution is a collection of technologies—software and infrastructure—that work together to aggregate a selected subset of information into a central location. From there, different employees can then easily access information that's relevant to their roles or business and personal requirements and in the process work more effectively with each other.

A *corporate portal* is usually structured around roles that are found inside your organization. An *enterprise portal,* by comparison, expands the corporate portal to include customers, vendors, and other roles outside your organization. The focus of this book is on the corporate portal. Though the issues and concepts discussed here can be expanded to the enterprise as well, the architecture and infrastructure of the enterprise portal is different and more complex than those defined for a corporate portal solution.

One of your first tasks to complete when considering a portal strategy is to establish a portal definition for your organization. You want to establish a standard definition along with a collection of portal objectives specific to your organization. You can then use this definition and list of objectives to evaluate the flood of jargon and software features available from portal vendors and other sources to find the best portal solution available for you and your organization.

THE BUSINESS PROBLEM

During the past several years nearly every new application and idea created by the software industry has made the jobs of employees more complex and difficult, rather than simplifying their responsibilities for them. This situation creates problems for employees making operational and strategic decisions. All employees have to access several applications to do their jobs. For example, to complete operational and transactional activities an employee has to check inventory status of a particular part and enter a purchase order. To simply complete the assigned responsibilities, your employee needs to open an enterprise resource planning (ERP) system and navigate through numerous screens. The ERP system allows the employee to review inventory and backlog information. A second application or system is launched to enter the purchase order. Any problems or issues that are encountered will require access to customer information that is housed in the customer resource management (CRM) system.

Employees responsible for strategic decisions have even more difficulty trying to do their jobs effectively. In many cases the data sources, systems, and applications located throughout your organization need to be combined to present the summarized information or desired report format that executives expect to review. Your IT department likely has several initiatives and activities associated with taking the information available from transactional systems and converting it to a format needed to maintain an enterprise information system (EIS) or decision support system (DSS), or the systems that provide the summarized information this group of employees needs to make strategic decisions. To find an answer to a question, make a decision, or take some action, employees spend an enormous amount of time traversing the maze of these disconnected applications and systems.

This is only part of the problem. Corporatewide systems are complex and designed for a specific purpose and function, so your IT department is required to deploy many different and often unrelated applications and modules to fill the information and processing needs of the entire organization. In addition, an incredible amount of training time is needed for an employee to learn how to effectively use such a complex suite of applications and all of the processes and steps involved to complete their assigned responsibilities. Only a small fraction of your organization's employees know how to use all of the functions of one system, much less all of the systems and databases that affect their job.

Corporate Intranets as a Partial Solution

The *corporate intranet* was originally designed and implemented to meet this need for shared information across the organization. Using the corporate intranet, employees are able to access corporate information using a web browser such as Microsoft Internet Explorer or Netscape Communicator to find forms, open applications to perform their jobs, and review a customer's project status, and for many other activities. The corporate intranet solution provides navigation to different enterprise systems and documents.

Corporate intranets everywhere are responsible for hosting a multitude of applications and an exponential growing number of documents. These applications, documents, related tools, and enterprise systems need to be made readily available for employees to use. This is a difficult task for IT departments, and it has created information access, knowledge-sharing, and security problems. As intranet sites grow larger, a new set of problems has been created. Various studies have researched the problems and issues currently facing corporate intranets and why they are in chaos.

Understanding these issues is the first step in your ability to recognize and categorize your intranet problems so that you can build a strategy to improve knowledge sharing and decisions made about information access throughout your organization. To summarize, the key problems the corporate intranet is likely to encountered include the following:

 • *Employees need to make more informed and consistent decisions.* Employees make operational (i.e., routine) and strategic decisions. To make routine decisions, people need to know when a state or condition exists and what the standard or expected decision and associated actions are. Strategic decisions require that all relevant data points be known and available to decision makers for the best decision to be arrived at. In many cases inconsistent, incomplete, uninformed, and wrong or no decisions are being made because employees cannot find or do not have access to the information or data points needed to make timely, consistent, and well-informed decisions.

- *Employees are asked to complete more activities online.* Enrolling in 401(k) programs, updating medical benefits, turning in hours worked on customer projects, and requesting software upgrades for their workstations and laptops are just some examples. Different systems, different applications, multiple document repositories, and multiple data marts manage these online intranet activities. When employees have to use these systems they are required to know where to find them and what to do once they have access.

- *Intranet sites contain thousands of pages and continue to grow.* Corporate announcements, updates to business processes, requests for reports, and numerous other pieces of information are added to your organization's intranet site every day. The task is to create an intranet site with well-organized content from an overwhelming amount of material that guides your employees to documents, applications, and data they need to do their jobs while continuing to be contributing, productive members of your organization. The intranet solution has difficulties, however, when it comes to managing, maintaining, and keeping information current.

- *Employees must still access information from multiple sources.* Some corporate information is made available through the corporate intranet. Other information and applications might still be accessed through legacy data systems, ERP systems, spreadsheets, and other systems and sources unique to your organization. Employees will become frustrated having to traverse the intranet, multiple systems, and multiple sources to complete their assigned tasks. In many cases an enormous amount of training and experience is needed to become familiar with the applications used to perform their jobs effectively.

- *Navigation through your organization's intranet becomes impossible.* Employees will have difficulty remembering how to find and access information buried layers deep or that is being constantly relocated within the corporate intranet. The problem is compounded by the fact that the ability to logically organize and then effectively navigate the continually increasing number of systems, data sources, and intranet pages requires conscious thought and a thorough understanding of the organization.

THE CORPORATE PORTAL SOLUTION

To begin to envision an intranet solution that can be implemented to deliver the type of features and services that you want to have available for employees, you have to establish an appropriate knowledge- and information-sharing strategy. Consider, for example, a fictitious tax and audit services company called Corporate Portal.com. It has several departments responsible for writing methodologies and compiling best practices for consultants to use on tax and audit projects. The objective of these methodologies and best practices is to provide information, techniques, tools, and learning opportunities for consultants (all with different skills and responsibilities during a project) to successfully perform their jobs. Employees, however, are having trouble finding the information they are looking for, and it has gotten so difficult that at times consultants do not know what information and other tools even exist for them to use. The solution CorporatePortal.com wants to implement is a central location that logically catalogs and organizes the material and information from enterprise systems that employees (i.e., the consultants) must have available to them.

Many organizations like CorporatePortal.com want an intranet solution that lets employees know the information that is available to them and allows them to interact seamlessly with the multiple sources of data and applications they need to use while performing their daily tasks any time of day or night. Employees need to be able to get documents and read processes. They want to see their mail, projects, customer updates, and any other requested information in a single just-in-time intranet window. They need to be able to collaborate with the appropriate people in your organization if they have questions or knowledge to share with them, and get answers or provide insight. Employees need to be able to easily organize any information available from this intranet portal solution according to categories defined for your organization and categories that they define for themselves.

There is an intranet concept that resolves these problems and issues your organization is currently faced with. The concept is to create a corporate portal. A portal is an intranet "window" that presents information to users and an intranet "door" that allows users to pass through to reach selected destinations. The corporate portal creates the central location where navigation services are available for employees to find information, launch applications, interact with corporate data, identify collaborators, share knowledge, and make decisions. The definition of a corporate portal is:

> A browser-based application that allows knowledge workers to gain access to, collaborate with, make decisions, and take action on a wide variety of business-related information regardless of the employee's virtual location or departmental affiliations, the location of the information, or the format in which the information is stored.

Corporate portals can provide a successful intranet strategy for your organization. Corporate portals have several features that are used to implement knowledge management initiatives in your organization. These include:

• *A Consistent View of Your Organization.* Employees must identify and interact with many different data sources. The corporate portal can provide access to an index of report catalogs and direct users to the right information source. The type of information your employees need to access might be structured (e.g., data marts, data warehouses), unstructured (e.g., e-mail messages, word-processing documents), transactional (e.g., creating a customer order, enrolling in the 401(k) program), or collaborative (e.g., scheduling a meeting, commenting on the department budget). The corporate portal is built on existing content repositories, applications, and data marts that users can immediately access without having to know the actual location of the data or which application is used to read or update the data. By creating an interactive environment with every aspect of the organization and every type of job-related activity represented, the result will be a better forum for making decisions, sharing best practices, and exploring new ideas.

• *Information Organization and Search Capabilities.* The corporate portal can provide a format to implement a common taxonomy and consistent semantics for your organization. To facilitate employee access to corporate information in a structured fashion, a corporate portal menu hierarchy is required so that employees can understand and quickly navigate the information. This navigation system creates a common naming convention for processes, procedures, and activities in your organization. This menu hierarchy also serves as a logical breakout of how information is "filed" in your organization and which part of the organization is responsible for keeping the information updated.

The corporate portal creates a central location for users to find and access corporate content. The portal is not designed to host information or to be a content store. The content presented in the corporate portal should continue to reside on the file server or in the host application that controls the data storage and business rules of the information or report that is displayed in the portal. Implementing a knowledge management solution that maintains the existing status quo for data storage and business rules and processes is critical to sustaining the integrity of the information presented in the corporate portal. The corporate portal solution creates a wrapper of services around the information that is hosted in the user interface. These services include user assistance, search facilities, identification of relevant information (e.g., related white papers, additional information about the customer, how other departments use the report or information being reviewed, who to contact if you have questions), facilities to create discussions and interact with a community of users, and the ability to drill down into more detail and add value as a navigation aid.

It is designed to provide a knowledge desktop with a user interface that displays or presents information in a browser client from data sources that reside throughout your organization. There are hundreds of ways that your organization affects your relationship with employees. Employees should be able to construct queries, search for correlation in the data, plot the data, and move the results into other applications such as spreadsheets and word-processing documents. This flexible access to data and the tools necessary to manipulate, navigate, and locate the data available to them is critical. Chapter 5, "Information Organization and Search Capabilities," discusses these considerations in more detail.

• *Direct Access to Corporate Knowledge and Resources*. This functionality gives employees and business professionals the means to communicate and collaborate with each other. To share knowledge throughout your organization, employees need to publish and distribute information that can be referenced and accessed from a central location. By providing an environment to share information, employees should be able to collaborate with each other and thereby improve processes.

You will want to establish communities or team rooms where employees regularly share information and ideas, examine and weigh options, act upon your organization's values and beliefs, and learn to improve the quality of their decisions. Communities provide the best context and most promise for addressing this challenge. The goal of incorporating communities in your corporate portal solution is to teach employees how to make choices that will sustain your organization over the long term. Establishing a growing sustainable communities movement that supports continuous interaction as part of your corporate portal solution creates an unprecedented opportunity for employees to learn from one another.

Employees need to communicate, collaborate, and coordinate with other employees and systems in your organization. These features can be implemented through the corporate messaging system, discussion forums, automated alerts and notifications, or the automation of approval processes and associated status information. All of these features are available from corporate applications and systems that are made available from the corporate portal solution. How each of these features is implemented into the corporate portal solution will differ, depending on the portal software selected by your organization. Some features can be implemented by simply configuring the portal software, while other features require custom development of the portal software development environment. Chapter 6 gives additional information to consider.

• *Direct Links to Reports, Analysis, and Queries*. Applications are built to support and maintain multiple groups of individuals throughout your organization. Corporatewide systems are complex and designed for a specific purpose and function, so organizations have to deploy many different applications and modules to fill the information and processing needs of the entire organization. The corporate portal directs users to locate and launch the right module of an application to do their job or complete a specific responsibility with the right security. This allows employees to be directed to only the components or screens of an application that are specific to their job.

As a consequence, the corporate portal solution has an additional benefit in helping to reduce training costs. Because the corporate portal removes the complexity of understanding the entire application functionality, users can concentrate on only the concepts and steps essential to completing their assigned responsibilities. Although employees may still require training classes and support from more experienced users to become proficient at using a complex suite of applications, training can be concentrated on the systems, applications, and data sources that directly impact their job. The training and cross-training challenge continues to expand as new employees, processes, and systems are integrated into your organization. By pushing selected information into a corporate portal solution, training requirements may be reduced and focused specifically to individual roles in your organization.

From within the corporate portal solution, employees should be able to search data sources, look for patterns in the data, create graphs and presentations from the data available, and move the results into other applications or other formats used to share new information throughout your organization. This flexible access to data and the tools necessary to manipulate, navigate, and evaluate data creates an environment that promotes enhancements and improvements to existing processes and services. Specific technical and data-related issues are covered in Chapter 7.

• *Direct Links to Relative Data and Knowledge Experts.* Employees are given an awareness of relevant information that is outside the immediate domain or department of their primary job requirements. Such information is generally presented as links that can be easily located on the corporate portal context pages. The purpose is to help employees make speedy decisions while doing their job without experiencing information overload. There may be business-essential information that is not directly a part of the decisions an individual employee makes. (e.g., related white papers, current industry information that might be helpful, customer account information, customer order information, how other departments use the information or report, where to find user assistance about the current process being followed, who to contact if you have questions). The information is nonetheless relevant to understanding how the employee's current activities affect other employees in the organization and how the activities of other employees directly or indirectly affect that person. This capability facilitates fast action, creative problem solving, and a better understanding of the entire company.

"If only we knew what we knew" is a common lament. The corporate portal can nip these complaints in the bud by directing knowledge experts to employees in the organization through a process of matching data with a corporate taxonomy or defined set of categories. To start, relationships that tie data-to-data, employees-to-data, and employees-to-employees need to be addressed. To establish a portal interface that provides seamless integration between data and employees in your organization, you must define and maintain several identity profiles or reference maps. These profiles and reference maps work together and cross-reference each other to present information and hyperlinks in the portal interface. The user thus has a personalized desktop that opens in a browser with your organization's corporate information, personal mail and calendaring information, and job-specific information. All of the information available in the corporate portal interface can become the central focus of the context window with a few simple clicks of the mouse. All the hyperlinks and drill-down features associated with the data in the content window should be context-sensitive. Using the identity profiles and reference maps to define these relationships, this type of access to relevant information can be made easily available in the corporate portal. The job of the IT department is to define, create, and maintain the data source that controls these identity profiles and reference maps. Chapter 8 discusses this cross-referencing of data and employees in more detail.

- *Individual Identity and Personalized Access to Content.* The corporate portal facilitates the important role of presenting the right and requested information to the user based on the access and security defined in the user profile. Employees are defined by their digital business identities that describe their roles, activities, skills, and positions in the organizational chart. Workflow processes, job-related functions, and corporate functions can be facilitated from the intranet through the corporate portal. The information presented to each user in the corporate portal also has certain useful characteristics: First, it can be context-sensitive based on the employees' role and responsibilities in your organization. Second, it can be personalized by each user to arrange and organize the information in the corporate portal to that individual's specifications through configuration.

There needs to be a balance between the information that must be constant in the corporate portal and the information or features that can be defined or configured by each portal user. The main portal menu hierarchy is an example of a piece of information that should remain constant for all portal users. Examples of information that should be configurable include adding favorites or bookmarks inside the corporate portal so a user can easily find information that is referred to frequently. Users should be able to configure a personal tabbed page from each menu option or some other feature that allows content pages to be organized and reorganized as required by the portal user. Chapter 9 gives additional information to consider when it comes to establishing context-sensitive content and personalization features.

CorporatePortal.com Case Study

CorporatePortal.com is an organization that provides tax and audit services to its customers. The company has several internal systems that are used by employees to complete their individual assigned responsibilities. Employees need to share or have access to available resource material, department information and procedures, training material and classes, feedback and collaborative tools, personal information management (PIM) systems, and corporate information. This information is available in several different applications and data sources.

CorporatePortal.com determines that employees are having certain problems with the current intranet and existing applications. Employees are not aware of material and manuals in the organization. Awareness and use of this material would allow employees with similar job descriptions to make consistent decisions and reduce the need to ask questions regarding current processes. The mission and objectives for CorporatePortal.com need to be incorporated into the objectives and daily activities of every employee. Measurements (e.g., scorecard information) defined for corporate and department objectives need to be centrally located and easily referenced to establish employee priorities. CorporatePortal.com wishes to provide all employees with a corporate taxonomy for the dual purpose of (1) creating a menu hierarchy to navigate available documentation and systems and (2) providing semantics to create a common vocabulary. The final benefit CorporatePortal.com hopes to take advantage of is better team communication and collaboration on customer projects and internal projects.

REASONS TO CONSIDER A CORPORATE PORTAL STRATEGY

The corporate portal is an excellent format to share information about each role or responsibility, process or activity, and department or workgroup throughout your organization. The process owners or business domain experts for each of the areas of knowledge in your organization can be designated to establish and maintain the information available for employees to access through the portal desktop. Whether you use business domain experts extensively or only to monitor documents and discussions that they have knowledge about, they need to be responsible for some of the content presented through the corporate portal. Employees should have access to information from all the areas of expertise needed to perform their assigned responsibilities. All employees in your organization should be required to access documentation and information about your organization. The corporate portal solution presents data available from enterprise systems and other information published by business domain experts together in the portal desktop; as such, it serves as a single point of access for users.

Your goal is to determine what published information is required by the proposed corporate portal system, identify the business domain experts, and determine how your IT department and these business domain experts can make information accessible. The implemented result should allow employees to get the latest information they need about the role, process, or department without having to search through several systems or make several phone calls. To accomplish this result you need to consider third-party applications and corporate portal software products. Creating the portal desktop required to achieve your defined objectives means establishing the correct combination of information and services required by your business domain experts, web-based services and technologies, and software applications.

Since 1999, magazines and trade journals began proposing portals as the solution to the intranet problem. Industry research analysts estimate that more than $14 billion will be budgeted to create corporate portals in the next six years. The first generation of corporate portals is already being planned, designed, and implemented in many Fortune 1000 companies or will be over the next two years.

Your organization needs to consider and build the corporate portal solution in stages. There are several universal features that are incorporated or built into a corporate portal solution. These universal features, shown in Figure 1-1, include:

- Self-service applications (i.e., access to discrete enterprise data)
- Corporate portal (i.e., aggregation of self-service applications)
- Comfort and familiarity (i.e., user personalization)
- Understanding and knowledge (i.e., navigation personalization)
- System intelligence (i.e., behavior assistance personalization)

The first generation of corporate portal solutions are self-service applications. Each self-service application is developed and added

Figure 1-1. Corporate portal universal features.

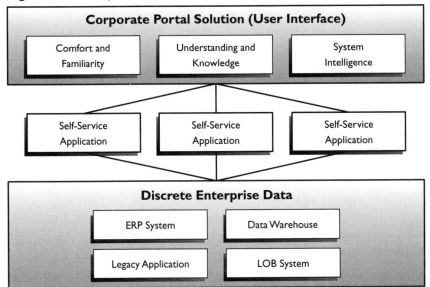

into a central knowledge desktop. These self-service applications collectively become the corporate portal. In many cases the personalization requirements of the corporate portal need to be globally or universally defined and implemented when the first self-service application is added. The personalization requirements can be enhanced and updated as the corporate portal evolves and grows. It is important that as you consider your corporate portal strategy, the universal features and corporate wide issues are identified and addressed.

Successful completion of the first self-service application makes the intranet content included in the corporate portal accessible to all employees complete with search, browse, navigation, and personalization services. Your second-generation implementation compiles or organizes several self-service applications into a collection of central corporate "windows" or portals. In effect, you are extending your self-service applications to incorporate corporate portal services that include additional applications, additional data points or data sources, collaboration, and workflow processes. The third generation of your corporate portal solution should complete as many universal features as possible, including personalization, decision making, and knowledge management initiatives as needed. These features are defined and included in the personalization aspects of the corporate portal. Personalization of your self-service applications and corporate portal services allows a user-defined and managed configuration of the information for each user's unique corporate portal experience. Some personalization features to consider include:

- Identifying of knowledge experts and data sources directly and indirectly related to completing each user's assigned responsibility.
- Pushing information to users on the basis of their responsibilities or interests.
- Configuring the corporate portal applications and information systematically based on tracking the preferences and behaviors of corporate portal users.

These corporate portal universal features are a way to outline and measure the capabilities to be included in your corporate portal and to determine what personalization capabilities to include in each development and implementation phase. Each of the corporate portal features and functions that need to be considered in your solution is explained in more detail in subsequent chapters.

The first step in building your corporate portal is presenting the appropriate business case to the decision makers in your organization. A corporate portal solution is a corporate application that is going to be made available to all employees and used to service all workgroups and individual department needs. To guarantee the success of the corporate portal initiative, senior management (including the chief information officer and IT management) should be involved in marketing the value of the corporate portal solution and understanding the associated financial metrics, budget estimates, procurement, and resource commitments and requirements. Other IT initiatives include:

- *Committing to a corporate portal infrastructure supplier.* Corporate portals are built using infrastructure technologies (e.g., web servers, data warehouses, application servers). Your organization must align your corporate portal investments and your thin-client (intranet and extranet) infrastructure commitments. Figure 1-2 is a list of some of the leading suppliers and their technology offerings.

• *Funding the corporate portal solution with knowledge management budgets.* In a few cases your organization may have a well-defined business case and knowledge management strategy. In most cases, organizations have knowledge management initiatives with vague project definitions and descriptions. Because of problems such as information overload and an inability to make decisions (problems that similarly plague intranet development), knowledge management solutions have tended to focus on a specific problem, such as creating and publishing corporate information, instead of on the implementation of a complete corporate knowledge management strategy. If this situation applies to your organization, corporate portals are the best way to make corporate content more available and more valuable for employees, and you should consider redirecting your knowledge management budgets into your corporate portal project.

• *Coordinating the corporate portal with extranet projects.* As you create the corporate portal strategy and business case for your organization, consider the expectations of your extranet customers and partners. Your extranet partners require the same knowledge experts, data warehouses, and access to applications to complete their activities and interactions with your organization. If you are able to establish extranet champions for your corporate portal strategy right away, you may want to consider an enterprise portal application as your first self-service application. The extranet portal demands cooperation between the corporate portal developers and extranet customers and requirements. Make certain that your corporate portal strategy includes directories and security plans to operate in concert with extranet systems and service requirements.

• *Making usability testing an information technologies competency.* When Microsoft Corp. first began conducting usability studies in the late 1980s to figure out how to make its products easier to use, its researchers found that out of every ten users, six or eight people could not understand the user interface and get to most of the features. Software portal products are being developed to provide the user interface and functionality requirements (e.g., naviga-

Figure 1-2. Partial list of portal vendors.

Vendor	Website	Headquarters
Application Vendors with Portal Tools		
IBM	www.ibm.com	Armonk, NY
Oracle	www.oracle.com	Redwood Shores, CA
PeopleSoft	www.peoplesoft.com	Pleasanton, CA
SAP	www.sap.com	Walldorf, Germany
Vendors with Decision Support or Knowledge Management History		
Brio	www.brio.com	Palo Alto, CA
Hummingbird	www.hummingbird.com	Toronto, ON
MicroStrategy	www.microstrategy.com	Vienna, VA
Sterling Software	www.sterling.com	Dallas, TX
Viador	www.viador.com	San Mateo, CA
Portal Start-Up Vendors		
2Bridge	www.2bridge.com	San Francisco, CA
Corechange	www.corechange.com	Boston, MA
CoVia	www.covia.com	Mountain View, CA
DataChannel	www.datachannel.com	Bellevue, WA
Epicentric	www.epicentric.com	San Francisco, CA
Hyperwave	www.hyperwave.com	Westford, MA
InfoImage	www.infoimage.com	Phoenix, AZ
Intraspect	www.intraspect.com	Los Altos, CA
Knowledge Track	www.knowledgetrack.com	Pleasanton, CA
Plumtree	www.plumtree.com	San Francisco, CA
Sagemaker	www.sagemaker.com	Fairfield, CT
Component Products		
Autonomy	www.autonomy.com	San Francisco, CA
Excalibur	www.excalib.com	Vienna, VA
InfoSeek	www.software.infoseek.com	Sunnyvale, CA
Semio	www.semio.com	San Mateo, CA
Verity	www.verity.com	San Francisco, CA
Miscellaneous		
Digital Dashboard	www.microsoft.com	Redmond, WA
IONA	www.iona.com	Dublin, Ireland
Radnet	www.radnet.com	Wakefield, MA
Sybase	www.sybase.com	Emeryville, CA
TIBCO	www.tibco.com	Palo Alto, CA
TopTier	www.toptier.com	San Jose, CA
Verano	www.verano.com	Mountain View, CA

tion, search, data connectivity) of portal solutions. Your organization must consider the user interface functionality and requirements equally as important as the back-end and security functionality and requirements of the corporate portal solution.

• *Identifying the corporate portal team members.* The corporate portal strategy team should include individuals whose combined backgrounds represent employee management skills, project management skills, business process analysis, and several years' experience with your organization. The executive sponsor of the corporate portal solution should be identified. This sponsor or champion needs to be directly involved in all aspects of the corporate portal solution. Some of the sponsor's activities include approving the requirements for the first phase of the corporate portal project, managing the corporate portal budget, and working directly with the corporate portal development team through the implementation of the solution. A senior project manager from the IT department must also work closely with the corporate portal sponsor and concentrate primarily on items such as the technical infrastructure, administration, managing risks, and establishing priorities for the project.

Normally the first phase or iteration of the corporate portal solution includes one or many self-service applications. A self-service application is a unique instance of an isolated job function, responsibility, or process that can be encapsulated as a system or subsystem that is defined as a part of the complete corporate portal solution. The corporate portal solution is deployed in several iterations or design phases in order to reevaluate universal or global features as the portal application incorporates functionality in the higher levels of personalization and navigation. This reevaluation process is important to make sure that all portal windows and self-service applications have consistent behavior and functionality throughout the corporate portal solution.

The task for you as the corporate portal strategist is to develop a plan for implementing a corporate portal solution that is a tailored configuration of the self-service applications identified for your organization. Each self-service application is a customized collection of several corporate portal software functions and the universal features to meet the objectives of your organization. The resulting business plan you create for your organization should describe the rich portal environment designed to meet the specific needs of employees throughout your organization.

The implementation of your corporate portal strategy results in a business case that documents how the benefits of the corporate portal solution are best deployed. Some deployment suggestions include:

- By roles and responsibilities of employees
- By the processes and activities performed by employees
- By department or workgroups of employees

In addition, there are some notable benefits associated with a staged delivery of the corporate portal design and implementation. They include:

- *Planning to deploy the most critical functionality earlier.* Identify the most important business functions and processes in your organization to be added to the corporate portal first. Employees who need these functions can begin using the corporate portal application while the next function or process is being developed, tested, and deployed. Staged delivery can be a valuable approach for gaining acceptance of the corporate portal solution in your organization.

- *Reducing risks early.* The business plan can outline how a staged delivery of the corporate portal solution emphasizes risk management throughout the project. Delivering the corporate portal solution in stages reduces the technical and political risks of unsuccessful integration of software, technology, and user acceptance. Management risks are reduced through frequent deliverables that demonstrate progress to everyone watching the project. Building opportunities to revise plans into each stage of the delivery further reduces planning risks.

- *Identifying problems earlier.* The more frequently new corporate portal functions are added into the corporate portal solution, the more frequently feedback is collected and forwarded to the planning team and the developers of the system from the employees using the system.

• *Making more options available sooner.* The planning team and the development team can consider addressing changes requested by the employees using the corporate portal solution. The staged delivery approach allows the planning team and the development team to guarantee that changes will be considered periodically by building opportunities for improvements into new delivery stages.

Specific business and technological advantages of a corporate portal solution include the following:

Business Advantages

• Planning and implementation at the roles and responsibilities, activities and processes, or department and workgroup level ensures a manageable deployment.
• Ownership at the roles and responsibilities, activities and processes, or department and workgroup level allows executives and managers to plan a corporate portal tailored to the unique needs of employees throughout your organization.
• Budgeting responsibilities can be clearly assigned at a roles and responsibilities, activities and processes, or department and workgroup level.

Technological Advantages

• Incremental investment allows bandwidth, hardware, administration, and other infrastructure costs to be distributed over time, keeping pace with the development and deployment of corporate portal services.
• Rollout provides a degree of flexibility in the implementation of functionality and connections between corporate portal services and data sources.
• Scalability lends itself to supporting a large variety of features, functions, corporate standards, and connected systems. This allows the corporate portal to provide a number of services (e.g., user assistance, search capabilities, discussion forums) that grow in complexity with the addition of self-service applications (e.g., sales force automation, cus-

tomer relationship management) and enterprise systems (e.g., Oracle Financials, Microsoft Office applications).
- Growth allows the corporate portal to evolve as the requirements and available technologies change.

Is your organization interested in taking advantage of these benefits? For executives and business professionals who want to embark on researching a corporate portal journey, the key points and checklist that follow are designed to help you explore concepts about corporate portals and develop a business case and a strategy for your organization. The strategy you define will outline a corporate portal solution that can improve the quality of decisions your employees make for your organization, your customers, and your future growth.

KEY POINTS

1. Corporate intranets continue to grow larger and are required to provide more functionality. To keep up with new intranet requirements, organizations need an updated corporate strategy.

2. The corporate portal strategy is a proposed solution to the intranet chaos in organizations today. Corporate portals create a central intranet "window" that presents information to users and an intranet "door" that allows users to pass through to reach other destinations.

3. Executives should consider a corporate portal solution for the organization providing employees with several benefits. These include:

- A consistent view of the organization
- Information organization and search capabilities
- Direct access to knowledge and resources
- Direct links to reports, analysis, and queries
- Direct links to relative data and knowledge experts
- Individual identity and personalized access to content

4. To implement a corporate portal with a desktop that can meet the expectations of employees in your organization, the solution must entail:

- Publishing relative information, best solutions, and best practices that can be continually recycled as knowledge.
- Creating a more responsive organization by creating a network of shared expertise that includes data and people.
- Cross-referencing ideas and promoting innovation.
- Creating the central deployment and administration of personalized knowledge desktops.

5. By considering several software functions in your corporate portal solution you can help ensure that the features required by employees in your organization are met. The software functions to consider include:

- Data points and integration
- Taxonomy
- Search capabilities
- Help features
- Content management
- Process and action
- Collaboration and communication
- Personalization
- Presentation
- Administration
- Security

6. The first step toward a corporate portal solution for your organization is to create a business case. The proposed corporate portal solution should be documented as a project to be implemented in several successive stages or deliveries. You also need to coordinate the corporate portal research activities with the IT department.

7. The purpose of this book is to provide you with a complete understanding of a corporate portal solution with enough information and checklists to build a corporate portal business case for your organization.

Use the following checklist to review or analyze the quality of information currently available to employees in your organization and their ability to share knowledge and ideas with other employees.

Evaluating Existing Data and Knowledge-Sharing Issues

☐ Do employees share common corporate semantics throughout your organization?

☐ Do employees have access to the data sources and knowledge experts needed to complete their jobs?

☐ When different groups of employees access data in your organization, do they all see consistent data values?

☐ Can employees easily find the information and data sources they are looking for?

☐ Are employees aware of what information or data sources are available for them to access?

☐ Can intranet and extranet data sources be searched to locate information or data sources employees are interested in?

☐ Can employees with similar job responsibilities share experiences and ask questions of each other in your organization?

☐ Are employees made aware of information, knowledge experts, and data sources in other departments or other employee roles that directly affect their specific responsibilities?

☐ Can employees easily navigate through information available in your organization?

☐ Can employees isolate issues and coordinate a resolution in a collaborative environment with other decision makers?

☐ Do employees with similar job responsibilities make consistent decisions?

☐ Can employees personalize their work environment?

☐ Does your organization foster a shared community?

☐ Do employees have easy access to summarized information and reports? Can employees drill into information available in these reports?

☐ Are employees made aware of information that would be helpful or relevant to their assigned responsibilities?

☐ Is information that is available to employees current and relevant to the decisions they need to make?

2

Corporate Portal Definitions and Features

Your organization can gain several advantages by implementing a corporate portal solution. These benefits include (among others):

- *Better Decision-Making Capabilities*. The structure and content available from the corporate portal desktop should provide the appropriate detail and direct access to information in your organization for employees to improve and enhance decisions they make while doing their jobs and completing their assigned responsibilities.

- *Improved Semantics*. The corporate portal solution provides the framework to create a consistent view of your organization through the use of consistent terminology and navigation hierarchies.

- *Improved Information Organization and Search Capabilities*. The portal solution focuses on the layout of individual desktop screens that are organized around the way employees work rather than around the applications they use. An additional feature is to provide search features to locate documents and information available inside your organization or on the World Wide Web.

- *Direct Access to Knowledge and Resources*. From a central portal desktop, employees can focus on the aspects of applications, data sources, and the experience of other knowledge workers to complete their assigned responsibilities.

• *Direct Links to Reports, Analysis, and Queries.* Summarized or status information that needs to be tracked, published, and presented is incorporated into the portal desktop. These reports provide several services that include (1) information to educate employees and (2) methods for evaluating and measuring the success of the organization's performance objectives and defined metrics.

• *Direct Links to Related or Relative Data Points.* This benefit encapsulates the ability to traverse content inside the portal desktop that is relevant to the primary responsibilities and interest of the employee.

• *Personalized Access to Content.* Personalization provides the ability and functionality required for each employee to organize, define, and rearrange the portal desktop to work effectively and efficiently.

These benefits are major elements or software functions that are built into the portal desktop used by your employees. These software functions work together in different combinations to achieve the portal benefits identified as important by your organization. Employees interact with the portal desktop, which allows your organization to address the corporate objectives identified to improve the entire decision cycle of employees throughout your organization. This decision cycle consists of three steps:

1. Gathering information.
2. Engaging in research and collaboration activities.
3. Taking action.

The corporate portal must provide features and content for each step in the decision cycle. The portal is a facilitator designed to draw your employees into a common community. It is a tool to exchange and improve your relationship with your employees and your customers. The goal of the portal desktop is to implement self-service, self-help, and self-discovery in aspects of your business where it makes sense. For example, employees that are experts using a specific application or spend most of their day using many aspects of a specific system to complete their assigned responsibilities will continue using these applications and systems. Your organization may decide that the portal desktop can provide two separate and distinct benefits to these knowledge workers. First, it provides access to information, applications, and interactions in your organization that they are often not aware of or familiar with. Second, it provides a format for them to publish their expertise, be recognized as experts, and be actively involved in improving processes directly or indirectly related to their responsibilities.

The concepts, advantages, and features of a corporate portal solution for your organization are undoubtedly worth consideration. This chapter outlines in more detail the following issues:

- The types of portals available from portal vendors, including their basic features and services
- The functions to include or incorporate as software requirements for your corporate portal solution
- The universal features your organization needs to establish as standards for your corporate portal solution
- A definition of the components in the user interface that represent the corporate portal software functions and universal features

CORPORATE PORTAL TYPES

Portal software vendors offer a collection of several features and functions that work together to provide the benefits your organization is expecting in the portal solution. A wide variety of products and vendors in the business intelligence, enterprise resource planning (ERP), document management, search engine, and other markets partially fill the definition of a "corporate" portal. A review of the portal market segment identifies at least nine different types of web-based applications that have labeled themselves portal solutions. A collection of these portal market segments must be combined to match our definition of a complete and scalable corporate portal solution.

The relationship of these nine corporate portal segments and the portal terminology used in our corporate portal definition is diagrammed in Figure 2-1.

Information Portal

This is the most general category and includes vendors that emphasize connecting to many classes of data sources. The two types of information portal vendors are:

- *Intranet Unstructured.* These vendors provide systems that automate the searching, categorizing, organizing, and publishing of intranet-based information. Examples of vendors in this market segment include Verity and InfoSeek. These systems are easier to install than enterprise reporting systems and have features similar to public or general Internet portals such as Yahoo! and Excite.
- *Enterprise Reporting.* These vendors have strong query and reporting applications. Most vendors in this category have come

Figure 2-1. Corporate portal market segments.

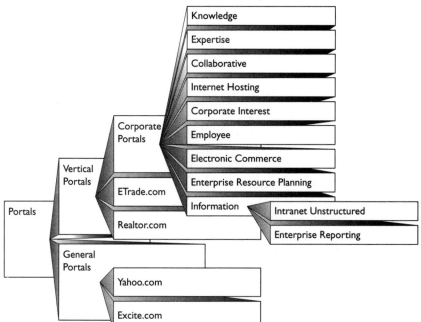

from the data warehousing or business intelligence space. Business intelligence vendors in this market segment have announced a subset of features found in their online analytical processing (OLAP) tools to provide data mining for the masses. Market segment vendors include Oracle and Brio.

Enterprise Resource Planning (ERP) Portal

This category primarily consists of browser front-ends to the vendor's own ERP system. Emphasis is on providing information from the ERP system to the casual user, using a web infrastructure. Every ERP vendor has announced a product in this category, including:

- SAP
- Oracle
- PeopleSoft
- Baan
- J. D. Edwards

There is some cross-functionality between portals in this category and e-commerce portals (discussed next) owing to the tight integration needed between back-office systems and front-ends of e-commerce customers.

Products in this portal category primarily connect to the ERP system for which they were developed. Thus, to take advantage of an ERP portal, your organization must have an installation of the ERP system. The ERP system is the data source that is presented in the ERP portal solution. Employees gain access to the enterprisewide capabilities of your ERP system while taking advantage of a web-based work environment. These ERP portal solutions provide the following features that allow individual employees to customize their ERP portal solution:

- *Personalization.* The workspace can be personalized for individual preferences and corporate roles that are applicable to each user.
- *Single Point-of-Access.* There is a website used to access screens, reports, and features of the ERP system. Included in this

website is the ability to add features that create links to launch or include aspects of third-party applications.

• *Administration, Maintenance, and Security.* There are administration and maintenance features to manage access and permissions to ERP data and business processes. Security features that are incorporated in the ERP system are used to control the web-based work environment with encryption and additional security requirements that are identified by your organization's information technology (IT) standards.

Electronic Commerce Portal

Electronic commerce (e-commerce) portals are aimed at customers for the sole purpose of online retail or procurement applications. These solutions create an Internet-based business relationship between your organization, customers, partners, and vendors. E-commerce portals use web browsers to create process and action, networked supply chains, and customer relationships and to establish new market activities.

Organizations concentrate on several goals and objectives for their e-commerce portals. One feature is to be able to tailor offerings through personal profiles. American Airlines was the first major airline to develop an interactive reservation system for passengers to plan and book trips and take advantage of the Web as an interactive marketing tool. Amazon.com concentrates on streamlining all of the business processes that affect customers to create a comprehensive set of retail services. The objective of the Dell Computer's e-commerce site is to let customers help themselves through the entire sales experience including pre-sales marketing through order entry and post-sales service and support. Creating a personalized service with community and convenience has allowed Dow Jones's *Wall Street Journal Interactive Edition* to charge customers a subscription fee for news feed services.

Employee Portal

This category has a definite human resources focus. Employee portals combine ERP and human resource information system (HRIS) access with the addition of work scenarios or scripts that lead users through the processes and routines of predictable daily work, rather than requiring users to piece it together themselves. The goal of employee portal products is to promote a high-level web-based work environment with assistance or help that assembles structured, unchanging processes into role-based routines. Services and functionality available for employees in your organization to take advantage of include:

1. Human resources functions, such as:

- Managing positions and associated compensation.
- Recruiting, hiring, and training employees.
- Promoting, relocating, and retiring employees.
- Incorporating local and international regulatory requirements.

2. Benefits administration

- Pension administration
- Payroll administration
- Stock administration

Examples of vendors providing employee portal solutions include PeopleSoft and KCS.

Corporate Interest Portal

This category consists of corporate line-of-business portals available from the Internet. The corporate interest portal provides listings of business-to-business resources, services, and business products that might be of interest to your organization. The information available directs users to online and offline sources. These Internet sites use search and directory hierarchies to direct users to the most relevant information they need without having to search the entire World Wide Web for the service or resource they are trying to locate. These corporate interest sites are often categorized into identified industry verticals that contain dedicated subject matter specifically focused to a line-of-business or specific business activity.

Examples of websites that allow access to information specific to a variety of industry verticals include Dow Jones and ISyndicate. There are also geographic verticals that provide useful information about events, news, weather, and other areas of interest for local employees. Your organization might want to use Citysearch.com, for example. Simple solutions are available to allow users to access the city of interest directly, without having to complete a series of questions from the website provider's home page. These corporate interest portal sites have personalization options as well to provide information about specific subjects of interest and preferred default settings to individual users.

Internet Hosting Portal

Internet hosting portals provide line-of-business–oriented application hosting in which the vendor runs the system on its infrastructure. AT&T WorldNet and MCI WorldCom are two of the largest Internet hosting services available. Services provided by Internet hosting vendors that can be made available to your organization include:

- *Download Services.* These services are used for distributing files (including software), white papers, and other material. This service saves an organization costs on printing, order entry, fulfillment, and shipping.
- *Application Hosting.* This service is typically for hosting Active Server Pages that are created and maintained by your organization and made available through the Internet hosting provider.
- *Internet Connectivity.* This service provides everyone in your organization access to the World Wide Web.
- *Security Services.* These services guarantee that downloads and mail messages and other Internet services are secure transactions so that your organization's data cannot be accessed or seen by any unauthorized users.

Even if your organization's website is hosted outside your internal network by a portal vendor, your organization should consider a unique domain name. The domain provides your organization with:

- A unique identity on the Internet for your organization to use
- A unique web address (e.g., www.yourdomain.com)
- The ability to route mail to the domain (i.e., web address)

Internet domain name services are available through vendors such as MindSpring, which allow you to research and register an Internet domain name online. Once your domain name has been selected for your organization it must be registered with InterNIC for a nominal annual fee that is mandated by the government to register the domain name.

Collaborative Portal

Collaborative portals are applications that focus on communication features such as team rooms, project management tools, discussions, chat rooms, and e-mail. These Internet sites and related applications or products are designed to support three key activities:

- *Communication.* This means creating an environment where team members can communicate and share information regardless of time zones and geographical boundaries.
- *Collaboration.* E-mail, electronic document storage and retrieval, corporate discussion forums and information distribution, and personal time management resources are included in this category.
- *Coordination.* Tools for creating and documenting processes that are shared with the whole organization provide the capability to analyze and simulate process and action or workflow. Business process modeling allows your organization to update workflow activities with the best possible solution being implemented.

Several applications are available to evaluate and purchase that are designed for teams to communicate and work more effectively together. Two of these products are eRoom (from eRoom Technology) and TeamRoom (from Lotus Development Corporation). The collaborative application used by your organization may or may not be available from a web browser client. If the solution is not completely available from a browser, you may decide to present a summary or report of team projects on the corporate portal content page with additional details available by launching the collaborative application software. Alternatively you can design a hyperlink that opens the collaboration application software from the corporate portal desktop and connects straight to the team project that the user is reviewing.

Expertise Portal

Expertise portals provide informed advice, decisions, or recommended solutions for a given situation or submitted question. These solutions are designed to incorporate knowledge and reasoning methods that are not easily represented in traditional computing approaches. Expertise portals extend the boundary of what can be automated to include tasks that require reasoning, symbolic processing, and problem solving. The goals of the expertise portal are to be accessed by many people, to represent knowledge that may reside with many individuals, to preprocess information to increase the availability of expert information, and to gain access to expertise immediately. The expertise portal fills a number of functions:

- *Librarian.* Helping employees find, organize, and interpret information required to carry out a task.
- *Advisor.* Sharing the specialized expertise that is needed.
- *Instructor.* Helping employees learn a task.
- *General Assistant.* Taking care of defined routine tasks.

The expertise portal is composed of two somewhat independent parts: an inference engine and a knowledge base. The inference engine is the control structure used to retrieve and submit requests to the knowledge base. The knowledge base is where the real power of the expertise portal exists. This is the coded pool of rules, insights, and knowledge that are available for employees to access. This structure provides two important features for the expertise portal. First, the expertise portal allows the knowledge base to be modified, updated, and expanded. This makes it easier to keep the information available current with changes in the industry, or with changes in user requirements. Second, an explanation of the reasoning behind a conclusion can be allowed. This feature is required to provide the credibility and confidence that employees will require before accepting the information provided into use. Acquire by Acquired Intelligence is an example of an expert system and expertise portal.

Knowledge Portal

A knowledge portal solution that completes our definition is a combination of all the aforementioned market segments with a concentration on the following capabilities:

• Retrieving core information from corporate IT systems and presenting it according to the preferences, roles, and specific tasks of individual users.

• Providing personalization and navigation features that allow users to create the working environment that best fits the way they need to work.

• Facilitating communication and collaboration between people who need information and the people who can supply the information.

Knowledge portal products incorporate a combined collection of the features and functionality outlined by these individual portal market segments. Portal products collectively should be evaluated as possible applications for your organization to use to establish your enterprise portal or corporate portal solution. When your organization is ready to begin to compare and contrast different software applications, there are several different types to choose from. For example, SAP is an application vendor with portal tools. Its portal solution is mySAP.com Workplace. An example of a vendor with a portal software solution that has experience in decision support systems is Viador. Another with experience in knowledge management is Semio. InfoImage is an example of an e-business consulting company that has become a knowledge portal vendor.

The features and benefits to look for in knowledge portal software solutions should include:

- A single point-of-access from a web browser to applications, business content, and services. You should, however, verify which web browsers and version numbers are supported by portal software applications. When multiple web browsers and versions are supported, they are not always supported with the same functionality or feature set.
- A personalized, role-based user interface that's customizable to individual needs.
- Simple maintenance that requires no additional client software or hardware. Be aware, however, that in many cases, there are minimum bandwidths and modem speeds that employees or users will need to connect to the web server to use the corporate portal solution.
- Access to enterprise applications and data sources using a development application programming interface (API).
- A single sign-on into the portal solution to access all the applications and data sources available in the portal desktop.
- Integrated communication and collaboration features with existing enterprise applications, systems, and hosted services.
- Bundled search engine or integration capabilities with third-party products to provide search features and functions.
- Bundled web-based business intelligence tools or integration capabilities with third-party business intelligence applications.

Portal software vendors use a combination of several programming interfaces and software functions or actions to implement the portal functionality in their products. Each of these portal software applications implements or supports portal features differently. The best process to select the appropriate portal software vendor is to determine the objectives and requirements of your enterprise or corporate portal solution and evaluate which product most appropriately matches your needs.

CORPORATE PORTAL SOFTWARE FUNCTIONS

The corporate portal software functions are the core services, actions, and building blocks that allow your organization's self-service applications to be included in the corporate portal solution. Your organization must review the software functions and determine how employees in your organization want to use these functions in their current processes and job responsibilities. The portal software application provides software functions that employees have not been able to take advantage of using their current business processes. In the process of reviewing the business functions and self-service applications for the corporate portal solution, you also want to consider how the software functions can be used to enhance or improve your organization's existing business functions.

Corporate portal software functions all contribute to creating a consistent view of your organization for every employee. By concentrating on how to implement these major software functions, the business processes and self-service applications used by employees are made available in the knowledge desktop unique to their role in these business functions. It is important that information that is presented be accurate and timely to provide the value necessary to make better decisions as an individual and more consistent decisions as an organization. The most common software functions that portal software solutions need to support include:

• *Data Points and Integration.* This element provides one of the fundamental functions to be supported by the corporate portal solution, including the ability to access information from a wide range of internal and external information sources and display the resulting information at the single point-of-access desktop. Your organization needs to verify that your applications and data sources can be integrated into the portal software solution selected.

• *Taxonomy.* The taxonomy or categorization element provides information context, including the organization-specific categories that reflect and support your organization's business. The taxonomy provides rapid recognition of common terminology used in your organization and improves semantics for users of the corporate portal solution. The taxonomy established for your organization should be logical and easily recognized or understood by employees that use the corporate portal. When evaluating portal software solutions, you should verify that your organization's naming and categorization standards can easily be implemented and maintained.

- *Search Capabilities.* The search element provides several services for the corporate portal users and needs to support searches across the enterprise, the World Wide Web, and third-party search engine catalogs and indexes. Users will want the portal solution to support search queries that can be run on a scheduled basis or as an immediate request. Make certain that the portal software solutions considered are able to support sophisticated search requirements and that the search element is flexible enough to meet future expectations as well as current requirements. As the portal solution grows in your organization, you can expect search requirements and functionality needed to expand.

- *Help Features.* The help element provides assistance when using the corporate portal solution. Help should be available for both corporate portal features and organization-specific features. Several different types of help functions should be available from the corporate portal desktop. Your portal solution may require simple pop-up help when a mouse is held down over a menu option, context-sensitive help for information entered in a specific field, or detailed help on a specific topic or issue. The help function allows portal users to do some self-discovery on an issue before having to contact a knowledge expert to assist them or answer a question. Take advantage of help features and functionality available in portal software solutions.

- *Content Management.* The publishing and distribution (or content management) element supports content creation, authorization, and inclusion in (or exclusion from) corporate portal content collections. As a rule, organizations have volumes of information and reference material to make available from the corporate portal. There are new policies, procedures, forms, templates, announcements, schedules, and much more that need to be pushed continually to employees. The content available from the corporate portal desktop should be available for distribution in multiple on-line, downloadable, or hard-copy formats. Content management and third-party integration features available in portal software products are important factors to review and match to your organization's requirements.

• *Process and Action.* The process and action element enables the corporate portal user to initiate and participate in your organization's business processes. Often there are two different implementation approaches to integrating workflow or process and action features in the corporate portal solution. The first is to integrate existing workflow solutions into the corporate portal desktop for users. The second is to design or script a solution using the development environment and tools available using the portal software product's programming interface. Make certain that the corporate portal software selected by your organization can support how employees need to work to complete their assigned responsibilities.

• *Collaboration and Communication.* The collaboration and communication element facilitates discussion, locating innovative ideas, and recognizing resourceful solutions. This element gives employees the ability to work together in a qualitatively better way by creating a shared, virtual desktop (collaboration), supporting electronic messaging (communication), and adding collaboration and communication features to business processes (coordination). Portal software functionality needs to include easy configuration and administration features to existing enterprise messaging, personal information management, and calendaring systems.

• *Personalization.* The personalization element is a critical component to create a working environment that is organized and configured specifically to each employee in your organization. Employees are empowered to work efficiently with the information needed to complete their jobs easily available. They can also work effectively by being allowed to define and organize their individual desktops. Decision-making capabilities are optimized to each portal user's working style and content preferences. The key is achieving balance between the features and information that need to be consistent and constant in the portal solution and the personalization and unique features needed by individual employees. Being able to control the content and structure of multiple desktops configured throughout your organization requires a portal solution that is easily configured and maintained. You need to research and review administration and configuration features available in portal software solutions to verify that your IT department can develop, deploy, support, and maintain the personalization of your portal solution.

• *Presentation*. The presentation element provides the knowledge desktop and visual experience to the corporate portal user that encapsulates all of the corporate portal's functionality. All of the software functions or elements mentioned previously must be supported in the presentation element in a format that is flexible enough to allow intuitive use and easy navigation throughout. The presentation element contains all the software functions or elements available from the corporate portal desktop. How this collection of software elements might be organized and displayed in a user interface is shown in Figure 2-2.

• *Administration*. The administration element provides two services. The first is the deployment and maintenance activities or tasks associated with the corporate portal system. The second is what can be uniquely configured by an administrator for the corporate portal system as well as by each user through corporate portal personalization.

• *Security*. The security element provides a description of the levels of access each user or groups of users are allowed for each portal application and software function included in the corporate portal. The types of access allowed include no access, reader access, editor access, or other. Your organization's IT security requirements for intranet applications need to be addressed and supported by the portal solution implemented by your organization. Research and review the security models of third-party portal software applications to make certain the security model included in the portal software application meets the IT standards defined for your organization.

CORPORATE PORTAL UNIVERSAL FEATURES

When all the software functions are integrated into a single desktop interface, there need to be additional portal features to moni-

Figure 2-2. Main components of the corporate portal user interface.

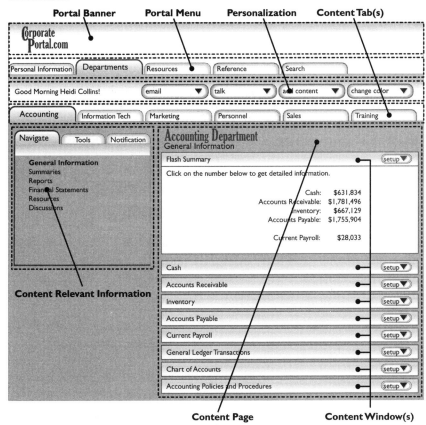

tor and control how these functions interact with each other. These universal features or control mechanisms are the consistent and pervasive user interface components that tie the software functions together in the corporate portal desktop. Your organization must review this set of features to define how they can be implemented in the corporate portal application.

Initial collections of the universal features for your corporate portal need to be defined in the first phase of your project and documented in the business case. This list of universal features can then be continually reviewed and enhanced as new phases of the corporate portal solution are implemented. These cohesive corporate portal universal features include:

• *Self-Service Applications (Access to Discrete Enterprise Data)*. All roles and responsibilities, processes and activities, and departments or workgroups that are elected to be part of the corporate portal solution need to be identified. The summary and scorecard information made available from the portal desktop usually originates in several different applications and systems throughout your organization. Additionally, you must establish the interaction or processes users will have available to them with the information presented in the portal desktop. Finally, you need to address usability of the information presented in the portal desktop. Users tend to want to be able to easily drill down into information, navigate to additional information or processes, leave the portal desktop to work in other applications when necessary, and return to the corporate portal desktop to continue their daily activities. Several business domain experts can be recruited to work with you and your team in making decisions about how employee roles, objectives, and goals should be incorporated into the corporate portal solution.

• *Corporate Portal (Aggregation of Self-Service Applications)*. The software functions and corporate portal universal features must behave consistently and be easily understood by users of the corporate portal self-service applications. To ensure this, the first step is defining or recognizing how these software functions will be incorporated or allowed to behave within each self-service application or staged delivery. The number of corporate portal users and the behavior of the software functions also need to be evaluated and possibly updated between staged deliveries to accommodate more users or expanded functionality. Your organization should create a main portal menu hierarchy that best outlines or defines how information can be located, which may be by a combination of responsibilities, activities, and departments. As an example, you might create an initial menu hierarchy system that works well for the first group of corporate portal users. All portal users can find information in less than four or five mouse clicks and have established a collection of bookmarks or favorite content pages that they can easily find. Over time, additional users and the information they need to access need to be included in the corporate portal solution. Your organization must decide whether to reevaluate the portal menu hierarchy with additional levels, create a second or third menu hierarchy that users can select from, or establish a corporate menu hierarchy that everyone must use combined with a personal menu hierarchy that can be configured by each user as the solution. Alternatively, you may choose a unique solution created to meet your organization's specific user requirements. You need to verify that the portal software solutions you evaluate can easily support whatever navigation and configuration features you decide on for your corporate portal solution.

• *Comfort and Familiarity (User Personalization).* Corporate portal users need to be able to customize and organize their knowledge desktop to work effectively from a single point-of-access. Icons, logos, and colors can be useful to distinguish information associated with your organization. Individuals with similar responsibilities from personal information management (PIM) to specific business functions may require a consistent set of available features in the portal solution so they can work together effectively. However, this set of consistent features needs to be supported with some level of individual personalization. This personalization might include allowing features or content to be rearranged on the desktop, bookmarks and favorites to be set, or personal folders or menus to be maintained and updated. The comfort and familiarity goal is to allow the user to think and work as efficiently as possible while making better, more informed, and consistent decisions for your organization. The flexibility and extent of the user personalization requirements must be outlined by your organization, reevaluated on a scheduled basis, and enhanced as the corporate portal solution matures.

• *Understanding and Knowledge (Navigation Personalization).* Presentation of relevant information and navigation through that information is another global consideration to be evaluated and included in the corporate portal solution. To facilitate navigation through an extensive information network without overwhelming the corporate portal users in your organization requires the implementation of corporate knowledge maps. The process of creating knowledge maps that translate into a cross-reference of resources and information in your organization is a valuable exercise. This experience should not be looked at as a one-time event but a continual process of looking at your organization's knowledge from different perspectives to address current and future issues. The final result is a road map of your organization. If you have created a set of maps that describe all the available routes from one piece of information to all other pieces of information, then by knowing exactly where you are on the map, you are able to get to every other location on the map. (Chapter 8 gives more detailed information on how to cross-reference documents, employees, roles, and other information in your organization.)

• *System Intelligence (Behavior Assistance Personalization).* Change will be the most notable constant throughout the design and implementation of the corporate portal. Each employee has a definite and adjusting perception of what should be available in the corporate portal. Your portal software solution should help you implement two strategies with respect to behavior assistance personalization:

1. *Tracking corporate portal enhancements.* As you are creating the corporate portal strategy, you may experience relentless or accelerating change. The corporate portal has to recognize and adjust to changing requirements in information needs throughout your organization. A successful corporate portal strategy should therefore incorporate a well-defined plan for evaluating and updating corporate portal software functions and universal features. Your corporate portal needs to include a learning process to adjust the parameters of each employee's requirements on a scheduled basis. This means that several of the set of consistent features and global elements included in your portal solution must be reevaluated, enhanced, and expanded as the portal solution is iteratively developed and deployed. The preliminary corporate portal strategy needs to outline the aspects of each self-service application, each software function, and the corporate portal universal features in order to document and provide change management procedures for each of these elements. These procedures allow your organization to continually recognize and adjust to ongoing change, in effect creating an intelligent system for your employees. Make certain that the portal software solution implemented in your organization supports a comprehensive API for your internal development team to take advantage of.

2. *Finding a way to identify employee behaviors and activities and learn from them.* You can create feedback processes and opportunities within the portal desktop and begin to use the results to help employees. Amazon.com uses this type of functionality to direct customers toward additional services and products that match previous buying preferences. Your organization can use this same type of pattern-matching and cross-referencing of information and knowledge experts to provide additional corporate portal benefits for your employees.

CORPORATE PORTAL USER INTERFACE

There are several layouts and implementations of the portal interface that combine all the components of the corporate portal software functions and universal features. One example of these user interface components is shown in Figure 2-2. The components available include:

1. *Portal Banner.* A graphic provides a visual representation of the page represented in the corporate portal.
2. *Portal Menu.* A persistent menu provides access to applications, functionality, and services throughout your organization.
3. *Personalization.* A persistent set of options is presented that allows users to modify the look and feel of the corporate portal user interface.
4. *Content Page Tab(s).* A collection of secondary menu options that are associated or related to the context of the current content page are also presented. These menu options provide access to additional content pages.
5. *Content Page.* This is the information presented in the main window of the browser associated with the portal menu option or other navigation option selected by the corporate portal user.
6. *Content Window(s).* The collection of information contained in the content page can be a single window or several windows of information contained in the same content page.

7. *Content-Relevant Information.* Several additional features may appear in the content-relevant information section of the corporate portal for easy access by users. These include:

- *Tools* (e.g., to access collaboration, communication, and applications that are standard in your organization)
- *Navigation* (e.g., to provide additional navigation options, including both data and knowledge experts, that are related or relevant to the information presented on the content page)
- *Notifications* (e.g., to provide important messages that are related to the context of the content page and need to be brought to the attention of the corporate portal user)

Portal software functions are integrated into the portal desktop in several different ways. All the portal software functions available in the desktop portal comprise the overall presentation of the portal desktop. The portal banner provides presentation features for branding and visual recognition by employees. The portal menu allows your organization to create a standard taxonomy with semantics that employees can easily identify with. Users have direct hyperlinks to topic help and search functionality through the portal menu. Employees have individual recognition and persistent access to all PIM applications, portal configuration features, bookmarks and favorites, and other employees through instant messaging from the personalization section of the portal desktop, which is also a good location from which users can easily participate in discussion forums throughout your organization. Each content page available in the portal desktop provides integration to information and applications throughout your organization. The portal software functions included in the main content page are data points and integration, content management features, process and action functionality, search functionality, and detailed help features that are available. There will also be personalization features available for users to interact with portal content pages. The content-relevant information is a dynamic section of the portal desktop that provides behavior assistance, additional navigation, and additional awareness of specific information that is of importance to the context of what is presented in the content page.

CorporatePortal.com Case Study

The corporate portal solution initially being considered needs to support integration with data sources in CorporatePortal.com that are responsible for financial systems, project (tax and audit) systems, customer satisfaction systems, document management systems, messaging and collaboration systems, search engines, and project management systems. A CorporatePortal.com menu hierarchy needs to be implemented in the portal solution to allow navigation to enterprise system information, Internet information, and knowledge experts. Help features must be identified, developed, and supported from the portal desktop. The portal solution also has to support the PIM expectations of employees. Your task as the corporate portal strategist is to research the feasibility of these requirements and determine if you should build a business case to move forward with a portal solution.

CorporatePortal.com has selected the InfoImage freedom knowledge portal software application to be evaluated for the purpose of the corporate portal business case. This application supports a scalable and distributed collection of portal servers and services. The data integration and connectivity support required for the initial data sources identified is available. The corporate portal platform proposed is capable of supporting the initial 350 employees. The web browser is standardized on Microsoft Internet Explorer version 5.0; bandwidths supported include LAN, ISDN, and cable modem lines.

The IT development team also benefits from the existing core features and software functions that are provided as part of the portal software application by using the software development kit to programmatically extend the base Freedom application to meet CorporatePortal.com's requirements. The development team can use its current Internet programming standards (i.e., HTML, DHTML, JavaScript, XML/XSL, and Active Server Pages) and Freedom's application programming interface to create objects and business functions for the portal desktop.

KEY POINTS

1. Corporate portals are designed to help improve all three stages of the decision cycle in your organization—gathering infor-

mation, engaging in research and collaboration activities, and taking action.

2. Portal products available from current vendors include
many or most of the features considered critical for a corporate
portal solution. The types of portal solutions include:

- Information portals
- ERP portals
- E-commerce portals
- Employee portals
- Corporate interest portals
- Internet hosting portals
- Collaborative portals
- Expertise portals
- Knowledge portals

3. Software functions to incorporate as part of your corporate
portal solution include:

- Data points and integration
- Taxonomy
- Search capabilities
- Help features
- Content management
- Process and action (workflow)
- Collaboration and communication
- Personalization
- Presentation
- Administration
- Security

4. Your organization should assess how the following universal
features can be included in a corporate portal solution:

- Self-service applications (access to discrete enterprise data)
- Corporate portal (aggregation of self-service applications)
- Comfort and familiarity (user personalization)
- Understanding and knowledge (navigation personalization)
- System intelligence (behavior assistance personalization)

5. The components in the corporate portal user interface that represent the corporate portal software functions and universal features include:

- Portal banner
- Portal menu
- Personalization
- Content page tab(s)
- Content page
- Content window(s)
- Content-relevant information

3

The Importance of a Corporate Portal Strategy

Creating and planning a corporate portal strategy is not easy. The job is to collect and analyze the information needed to formally propose a corporate portal solution. The process can be approached in a systematic way to increase the probability of success. You need to determine if your organization has several identifiable and measurable business reasons to build a corporate portal solution. Consider whether these problems exist in your organization:

- Employees in your organization need consistent information to make routine decisions.
- Employees need information from many different systems to make strategic decisions.
- Employees must complete most company-related activities online.
- Employees need to be able to access company information from an intranet site through a browser.
- Employees must access company information from multiple data sources and applications to complete their assigned activities.
- Employees cannot locate or navigate efficiently through company information or the intranet site.

- Employees are not aware of information or resources available in the company to complete their responsibilities.
- Employees require extensive training to use portions of the applications and systems they need to use to complete their responsibilities.

If your first impression is that a corporate portal solution would provide several benefits or resolve several known issues for your organization, then the development of a corporate portal strategy and the completion of additional analysis activities would be beneficial.

THE CORPORATE PORTAL STRATEGY

The corporate portal strategy is a collection of identified activities that, once completed, determine the feasibility of implementing a corporate portal solution in your organization. In most cases a good place to start is (1) to evaluate your information technology (IT) environment and (2) identify the most critical business challenges in your organization. You should consider first the business functions and self-service applications selected for implementation in the corporate portal solution from both the IT and end-user perspectives. Once the initial ideas have been selected, the business processes are outlined and presented as a series of screens that represent a visual model or storyboard of the proposed corporate portal solution. Other activities that need to be completed as part of the corporate portal strategy are an analysis of the financial impact and a project development timeline to deploy the corporate portal. This collection of activities is described as the discovery process to help you identify, prioritize, and define the business functions, self-service applications, and corporate portal features to document in the business case. The activities within this process include:

- Information technology review
- Preliminary identification of corporate portal business functions
- Storyboarding

- Financial analysis
- Creation of a corporate portal project plan

The objectives of your corporate portal strategy include the following:

- Defining a high-level overview of corporate portal concepts and technologies.
- Understanding the IT environment.
- Identifying and defining the highest-level business requirements.
- Determining the corporate portal solution overview.
- Defining the corporate portal solution storyboard.
- Defining the financial analysis.
- Defining the preliminary project plan.
- Building the corporate portal business case.

The documentation deliverables of your corporate portal strategy include:

- Business case document (i.e., the corporate portal proposal)
- IT assessment
- Preliminary storyboard
- Financial metrics analysis
- Preliminary project plan

DEFINING A HIGH-LEVEL OVERVIEW OF CORPORATE PORTAL CONCEPTS AND TECHNOLOGIES

You want to outline the primary strengths of the corporate portal solution that provide the inspiration for a successful implementation. What are these strengths? They may be unique for your organization. Combining knowledge of corporate portal software functions and the corporate portal universal features with the knowledge you have regarding the initiatives and requirements of your organization should provide enough information for you to evaluate and identify your corporate portal strengths and benefits. (Chapter 2 includes a complete listing of considerations for the corporate portal solution in your organization.) Corporate portals are designed to improve decision cycles in your organization and can incorporate knowledge sharing into all decision-making activities completed by employees. The corporate portal solution you implement should improve how employees gather information, research and collaborate, and take action.

A corporate portal solution must be approached and built in a hierarchical fashion. There are at least three generations of requirements that continue to build on each other when implementing a corporate portal solution. The three generations of corporate portals and the universal features and objectives of each are as follows:

Implementation of Corporate Portal	Objectives/Features
First generation	Build and present the core content Identify and develop self-service applications (i.e., access to discrete enterprise data)
Second generation	Extend the solution to all intranet activities Develop the corporate portal (i.e., aggregation of self-service applications)
Third generation	Create a personalized environment with focus on: • Comfort and familiarity (i.e., user personalization) • Understanding and knowledge (i.e., navigation personalization) • System intelligence (i.e., behavior assistance personalization)

An agreed-upon corporate portal definition should be comprehensive enough for anyone reading the business case to understand the purpose of the solution being proposed. The definition should also be concise enough to provide direction for your organization.

Over time, your organization may change its corporate portal
definition, which may lead to new opportunities. As employees in
your organization begin to use the corporate portal and the corporate portal environment becomes more complex and competitive,
you may want to expand the definition. For the purpose of the first-
generation corporate portal solution and its business case, the following questions must be answered by your corporate portal definition:

Documenting the Corporate Portal Definition

☐ Why should a corporate portal be implemented?
☐ What unique solution(s) will it provide?
☐ Why hasn't another business solution provided these unique so-
lution(s)?

CorporatePortal.com Case Study

A corporate portal solution offers several business advantages for
our fictitious tax and audit services company CorporatePortal.com.
Employees use many different enterprise applications and systems
to complete assigned tasks throughout the organization. Employees are only responsible for understanding and using the systems
that directly affect their responsibilities. This means users must
navigate through large amounts of material, and it becomes the
users' job to discard unwanted material, such that they may miss
the material they are trying to find. In order to streamline communication and processes, employees must be familiar with applications, documents, manuals, and the expertise areas of other
knowledge workers. CorporatePortal.com is evaluating a corporate
portal solution with the primary purpose of making a wide collection
of relevant information and data sources available to all employees
and the secondary purpose of improving communication and interaction among these employees.

Several objectives and unique opportunities are offered by the
corporate portal solution. These include the ability to:

- Retrieve information from corporate IT systems and present the results according to the roles, specific tasks, and preferences of individual employees.
- Present employees with information relevant to their daily tasks without making them search for it.
- Gather information about each employee, facilitating communication between the people who need information and the people who can supply the information. For instance, an account manager may need to learn the details of a customer's tax audit from the consulting team leader who was responsible for composing and documenting the results. By knowing the name of the customer, the account manager would be able to use a few mouse clicks to locate the name of the team leader and contact him through e-mail, telephone, or other tools available.
- Allow employees to act on the information presented in the desktop without requiring them to switch to a different system or interface for the purpose of sharing the information and collaborating with other employees.
- Present a desktop interface through a web browser that requires minimal technical training.
- Support multiple business processes for a single department, a single process across multiple departments, or multiple processes across multiple departments.

No other solution available at CorporatePortal.com provides a desktop interface to consolidate a complete collection of corporate information, content management, team collaboration and coordination, and personal information management. The corporate portal centralizes enterprise information and coordinates business functions for all employees. The services and self-service applications facilitated through the corporate desktop allow employees to share knowledge and find answers they need to make informed decisions.

The corporate portal is a new working environment for CorporatePortal.com employees. The software functions and features available from the portal desktop need to provide several benefits for employees to accept and continue using the application. There need to be usability walkthroughs and reviews to make sure that

the corporate portal creates an easy-to-use workspace that satis-
fies the objectives and critical success factors identified. The usability is twofold: first for content and second for features. The portal
desktop provides a unique set of objectives for the different user
roles in the CorporatePortal.com organization. The content and
pages available can be customized for each role while the software
features and portal functions remain consistent. The information
and reports presented to different roles through the portal desktop
need to be accurate and timely. Employees should be able to make
more informed decisions with access to relevant information that
they can easily find. The content, systems, applications, and other
material selected to be included in the portal desktop should be well
established, managed, and maintained separately from the corporate portal. For example, the messaging system, Oracle Financials,
and other applications are all maintained and administered as existing systems or projects. The corporate portal solution can only be
as accurate as the systems that are served by the portal desktop.

UNDERSTANDING THE IT ENVIRONMENT

A review of existing initiatives in your IT department or other departments needs to be completed. This is accomplished by reviewing projects in development or those scheduled to be developed
throughout your organization. After completing this analysis, you
may want to consider integration of the corporate portal solution
as a component of an existing initiative. This might prove to be
more cost- and budget-effective than having to establish a new project initiative or locate new funding and budget sources for the corporate portal solution. The corporate portal could prove to be
easily included in intranet, extranet, or knowledge management
initiatives.

The more information you uncover or become familiar with
about your organization and your IT department, the more effective you will be in managing and planning a corporate portal solution business case. A review of the IT infrastructure must be
conducted as part of the discovery process. The purpose of this
review is to determine how to take advantage and leverage the existing IT infrastructure as part of the corporate portal solution. It

is also critical to understand where technical limitations exist and what improvements of existing enterprise systems or infrastructure need to be included as part of the corporate portal business case. This documentation is collected from the IT department and business domain experts to provide insight into the strategic direction, business processes, goals, and critical success factors for the corporate portal solution being proposed in the business case.

There are many IT projects and administrative duties that contribute to a corporate portal solution. The intranet, data warehouse, relational database management system, reporting system, enterprise resource planning (ERP) system, financial system, messaging system, and multitude of other systems and applications— all provide data and user interface screens to employees from the corporate portal desktop. As self-service applications are added to the corporate portal, you must verify that the data sources and appropriate applications are fully implemented. The IT department must already have complete implementation and support procedures available for the information or application that needs to be included in the portal desktop. The portal desktop only serves as a window or gateway to existing data sources, systems, and applications. Chapter 10 provides additional information regarding research and analysis activities to understand your IT environment.

CorporatePortal.com Case Study

A review of the corporate infrastructure has been completed. This information provides valuable information about the current state of the corporate wide area network. A preliminary estimate of how many corporate portal users are to be supported in the first phase of the portal solution has been determined. These users need to have workstations with web browser software and access to the applications, systems, and data sources that are going to be used through the portal desktop. The first implementation of the corporate portal targets approximately 350 users and needs to be supported by two IT employees once the corporate portal solution has been deployed. The IT employees are responsible for portal development, deployment, maintenance, and administration of the corporate portal solution.

CorporatePortal.com is interested in recruiting employees in six departments of the organization to establish a set of corporate objectives and measure their performance. The systems that have been targeted to provide data for these metrics are the current financial system (Oracle Financials), the tax and audit project management system (Oracle RDBMS), and customer satisfaction reports (Oracle RDBMS). These Oracle-based systems are well established and supported by the IT department. The portal desktop can present reports and query results from available Oracle databases and views to present performance results to employees.

Several other data sources are available throughout CorporatePortal.com to find documents. The documents consist of Microsoft Word documents, Excel spreadsheets, PowerPoint presentations, e-mail messages, project files, Adobe Acrobat files, and others. These documents are shared through the CorporatePortal.com website and Microsoft Exchange public folders and reside on network file servers. A content management application and search engine needs to be evaluated and implemented at CorporatePortal.com to consolidate and easily locate structured and unstructured information throughout the organization. Employees can then share and interact with information available in enterprise systems and the corporate document repository from the portal desktop.

Microsoft Outlook is the messaging and e-mail system implemented at CorporatePortal.com. The company requires structured discussion forums and project team knowledge sharing. Employees infrequently use the current feedback and bulletin board applications at CorporatePortal.com. The portal desktop is intended to provide centralized access to instant messaging (i.e., online chat) and discussion forums at the desktop for employees. A project team collaboration application will be evaluated and included as part of the corporate portal solution to coordinate specific tax and audit project knowledge and associated activities.

IDENTIFYING AND DEFINING THE HIGHEST-LEVEL BUSINESS REQUIREMENTS

After determining the most significant IT factors that will have an impact on a corporate portal solution and locating sources of information about these factors, the corporate portal strategy team's judgment must play the deciding role. Decision makers must be convinced that the corporate portal solution is relevant for the organization and continue moving forward with the implementation of the corporate portal business case, otherwise the process will be concluded. It is important to work with as many business domain experts and employees in your organization to identify the business functions and self-service applications to include in the corporate portal solution.

Working together, the business domain experts and the corporate portal strategy team identify and prioritize critical business information or processes. The business domain experts from across your organization are responsible for brainstorming what the most important information business functions are. Their analysis assists in identifying the areas where the highest corporate portal opportunities exist. You should include some high-level concepts and the specific range or functionality required by the business processes included in the corporate portal solution. As this step in the process is completed, a collection of information regarding the self-service applications and corporate portal features is studied, then the priorities for the first phase of the corporate portal solution can be decided and documented in the business case. (Chapter 11 covers in detail the research and analysis activities you need to undertake to identify and define the highest-level business requirements.) Successful corporate portal initiatives should include business functions and corporate portal features that facilitate several types of user functionality, such as:

- Identifying a consistent set of portal desktop features for the roles and responsibilities of users throughout your organization and their target activities.

- Letting users make decisions and do their jobs by making the information, knowledge experts, and enterprise applications available from the portal desktop.

- Identifying the initial features, business functions, and self-service applications or processes to be included in the portal solution for the identified roles.

- Providing a complete view of the detail or supporting information that hyperlinks the user into additional areas of knowledge associated with the initial features, business functions, and self-service applications or processes included in the portal solution.

- Streamlining business functions and processes of the identified roles through information organization and search capabilities.

- Letting users help themselves by providing intuitive navigation capabilities throughout the portal solution.

- Delivering personalized service to your employees.

- Fostering community.

CorporatePortal.com Case Study

Three key metrics are used to measure the success of the CorporatePortal.com organization: financial information, current project (i.e., tax and audit) status information, and customer satisfaction metrics. Several versions of these reports need to be summarized and made available for different departments and user groups in CorporatePortal.com. These "scorecard" reports need hyperlinks to drill down into more detailed information or reports. Executives and managers need to assign grade information (e.g., on target, off target, at risk) and additional comments to accompany the scorecard reports presented in the corporate portal desktop.

A shared corporate document repository needs to be available and easily traversed from the corporate portal. Multiple document formats (e.g., Word documents, Excel spreadsheets, graphic files, PDF files) will be accessible from the same taxonomy in the portal desktop. Other features that need to be included in the content management aspects of the corporate portal include mechanisms that allow documents to be checked in and out by users, version control, and revisions layering (i.e., the ability to see comments on documents and who the writer of the comments is).

Project teams need to be able to collaborate and coordinate their activities in a shared portal workspace. Their online activities include sending e-mail notifications, scheduling meetings, and presenting a calendar of events. Employees need access to discussion forums and instant messaging features to facilitate additional team activities. An expert locator needs to be provided to find knowledge workers with the appropriate skills to help resolve issues and respond to frequently asked questions.

The benefits of a corporate portal solution have been discussed with business domain experts at CorporatePortal.com. These discussions have allowed business experts to review their current work processes and consider how a corporate portal can improve the working environment of their employees. The preliminary self-service applications have been identified to benefit CorporatePortal.com employees. For example:

- Key financial information, current project (tax and audit) status information, and customer satisfaction metrics should be summarized and easily available in the corporate portal desktop.

- A corporate document repository needs to be accessed from the corporate portal. This information needs to be accessed from both a standard menu hierarchy and a search engine.

- Project teams need to be able to collaborate and coordinate their activities in a shared portal workspace.

- An expert locator is needed to allow employees to locate other knowledge workers for their assistance in resolving identified problems.

- Discussion forums and instant messaging must be available from the portal desktop.

- A desktop interface should be designed that consolidates these identified self-service applications with the ability for employees to choose and personalize how this pertinent information is organized and presented.

IDENTIFYING ADDITIONAL CORPORATE PORTAL SOLUTION RESEARCH ACTIVITIES

There are additional areas to explore, research, and evaluate for inclusion in the corporate portal business case. Depending on the structure and politics of your organization, this final list of activities will be unique. Some suggested activities include:

- Determining the corporate portal solution overview.
- Defining the corporate portal solution storyboard.
- Defining the financial analysis.
- Defining the preliminary project plan.

Your organization will want to want to understand how to estimate time and resources to establish the initial phases of the corporate portal, understand the criteria to accept or reject future enhancements to be included, create a process to optimize corporate portal features and functions, and track the development and implementation progress of the corporate portal. They will want to know how to recognize successes and completed milestones for the corporate portal, keep track of the schedule and status information of the project, and be able to divert and allocate resources as needed. It is important to determine what analysis and documentation needs to be created to respond to the information required to create an overview of the corporate portal solution. In most cases, your organization's requirements can be met by creating a storyboard that visually models how the corporate portal solution will look and work (covered in Chapter 12), a collection of financial reports that establish the investment required and when the return on that investment will be realized (covered in Chapter 13), and an initial project plan that outlines the resources, activities, employees, and milestones that compose the corporate portal (covered in Chapter 14). Before the more complex aspects of the corporate portal solution can be analyzed and presented in the business case, the basic details of how this solution fits in your organization needs to be addressed. Three considerations are:

1. Strengths associated with the implementation of a corporate portal solution
2. Weaknesses associated with the implementation of a corporate portal solution
3. Identification of critical success factors for the corporate portal solution

Corporate Portal Solution Strengths

Your research will establish corporate portal strengths for your organization. The corporate portal solution will evolve from its initial focus to connect employees to many information sources into a knowledge gathering and analysis solution that facilitates the ability to make intelligent business decisions. There should be easily recognized benefits in the areas of data integration and distributed user communities. By creating a network of applications and data sources for employees to access in corporate portal content pages, employees can quickly locate information without having to switch between several enterprise systems and applications. Providing access to structured and unstructured data—often on the same content page—is important. The ability to establish and promote user communities that break geographic and time zone barriers is a strength that could be important to your organization. The design of these corporate portal communities is to allow employees the ability to easily interact with their coworkers. Additional benefits include integration with existing authentication schemes to reduce the time to deploy and administrate the corporate portal solution, and taxonomy and metadata features that help classify corporate resources and data sources for easy reference and retrieval. Here are some questions you can ask to identify strengths:

IDENTIFYING CORPORATE PORTAL SOLUTION STRENGTHS

- ☐ Does the corporate portal solution being proposed create a consistent view of your organization that employees can easily understand?
- ☐ Does the corporate portal solution being proposed enhance information organization and search capabilities for your organization?
- ☐ Does the corporate portal solution allow direct access to corporate knowledge experts and other important resources?
- ☐ Does the corporate portal solution allow direct access to reports, analysis, and queries that employees need to perform their jobs?
- ☐ Does the corporate portal solution allow direct access to relevant information that will provide additional knowledge to employees as they perform their jobs?
- ☐ Does the corporate portal solution provide identity profiles that allow employees personalized access to their knowledge desktop?

Corporate Portal Solution Weaknesses

One of the most important research activities is to identify the weaknesses associated with the implementation of a corporate portal solution in your organization. Why? Because these weaknesses identify the reasons a corporate portal solution would fail in your organization. In most situations, the process of outlining the weaknesses is the reverse of specifying the strengths. Here are some questions you can ask to ascertain weaknesses:

IDENTIFYING CORPORATE PORTAL SOLUTION WEAKNESSES

☐ Is the corporate portal solution unique from other products or services available in your organization? If not, this lack of differentiation may be a fatal weakness.

☐ Is there so much competition among projects or funding that it may be impossible to create a corporate portal solution in your organization? If so, the lack of being able to integrate a corporate portal into an existing initiative within your organization may be an important weakness.

☐ Is it possible to identify and get consensus on the information or features to include in the corporate portal? If a consensus cannot be gained for the first implementation of the corporate portal information, this may be a major weakness.

For many new proposals, the primary weaknesses are associated with the newness of the solution itself. Potential users of the corporate portal may not realize the goals or purpose of the corporate portal solution. A marketing and communication strategy may need to be considered as part of the business case to help overcome this lack of awareness. The identification and documentation of a staged delivery process should also be considered. As identified issues are resolved and employees begin to accept the corporate portal solution, this weakness will be eliminated.

Corporate Portal Critical Success Factors

After analyzing the nature and contemplating the future of a corporate portal solution for your organization, the strategy team must determine the critical success factors that affect successful performance. Critical success factors to include in the business case should be focused on the internal variables that influence the risks associated with the entire organization. These factors need to be identified early in the process and referred to regularly throughout the implementation of the corporate portal strategy. The critical success factors should identify how a corporate portal solution addresses the organization and corporate portal mission statement outlined at the beginning of the business case documentation. The critical success factors will be unique for different departments and users of the corporate portal solution. For this reason it is important for the strategy team to understand the nature of the volatility between the different factions and use this information to categorize and prioritize the critical success factors in the business case documentation. The primary reason to formally post the critical success factors and objectives is to preclude the pursuit of strategies designed to achieve mutually exclusive (or conflicting) goals. It is appropriate to have all primary goals and critical success factors listed as long as any inconsistent secondary critical success factors are acknowledged in the business case documentation.

CorporatePortal.com Case Study

The CorporatePortal.com mission defines our organization and is continually referenced to successfully identify and measure our goals and objectives. The internal infrastructure and systems implemented at CorporatePortal.com are designed to assist in the execution of this mission. A corporate portal solution has been analyzed, and is being proposed to improve the ability of employees to understand and complete corporate objectives, fulfilling the organization's mission.

Corporate Portal Critical Success Factors

After completing the internal evaluation of existing systems and solutions, the company realizes that several corporate objectives are only partially being met. CorporatePortal.com is interested in taking advantage of existing technologies, systems, and applications. The corporate portal solution is being evaluated to enhance how decisions are made and provide knowledge-sharing aspects to existing processes. The goals and critical success factors identified for the company's corporate portal solution include providing:

- Improvements and enhancements to the decision cycle
- A consistent view of the organization
- Information organization and search capabilities
- Direct access to corporate knowledge and resources
- Direct links to reports, analysis, and queries
- Direct links to related or relative data
- Personalized access to content

Additional research and interviews need to be completed to determine how a corporate portal solution can address the list of critical success factors. The software functions and universal features that describe how each of the critical success factors can be measured also need to be included in the business case documentation. In addition, CorporatePortal.com will have a better idea of the risk associated with each of the critical success factors once the strengths and weaknesses of the corporate portal solution have been identified. The company identifies the following strengths for this first implementation of the portal solution:

- The portal desktop interface runs within a web browser and gives employees access to information, experts, and other features made possible from a central location.
- The portal desktop allows data from multiple sources (e.g., enterprise IT systems and databases, collaboration systems, the intranet, and the Internet) to be combined into a tailored display for each user.
- Personalization features allow users to choose the information presented in the portal desktop. The user also has control over the appearance (i.e., layout and colors) of their personal desktop.
- All users have unique identities that describe their roles, activities, skills, and organizational objectives. A subset of this business identity can be used to drive the presentation of information tailored to an individual user's tasks. This unique identity can also

be used to link individuals as knowledge workers to information throughout CorporatePortal.com.

- Notifications are provided regarding exceptions to current processes and alerts that need to be communicated or highlighted. These notifications are available to users automatically and brought to the attention of the portal desktop user when the related data source or application is accessed.

- The pages and reports available in the portal desktop can be turned into discussion topics, meeting invitations, and e-mail messages, or they can be added to the document repository.

BUILDING THE CORPORATE PORTAL BUSINESS CASE

Only when all the corporate portal strategy activities have been completed and your final analysis is done will you have the information needed to explain the real demand for a corporate portal by employees throughout your organization. The final analysis and the feasibility study are documented as a corporate portal business case. This document includes an explanation of the demand and an associated cost structure that yields a sufficient return on investment (ROI) to justify the investment in time, human resources, and money that must be made by your organization to deliver a corporate portal solution. The time investment is presented as a project timeline and plan. The corporate portal project plan must address the planning, architecture and design, development, and deployment activities for the first phase of the corporate portal solution. The business case is based on preliminary decisions coming out of the research and analysis activities. The actual corporate portal project will require the consensus and approval of the user community, business domain experts, and project sponsors regarding the business functions, self-service applications, IT environment, and software applications before development of the corporate portal solution begins.

A complete business case should be prepared that provides a description of the corporate portal solution and its impact on your organization. The research required to build the business case provides most of the information required to prepare the documentation. The business case must be specific and well written. The executive summary section must address and answer the most important issues that approvers of the corporate portal solution are interested in. Once the business case has been completed, the corporate portal strategy team must consider several presentation methods. They range from printed copies to be distributed to PowerPoint presentations, a demonstration, collaborative discussions, and question-and-answer sessions, among other methods. First, it should be recognized that all plans are subject to change depending on circumstances and the passage of time. What was a reasonable case last quarter may no longer be reasonable this month. The business case documentation should therefore be version controlled so that it can be updated on an as-requested basis. Chapter 4 gives more details on preparing the business case for your corporate portal project.

CorporatePortal.com Case Study

CorporatePortal.com has determined that its corporate portal solution is consistent with the existing knowledge management initiative. If the executive decision is made to move forward with the corporate portal project based on the results of the financial metrics and analysis included in the business case, the corporate portal project will be categorized as an enterprise project to be funded as part of the knowledge management budget. The material and conclusions in this business case are developed as CorporatePortal.com case study examples throughout the course of the book; Chapter 15 describes the complete "CorporatePortal.com Business Case."

KEY POINTS

1. The corporate portal strategy is the process that provides a road map for the creation of the corporate portal solution business case. The activities that are included as part of this process include:

- Information technology review
- Identification of preliminary corporate portal business functions

- Storyboarding
- Financial analysis
- Creation of the corporate portal project plan

2. The objectives of your corporate portal strategy include:

- Defining a high-level overview of corporate portal concepts and technologies.
- Understanding the IT environment.
- Identifying and defining the highest-level business requirements.
- Determining the corporate portal solution overview.
- Defining the corporate portal solution storyboard.
- Defining the financial analysis.
- Defining the preliminary project plan.
- Building the corporate portal business case.

3. The documentation deliverables of your corporate portal strategy include:

- Business case document (corporate portal proposal)
- IT assessment
- Preliminary storyboard
- Financial metrics analysis
- Preliminary project plan

4. Several key elements of information about your organization need to be identified, defined, and documented as part of your corporate portal strategy research. These include:

- Strengths associated with the implementation of a corporate portal solution
- Weaknesses associated with the implementation of a corporate portal solution
- Identification of critical success factors for the corporate portal solution

4

The Corporate Portal Business Case

The purpose for creating a business case is to build a proposal for a corporate portal that can convince your organization to move forward with this initiative as a knowledge management solution. The business case documentation should be used as a tool to support the planning and decision-making activities required to move forward with a corporate or enterprise portal. The business case documentation outlines the infrastructure requirements, the self-service applications and features requirements, suggested standards and best practices, discounted cash flow, payback period, and internal rate of return that a corporate portal solution can offer your organization. As you collect information and complete the research and analysis activities, you can reach conclusions regarding the financial and other business consequences of a corporate portal solution. Once you have determined that a corporate portal business case is a necessary tool to present the corporate portal as a knowledge management initiative to decision makers in your organization, a wide spectrum of detailed information needs to be collected from almost every source in your organization. The process may seem overwhelming. There are five fundamental steps to be completed:

1. Laying out the basic corporate portal concepts.
2. Gathering data on the feasibility and specifics of the corporate portal concepts.

3. Focusing and refining the corporate portal concepts based on the data compiled.
4. Outlining the specifics of your proposed corporate portal solution.
5. Putting your business case in a compelling format.

CORPORATE PORTAL SOFTWARE FUNCTIONS AND UNIVERSAL FEATURES

You are not required to create exhaustive research activities; your goal is to locate information that answers basic questions about the purpose and need for a corporate portal in your organization. Your research needs to be thorough enough to give the strategy team and executives in your organization the confidence that the answers provided are accurate and from reliable sources. The final results of the research are compiled into the business case, supporting documentation, and presentations. You want to outline the benefits that a corporate portal solution can provide your organization as you presently conceive the value. Consider the following checklists:

IMPROVING AND ENHANCING THE DECISION CYCLE

☐ Are there many exceptions to defined processes?
☐ Are decisions made consistently throughout your organization?
☐ Do employees know where to look up standard procedures or answers to frequently asked questions?
☐ Are decisions made quickly and accurately?
☐ Are processes changing quickly, making correct or consistent decisions difficult?

PRESENTING A CONSISTENT VIEW OF YOUR ORGANIZATION

Determine whether there are current IT projects, issues, and standards for the following software functions:

☐ Data points and integration
☐ Taxonomy
☐ Search capabilities

☐ Help features
☐ Content management
☐ Process and action
☐ Collaboration and communication
☐ Personalization
☐ Presentation
☐ Administration
☐ Security

THE CORPORATE PORTAL BUSINESS CASE COMPONENTS

Once you have established a first pass of your corporate portal concepts, the next step is to verify or compile additional information to reevaluate your concepts so you have enough information to actually write the business case. A suggested business case outline for a corporate portal solution follows:

Corporate Portal Business Case Outline

   I. Mission Statements
      A. Organization Mission
      B. Corporate Portal Mission
  II. Executive Summary
      A. Business Need and Opportunity
      B. Corporate Portal Definition
      C. Financial Metrics Statement
      D. Key Characteristics of a Corporate Portal
      E. Structure and Important Features of the Corporate Portal Solution
 III. Corporate Portal Solution Overview
      A. Critical Success Factors
         1. Business Factors
         2. Infrastructure Factors
         3. Other Factors
      B. Information Technology Analysis
      C. Business Process and Information Needs Analysis
 IV. Corporate Portal Team Members and Business Domain Experts

    V. Corporate Portal Storyboard and Script
   VI. Financial Metrics Analysis
  VII. Staged Delivery Analysis
      A. Staged Delivery Proposal
 VIII. Preliminary Project Plan and Timeline
   IX. Appendices (Optional)
      A. Information Technology Analysis and Results
         1. Organizational Environment
         2. Network Infrastructure
         3. Messaging Infrastructure
         4. Collaboration Systems
         5. Intranet Strategy
         6. Data Sources
            a. Messaging Infrastructure
            b. Collaboration and Groupware Systems
            c. Intranet and Internet Strategies
            d. Portal Software Applications
            e. Enterprise Resource Planning (ERP) Systems
            f. Enterprise Systems and Applications
            g. Cultural Considerations
      B. Business Process and Information Needs Analysis and Results
         1. Self-Service Application(s) Identified (Discovery)
            a. Processes
            b. Roles
         2. Corporate Portal Software Functions
         3. Corporate Portal Universal Features
      C. Financial Metrics Analysis and Results
         1. Analysis Methods
         2. Risk
         3. Quantifiable Benefits
         4. Quantified Costs
         5. Financial Metrics Summary

With accurate information and a solid understanding of your organization you should be able to make a persuasive presentation of the business case when meeting with decision makers in your organization. To begin the information gathering efforts, you should locate the business domain experts and create interviews or schedule meetings to collect the information needed. Determine what is to be included in the corporate portal business case and establish the interviews around the areas of expertise of the individuals being interviewed. As you progress through the interview process, you must determine the areas that need additional focus. Continue to probe into issues that have significant risk associated with them to compile the information necessary to make functionality, operational, and financial decisions that can be documented and included in the business case.

MISSION STATEMENTS

The corporate portal strategy team is responsible for documenting how your organization will benefit from a corporate portal solution. It's critical to review your organization's mission statement to verify that the corporate portal solution assists in the execution of the overall mission. You can write down the reasons in a short narrative statement that reflects your motivations and the benefits that would be realized by your organization. This short narrative statement is called a mission statement.

There are two mission statements included in the corporate portal business case:

1. The organization's mission statement that should concisely describe the goals, objectives, and underlying principles of your company. It is designed to articulate and clarify the philosophy of the organization.
2. The corporate portal mission statement that describes how a corporate portal solution adds value to the mission of the organization.

Both mission statements should be at or near the beginning of the business case to set the tone regarding the aspects of the corporate portal solution that are aimed at achieving the overall purpose of your organization. You should be able to document the basic objectives of the corporate portal in just a few sentences. One statement should describe the nature of the corporate portal solution in your organization, the philosophy, and the guiding principles of how the corporate portal helps the organization. A possible corporate portal mission statement might be:

> Implement a knowledge management initiative through a corporate portal application by providing immediate access to essential companywide information and allowing the users of that information to analyze and act upon the information to make consistent and timely business decisions.

You will want to map the corporate portal mission statement into the philosophy and purpose of the organization's mission. Consider the following checklists:

MAPPING THE CORPORATE PORTAL MISSION TO KEY COMPONENTS OF THE ORGANIZATION'S MISSION STATEMENT

- ☐ What is the range of products or names of services offered by your organization?
- ☐ What is the quality standard for your organization?
- ☐ What are the pricing standards for your organization?
- ☐ What are the details regarding products or services provided by your organization?
- ☐ What is the overall relationship to customers?
- ☐ What is the management style or relationship to employees?
- ☐ What is the nature of the work environment?
- ☐ What makes your organization unique in the industry?
- ☐ What is the philosophy regarding incorporating new technology or other new developments?
- ☐ What are the growth or profitability goals?
- ☐ What is the relationship to the community, customers, environment, or others?
- ☐ What are other management goals?

THE CORPORATE PORTAL VALUE PROPOSITION

Value propositions that can be mapped to the key components of the organization's mission statement include:

☐ Improvements and enhancements to the decision cycle
☐ A consistent view of your organization
☐ Information organization and search capabilities
☐ Direct access to corporate knowledge and resources
☐ Direct links to reports, analysis, and queries
☐ Direct links to relative data and knowledge experts
☐ Individual identity and personalized access to content

EXECUTIVE SUMMARY

The single most important section of your corporate portal business case is the executive summary. This portion of the document must be clear, concise, and a compelling condensation of your corporate portal proposal. The executive summary is the most-read section of the business case and, based on it, executive decision makers will determine whether they are going to spend the time to evaluate the proposed corporate portal solution.

The executive summary should be written last. This portion of the business case reflects the results of all your research and planning and should be documented only after careful consideration of all aspects of your corporate portal business case have been identified. If executives in your organization are only interested in a "concept paper" to gauge project proposals before requesting a complete business case, the executive summary should be able to serve as that document.

The executive summary allows readers to understand the purpose of the corporate portal business case quickly and decide whether to review the entire proposal. The executive summary should include the following types of information:

- Reasons a corporate portal solution makes sense for your organization
- Verification that the corporate portal solution has been thoroughly planned
- Description of the capabilities of the corporate portal strategy team and proposed project team
- The goals, critical success factors, and significant competitive advantages that the corporate portal solution provides

- Realistic return on investment (ROI) or cost/benefit projections

There are two types of executive summaries. The synopsis is more straightforward and simply relays in an abbreviated fashion the conclusions of the sections included in the business case. The narrative summary is designed to tell a story and can be organized in any order, with emphasis placed on the concepts and distinctive features of the corporate portal solution and less attention given to operational details. The executive summary can be one page in length and should be no longer than two or three pages. The highlights from each section of the business case should be summarized in one or two sentences. The following checklist can be used as a guide in summarizing a business case:

Writing the Executive Summary

☐ *Corporate Portal Mission.* Write the concise corporate portal mission statement.

☐ *Corporate Portal Solution Overview.* List the corporate portal value propositions, goals, and critical success factors that provide knowledge management solutions to employees throughout your organization.

☐ *Corporate Portal Business Domain Experts.* Briefly describe the histories and capabilities of the management team that is proposing the corporate portal solution.

☐ *Information Technology Analysis and Results.* Describe the infrastructure, software, and hardware resources to support the corporate portal solution.

☐ *Business Process and Information Needs Analysis and Results.* Describe the full range of services that are offered by the corporate portal solution, the proposed business functions, and the self-service applications to be included in the first phase of the corporate portal project.

☐ *Financial Metrics Analysis and Results.* Indicate the expected return on investment or the results of the cost/benefit analysis for the first phase of the corporate portal solution in the first year.

☐ *Staged Delivery Analysis and Results.* Describe the histories and capabilities of the proposed corporate portal project team; include a list of the milestones to be used to measure the success of the corporate portal solution and the dates you expect to reach them.

CORPORATE PORTAL SOLUTION OVERVIEW

The corporate portal solution overview is primarily straightforward information about the proposed solution. If you have evaluated the corporate portal concepts and how they apply to your organization, then this research is the basis of the information that needs to be included in this section of the business case. Before you discuss the more complex aspects of the corporate portal solution, a section about corporate portals in general is useful. You can create a synopsis of knowledge portals or corporate portals, the benefits they provide, and the shortcomings your research identified. Consider the following checklists:

WRITING THE CORPORATE PORTAL SOLUTION OVERVIEW

☐ Define the corporate portal and identify the business need and opportunity.
☐ Identify the impact of external factors on the corporate portal.
☐ Include any internal analysis of corporate portal needs in your organization.
☐ Determine the corporate portal primary benefits.
☐ Identify corporate portal strengths for your organization.
☐ Identify corporate portal weaknesses for your organization.

CORPORATE PORTAL BUSINESS DOMAIN EXPERTS

The quality of the employees involved in the creation of the corporate portal strategy has a significant impact on the success of the corporate portal solution. Decision makers in your organization know that the experience, skills, and personalities of the employees selected for your corporate portal teams will have great impact on the success of the project. You may be surprised how many executives are likely to review the business domain experts to scrutinize whom the business case originated from. When selecting the business domain experts and developing your business case, you should focus on and identify two main areas that represent the core of your management system:

- The employees that run your business
- Your organization's management structure and style

You need to create a summary of the contributions and skills of the corporate portal strategy team and business domain experts that contributed to the corporate portal business case. Consider the following checklist:

IDENTIFYING THE CORPORATE PORTAL STRATEGY TEAM AND BUSINESS DOMAIN EXPERTS

For each employee, include the following information:

☐ Employee name
☐ Role and title
☐ Experience
☐ Successes
☐ Strengths
☐ Areas in which employee lacks strength

INFORMATION TECHNOLOGY ANALYSIS AND RESULTS

The ability to implement a corporate portal solution or any other knowledge management initiative depends on the information technology (IT) department's contribution of knowledge, time, and resources to the project. A survey should be created by the corporate portal strategy team, and submitted for the IT department to complete (information to consider and use to create the IT survey is available in Chapter 10). Once you have worked with members of the IT department to complete the IT interview questions, you must analyze the results for your internal planning purposes, coordinate that information, and document the results. The summary you create is then added to the corporate portal business case. Consider the following checklist:

PREPARING THE INFORMATION TECHNOLOGY ANALYSIS AND RESULTS SYNOPSIS

Summarize sections from the IT analysis and include the following information in the business case:

☐ Background
☐ Messaging infrastructure
☐ Collaboration systems
☐ Intranet strategy
☐ Internet strategy
☐ Search systems
☐ Online help systems
☐ Content management systems
☐ Enterprise resource planning (ERP) systems
☐ Line of business (LOB) systems
☐ Legacy applications
☐ Data warehouse and data mart systems
☐ Business intelligence and executive information systems
☐ Knowledge management systems
☐ Cultural considerations (acceptance of the corporate portal solution by employees)
☐ Corporate portal management
☐ Administration
☐ Technical staff and support

BUSINESS PROCESS AND INFORMATION NEEDS ANALYSIS AND RESULTS

Any meetings and sessions that focus on establishing business process and information needs should include key representatives from your organization's IT department and several business domain experts. Business domain experts include managers of different departments, network and applications development personnel, and support staff. Business domain expert representatives should be drawn from groups that have expressed an interest in intranet technology to further their knowledge management and business goals. The corporate portal business functions and self-service applications considered and selected are reviewed and documented. The summary you create is added as a section in the corporate portal business case. Use following checklist as your guide:

PREPARING THE BUSINESS PROCESS AND INFORMATION NEEDS ANALYSIS AND RESULTS SYNOPSIS

Summarize sections from the business process and information needs analysis, then include the following information in the business case:

- ☐ Self-service applications and business functions identified
- ☐ Goals and critical success factors
- ☐ Application functionality described
- ☐ Data sources identified
- ☐ Search requirements
- ☐ Online help requirements
- ☐ Collaboration requirements
- ☐ Navigation features
- ☐ Relevant information features
- ☐ Personalization features
- ☐ Security requirements
- ☐ Corporate portal users identified
- ☐ Documentation requirements
- ☐ Content management requirements
- ☐ End-user training requirements

CORPORATE PORTAL STORYBOARD

It's recommended that storyboards and associated scripts also be included as a section of the business case. A visual representation of the corporate portal user interface can clarify the value propositions of the corporate portal solution. A series of storyboards accompanied by a script can establish how activities, tasks, responsibilities, and corporate information can be combined in a single user interface that allows a user to work effectively, with personalization features that provide organization and structure unique to each employee. You need to make the storyboards available in a variety of formats (e.g., black-and-white for making copies of the business case and color for presentations). The following checklist is a guide for creating a storyboard and script summary.

CREATING A STORYBOARD AND SCRIPT SUMMARY

Summarize a defined subset of the business processes and self-service applications as a visual representation or model; include these elements in the business case:

- ☐ The site map defined (navigation overview)
- ☐ The roles included in the storyboard
- ☐ The content pages included in the storyboard
- ☐ The content windows included in the storyboard
- ☐ The content-relevant information included in the storyboard
- ☐ The personalization features included in the storyboard
- ☐ The storyboard scripts defined

FINANCIAL METRICS ANALYSIS AND RESULTS

There are different approaches, each with a variety of definitions, that can be used to evaluate the financial consequences of implementing a corporate portal solution. It is important that the strategy team includes and documents the line items that are included in the corporate portal business case, the time period evaluated, and the assumptions used to calculate the financial metrics. An effective conclusion needs to be documented and should concentrate on supporting the objectives of the corporate portal solution. The conclusions and formal recommendation should be included in the executive summary of the business case and can be used to remind the decision makers to give special consideration to the important contingencies and dependencies regarding your corporate portal proposal. The financial metrics information you create should be added as a section in the corporate portal business case.

The analysis is based on a comparison of the total benefits of the application with the total costs. For example:

Total Benefits

- Direct increases in revenue
- Direct reduction in expenses
- Increased satisfaction of key stakeholders (measured through surveys and usability acceptance of the portal desktop)

Total Costs

- Direct costs (e.g., software, services, training, hardware)
- Indirect costs (e.g., decreased productivity during system changeover, parallel system support).

Return on investment analysis is used to determine the ratio of the estimated total positive benefits to the estimated total costs of a project. Usually you create the ROI analysis for the first year of the corporate portal solution. The ROI analysis consists of two calculations: ROI and payback period. Each is defined as follows:

- *Return on investment is the percentage of benefit relative to total cost over a period of time (usually a year).* Most organizations look for at least an annualized ROI of 20 percent, although some ROI calculations may reach 100 percent or more. The calculation is as follows:

ROI = Estimated Total Positive Benefits / Estimated Total Costs

- *Payback period is the length of time required for the benefits to exceed the costs.* It depicts the rate at which the organization realizes the return. Since companies often make decisions based on a budgetary cycle or available cash flow, the payback period calculation is often valuable in helping your organization decide when to begin a project. Also, the payback period is beneficial when discussing the beginning of any subsequent stages of the application. A very rapid payback period is three to four months; most organizations will expect a payback period of nine to ten months.

A second ROI analysis is conducted at the conclusion of the project (once the corporate portal system is in production) to verify that your organization is receiving the benefits that were originally estimated. On large projects, an interim ROI analysis is also run in order to:

- Evaluate if project costs are rising.
- Reevaluate if the business requirements or environment is changing.
- Determine if the benefits for the project are over- or under-estimated.

Use the checklist that follows as a guide to preparing a financial metrics synopsis.

PREPARING A FINANCIAL METRICS SYNOPSIS

Summarize a defined subset of the financial metrics and include the following information in the business case:

- ☐ Cost of ownership (COO)
- ☐ Return on investment (ROI)
- ☐ Cost/benefit analysis
- ☐ Net cash flow
- ☐ Discounted cash flow
- ☐ Internal rate of return (IRR)
- ☐ Payback period
- ☐ Cost and benefit models
- ☐ Assumptions
- ☐ Boundaries
- ☐ Data sources and methods

STAGED DELIVERY ANALYSIS AND RESULTS

Building an enterprisewide corporate portal solution is an extremely complex task that requires the commitment of several key employees within your organization. In contrast, planning a corporate portal solution that can successfully approach and meet your knowledge management initiatives is possible. The corporate portal solution should be defined as an iterative development project with well-organized phases using well-defined processes. The entire collection of corporate portal project phases with defined functionality and features is the complete enterprisewide solution. This process allows you to present a business case that addresses the larger issues while focusing on the initial resources, budgets, and efforts of the corporate portal project.

When determining what to include in the initial phases of the corporate portal, you should define the discovery strategy used to establish the requirements for the corporate portal solution. This strategy in effect organizes requirements by responsibilities, activities, or workgroups. The final collection of material identified during discovery is used to define the scope of your organization's business case. The discovery strategy entails the following activities:

- *Identifying existing functions.* The functions initially selected must have well-defined data sources, business processes, and user interface requirements. Use templates and diagrams to logically present the required functionality and the corporate portal software functions that need to be included to facilitate the value propositions a corporate portal solution offers.

- *Using techniques and tools.* It is important that you select techniques and tools that help the corporate portal strategy team walk through the discovery process so that you will know with some degree of certainty that the majority of the information needed to build a solid business case has been collected or identified and documented.

- *Building the corporate portal solution incrementally and iteratively.* Building the system incrementally provides the opportunity for the decisions or requirements initially identified to be reevaluated, so enhancements and other approved changes can be fed into the next iteration or phase of the corporate portal development process.

- *Using a software development methodology.* Your internal IT department has probably identified a software development methodology to follow when implementing solutions in your organization.

Methodologies and Models

You will want to establish a methodology that can be followed for the corporate portal project. A methodology is a collection of techniques for building models that are applied across the development of a software system (i.e., software life cycle). Your IT department should have standards for creating models used for software projects. Verify with your IT department that your corporate portal development team agrees on how the software life cycle, tools, techniques, methodologies, and other software development activities and processes will be used and followed.

The corporate portal solution uses models to describe the systems. A good software design methodology should provide several models to describe the solution. These models are used by different groups of users for different reasons, and they substantiate each other and verify that the corporate portal project has been well planned. The types of models your team might want to consider are:

Logical Model

- Defines what the business rules and self-service application requirements are.
- Defines how the business processes and corporate portal features are related.

Structural Model

- Defines the structure of the system.
- Defines the objects and how they are related.

Functional Model

- Defines the functions of the system.
- Defines how data flows through the system.

Control Model

- Defines how the system reacts to external events.
- Defines how each event flows in the system.

Each model uses a different type of diagram to document and illustrate the composition and flow it's designed to illustrate. These are:

Logical Model Diagrams

- *Entity Relationship Diagrams.* Describe the objects of the system in terms of their attributes and how they are related.

Structural Model Diagrams

- *Class Diagrams.* Describe the structure of the system in terms of classes and objects.

Functional Model Diagrams

- *Case Diagrams (Scripts).* Describe the external behavior of the system from the point of view of the functions performed.

Control Model

- *Sequence Diagrams.* Describe the dynamic interaction between objects identified in the structural model.
- *Activity Diagrams.* Describe the dynamic behavior of a single object.

PREPARING A STAGED DELIVERY ANALYSIS AND RESULTS SYNOPSIS

Summarize the staged delivery or iterative development process being used to implement the corporate portal solution. It should yield the following information to be incorporated into the business case:

☐ Software life cycle description
☐ Methodologies and models description
☐ Tools and techniques description

PRELIMINARY PROJECT PLAN AND TIMELINE

The preliminary project plan and timeline can easily be created from a third-party project management software application such as Microsoft Project. The overview of the initial tasks, milestones, and resources compiled to achieve the implementation of the first phase of the corporate portal solution needs to be included in the preliminary project plan and timeline section of the corporate portal business case. The types of information you want to incorporate include:

• *An assessment of your corporate portal solution and description of project objectives.* Define the complexity of the first phases of your corporate portal solution and identify any constraints that must be included. Formulate objectives that are specific to the scope of the corporate portal project, the user community that is affected, and the timeline that needs to be met.

• *Identification of project tasks, milestones, and resources.* The goal is to generate a list of the initial key tasks and their durations. You should concentrate on the relationship between tasks (e.g., which tasks depend on each other, which tasks occur repeatedly, what milestones and resources are required to complete identified tasks).

• *Refinement of the project plan.* The initial outline of the corporate portal solution needs to be created. The strategy team must identify the skills and procedures required to implement the first phases of the corporate portal solution. Any constraints identified (e.g., fixed costs, deadlines, or problems in communication about the project status) need to be documented.

APPENDICES (OPTIONAL)

There is a limitation to the amount of information that can be included in the corporate portal business case. You may be unable to expand on several items of interest in much detail in the business case documentation. In this case you can prepare an appendix that includes additional information that supports, confirms, and reinforces conclusions that are identified in the business case. An appendix is not required; the only reason to include one or more of this element is if the additional information is compelling or can be used as reference material.

KEY POINTS

The purpose for creating a business case is to build a proposal for a corporate portal that will convince your organization to move forward with this initiative as a knowledge management solution. The business case documentation should be used as a tool to support the planning and decision-making activities required by your organization. The main sections of the business case documentation are as follows:

- Corporate portal software features and universal features defined
- Corporate portal business case components
- Mission statements (for the organization at large and the corporate portal project in particular)
- Executive summary
- Corporate portal solution overview
- Corporate portal business domain experts
- Information technology analysis and results
- Business process and information needs analysis and results
- Corporate portal storyboard
- Financial metrics analysis and results
- Staged delivery analysis and results
- Preliminary project plan and timeline
- Appendices (optional)

5

Information Organization and Search Capabilities

The charter of the corporate portal is to provide a single point-of-access to information across your organization through a browser-based interface that encapsulates all of the corporate portal's functionality. Typically these are multiple, disparate sources feeding information into the portal desktop. The presentation design plays a critical role in the self-service applications deployed as a part of the complete corporate portal solution. The employee's experience with the corporate portal ultimately determines the effectiveness of the deployed self-service applications. As new applications are incorporated, the strategy created for the corporate portal needs to address how the presentation layer is affected or updated. When developing a presentation layer strategy, you need to keep two issues in mind:

• The corporate portal is accessing several different types and sources of information and many of them need to be designed or summarized and displayed in a small space.

• The appearance of the corporate portal must communicate effectively to each employee in your organization.

The key elements to include in the corporate portal presentation layer strategy are:

- *Information Gathering* (i.e., clarity of information and features presented to the employee)

- *Decision Support* (i.e., strength of context from an organizational and functional perspective)

- *Easy Access and Configuration* (i.e., full support for portal desktop—or interface—personalization to improve individual communication, quality of information, navigation, and the user's ability to take action or make decisions)

The corporate portal solution requires that all the software functions work together in a way that provides structure to the information and features available. You should have an overview of the benefits your organization is looking for in a corporate portal solution and a rough idea of some software functions and features to incorporate into the solution. The next step as a corporate portal strategist is to look closer into how enterprise information can be organized, presented, and easily found from the portal desktop. The corporate portal user-interface components include:

- Portal banner
- Portal menu
- Personalization
- Content page tab(s)
- Content page
- Content window(s)
- Content-relevant information

You can employ several user-interface and design features to enhance the corporate portal user-interface components to make the solution user-friendly so it's easy to find information with minimal training requirements. Portal software vendors provide a desktop that contains these user-interface features. Each vendor uses different names and marketing terms for these user-interface elements. The idea, however, is that these desktop elements work together to incorporate the software functions and universal features needed to fulfill your corporate portal objectives. Consider the portal desktop available from InfoImage (see Figure 5-1). The user interface components are integrated as follows:

Figure 5-1. InfoImage portal desktop.

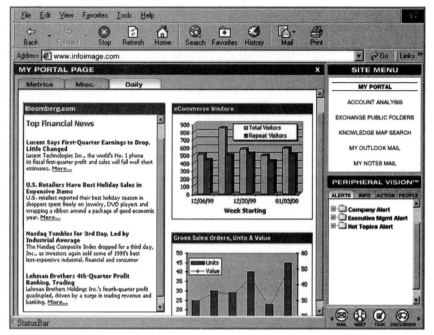

- *Portal Banner*. This feature is integrated in the content page and content windows as company logos and titles.

- *Portal Menu*. This is the main menu hierarchy referenced as the Site Menu.

- *Personalization*. This functionality is available from the Personalization Site Menu option (not shown). The Personalization content page allows users to set global features that will be available on every content page as well as define and organize the content windows that will appear on each content page.

- *Content Page Tab(s)*. This feature is part of the content page used to create subsets of the larger collection of content page information. The content page tabs include metrics, miscellaneous, and daily.

- *Content Page*. This is the largest window or frame. It contains one or many content windows, content page tabs, and content-relevant information (peripheral vision).

- *Content Window(s)*. This is a content window that constitutes a data object in your organization. Collections of related content windows are often grouped together and presented in a content page. The content windows on the daily content page include Bloomberg.com; e-commerce visitors; and gross sales orders, units, and value.

- *Content-Relevant Information*. These are reflected in the Peripheral Vision section of the desktop. This section of the portal desktop contains notifications and hyperlinks to important information that the user needs access to within your organization.

A second portal desktop example with a different look and layout can be seen in the TopTier user interface (see Figure 5-2). The same elements are available as follows:

- *Portal Banner*. This feature is located at the top of the portal menu information and can be customized to your organization's logo.

Figure 5-2. TopTier portal desktop.

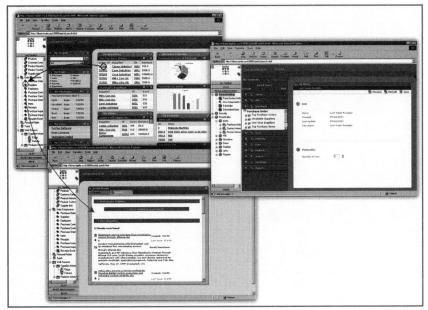

• *Portal Menu.* This is the main menu hierarchy referenced as My Toolbar. There are several menus available that are expanded and collapsed along the left-hand column.

• *Personalization.* This functionality is available from each portal desktop object for the user to change each element individually. Global personalization features are available from the Portal Administration menu option located below My Toolbar.

• *Content Page Tab(s).* This feature (not shown in Figure 5-2) is available as part of the content page as a second option to create subsets of the larger collection of content page information.

• *Content Page.* This is the context window or frame to display your organization's data, reports, and other information used by employees. The content page focuses on a single window or frame of information or can contain a collection of content windows.

• *Content Window(s).* This is a single data object in your organization to present summarized information to portal users.

• *Content-Relevant Information.* A collection of corporate notifications and hyperlinks (indicated by the arrows in Figure 5-2) to important information is reflected throughout the portal desktop; information is available from portal menu options, content windows, and e-mail notifications.

Search capabilities are included in this chapter as an additional navigation software function. The search element provides a centralized facility for refined and defined access to specified collections of data points and documents available throughout the enterprise and Internet. There is too much information in the enterprise for employees to know all the material and documents available to them as they perform their daily activities. To compound the problem, the number of systems and content published continues to expand and be relocated at an amazing rate. Additional tools and techniques are used to help employees identify and locate or relocate information specific to individual needs and tasks. Search is a simple research tool for employees when they need information on a topic or issue but do not know where to locate the information inside the organization. Search results and query functions should be included in the corporate portal solution. The search features included in the corporate portal are used several ways. They may be:

- Incorporated as predefined requests, with the result set displayed in content windows on content pages
- Ad hoc query screens that allow employees to submit a request and hyperlink into the result set returned

CORPORATE PORTAL INFORMATION ORGANIZATION

During the process of defining the self-service applications and functions for the corporate portal solution, you need to consider several issues regarding the layout or storyboard of the user interface. These include:

- Purpose and audience
- Content and navigation
- Quality and usability

Purpose and Audience

The user interface is the most important part of the corporate portal to the user. It is the most visible element and will make the biggest impression on employees. The usability of the portal desktop depends on users' acceptance of the interface. A number of decisions must be made about the interface. As you evaluate the self-service applications and business functions you want added to the corporate portal, you also want several features in the user interface to be consistent. These requirements are different for self-service applications whose primary purpose is displaying information and those self-service applications that gather information or provide data input screens. The employee roles intended to interact with each content window or data object also influences the design of the user interface. A self-service application that is aimed at employees less familiar with a task in your organization will require more help features than a self-service application designed for use by experienced employees. If the corporate portal solution is meant to be distributed internationally, language and culture considerations need to be considered. The design of the user interface is best approached as an iterative process. The perfect design will evolve over time. The main aspects of the user interface to consider are:

1. *Interface Styles.* The two most common user-interface styles: a multiple document interface and an expandable outline-style interface. The corporate portal often integrates both of these user-interface styles into the portal desktop. The multiple document interface allows you to display multiple documents at the same time. Each document is displayed in individual content page windows. The expandable outline-style interface is a single window containing two frames with a hierarchical view of folders on the left and a display or content page on the right. This type of interface is useful for navigating large numbers of documents, pictures, or files.

2. *Menu Options and Naming Guidelines.* Menu titles or captions should follow several guidelines:

- Menu names should be unique within a menu and may be repeated in different menus to represent the same action in another location or second menu.
- Menu names may be single, compound, or multiple words. Each menu name should have a keyboard access character. The access character should be the first letter of the menu title (each menu title needs a unique keyboard option per menu).
- An ellipsis (. . .) should follow menu items that require more information before they can be completed.
- Menu names need to be short.

3. *Submenu Guidelines.* A submenu branches off from the higher-level menu to display a new collection of menu items. You might create a submenu when the primary menu is full, to provide a function or feature that is used infrequently or to emphasize the relationship between menus.

4. *Toolbars.* A toolbar contains buttons that provide quick access to frequently used commands in an application and can enhance the menu interface of the corporate portal solution.

The implementation of the comfort and familiarity features in the corporate portal solution determine the level of knowledge and understanding users stand to gain from their experience using the solution. The consistency of menus and toolbars from content page to content page is important. Employees in your organization will view the corporate portal as the solution to accomplish a set of tasks and will insist that the tasks are easy to understand and perform. Your goal is to determine what controls are needed, the relative importance of the different elements, and the relationships between controls. The composition of the corporate portal needs to be established. Key composition issues to consider include:

- *Positioning of Controls.* Not all design elements are of equal importance in the corporate portal. The focus of your design ensures that the most important elements are apparent to corporate portal users. Important or frequently accessed elements are included on the portal menu. Less important elements are available in the relevant information section or through content page tabs. How the elements and controls are grouped together is important and should be established logically according to function or relationship. Buttons used for navigation should be grouped together to indicate their relationship to each other.
- *Consistency of Interface Elements.* A consistent location, look, and feel in the corporate portal creates a sense of familiarity and harmony, which adds a sense of order and everything fitting together. A lack of consistency in the user interface will create a sense of disorganization and confusion. The types of design elements that should be predefined include the types of controls to be included. You want to establish standards for size, font choices, and groupings. You should create prototypes of possible layouts and designs to help business domain experts make decisions regarding the consistency of interface elements.
- *"Form Follows Function" Design.* The user interface should include visual clues to the function of the elements included. You might include buttons that have a three-dimensional effect, to suggest they should be pushed. All the

buttons should have the same form throughout the corporate portal solution.

- *Use of White Space.* To emphasize elements and improve usability, blank space (referred to as white space) should be used effectively. The use of white space removes clutter from the user interface and adds focus to design elements. Consistent spacing and alignment of vertical and horizontal elements makes the design more appealing and readable.

- *Simplicity.* Divide the functionality throughout menus, submenus, toolboxes, and content page tabs to keep the individual content pages simple to use. A simple, logically organized design is always preferable. Creating groupings of information with similar purpose or functionality and with minimal scrolling requirements also reduces the amount of searching and typing that corporate portal users need to do.

- *Use of Color and Images.* A corporate portal application is going to be used by a large number of users, so it is usually best to use neutral (i.e., conservative) colors. Small amounts of bright color can be used to emphasize or draw attention to important areas on content pages. You should limit the number of colors in the corporate portal to create a consistent color scheme. Corporate portal users need to readily identify a function that is represented by icons or images.

- *Readability.* The font selected for use in the corporate portal solution should be readable at different resolutions and on different types of displays. Avoid decorative fonts since they are hard to read at smaller point sizes. Once again, consistency is important in the choice of fonts. Try to stick to one or two fonts in two or three different point sizes to make the corporate portal look cohesive.

To design the user interface for your corporate portal, you should review potential knowledge portal products, other standard user-interface options, and best-selling applications to determine what is appealing about them. You will probably find several common elements between applications such as toolbars, status bars, context-sensitive menus, and tabbed dialogs. You can also include your own experience as an end user to determine what you like most about user interfaces available in your favorite applications. Make sure that several members of the organization are included in making user-interface recommendations and decisions.

Content and Navigation

Depending on the roles, activities, and departments that employees belong to, their computers may need to be set up and configured so they can access the corporate portal and see the content pages and content windows they specifically need to complete their responsibilities. There should also be a collection of optional or user-selected content pages. Employees should be able to customize their portal desktop with content pages and content windows that interest them and add value to the way they work. These content pages should have consistent features, color themes, and other user-interface expectations. The goal of the content pages is to establish content aggregation and coordination of information. This is the idea that information follows a taxonomy and logical integration into the corporate portal solution.

The implementation of the self-service applications requires joint planning, development, and administration to successfully complete. The corporate portal strategy needs to be mapped out in terms of short-term and long-term business objectives. These corporate portal business objectives establish how structured and unstructured information needs to be presented for employees to use. There are several advantages the corporate portal solution can offer your employees. For example, the portal application permits:

- Collection of data from many sources
- Distribution of data in reports
- Collation of the data to provide employees a simplified view of complicated or overwhelming information
- Reduction of training and calls into the information technology (IT) department for personal assistance, provided the appropriate level of online documentation is available for employees to locate the answers they need

You need to work with business domain experts to define the information access requirements of employees in your organization.

The corporate portal is used to display reports in a format that combines ease of use and simplicity of presentation. Employees must be able to navigate through sections of reports using hyperlinks that allow them to move quickly from summary data to detail data or from one report to another. Each report is accessed online (i.e., not downloaded onto a hard drive) to ensure that the latest information is available and the response time can remain constant by incrementally updating displayed report contents. Administrators control permissions, security, report production, and maintenance to manage these reporting requirements.

When evaluating your organization's reporting infrastructure and identifying the technologies that can satisfy the needs of numerous user roles, there are a variety of different business questions to address. The final result, however, should provide a consistent and easy-to-use solution that supports a variety of different skill sets using the information provided. The types of reports employees will be most comfortable with (from most used to least used) include:

• *Predefined Reports*. There are reports that are created and updated with the most recent data on a schedule (e.g., hourly, daily, weekly, monthly) and distributed to employees.

• *Ad Hoc Reports*. These predefined report formats are only produced and distributed to employees when requested.

• *Parameterized Reports*. These are a collection of report formats that can be customized to accept different value ranges or selections. These parameters can include time (e.g., year, quarter, month), geography (e.g., state, county, city), or other available options.

• *Sophisticated Queries*. These are reports that are not currently predefined in the system. Users identify the data they need and the report format required. These report requests are submitted to the reporting system, created, and distributed.

• *Data Mining*. These reports are not based on existing report formats. This type of report request is designed to analyze data for the purpose of identifying and evaluating patterns and trends.

There are several existing projects or implemented systems in your organization that can provide information to the corporate portal to create this central knowledge desktop. They include:

- *Operational Data.* Data that is optimized for transactional processing. It is data that is updated often through online transactions. The data is not more than three to six months old (nonhistorical). Operational data is highly normalized (duplication has been minimized) for easy update, maintenance, and integrity.
- *Informational Data.* Data that is optimized for decision support applications. It is summarized operational data, and infrequently updated. Informational data is often stored in data warehouses or data marts.
- *Web Access.* Internet and intranet web sites that have been identified as useful or helpful to employees.

Creating consistent reports and providing access to this corporate warehouse of data through the corporate portal builds business intelligence and a better understanding of your organization's performance for employees.

The goal of the solution's taxonomy is to provide a corporate portal interface with the necessary breadth of information sources required without overwhelming the employee with too complicated an environment. There are two separate taxonomy issues that have to be addressed. One is the portal hierarchy menu that provides navigation through the portal desktop. The second is to create business intelligence among the information available and corporate portal users. This business intelligence is made available in the content-relevant information section of the portal desktop as a collection of hyperlinks. Employees can easily drill into additional material by clicking on these business intelligence links to get to new information that they would otherwise not have been aware of. While both issues are included in taxonomy, they need to be researched and solved independently.

The corporate portal menu, for example, is one of the few constants in the portal desktop. The purpose of the menu hierarchy is to create a high-level layout of your organization using semantics that all employees can understand. You must determine whether a single main menu hierarchy is called for or whether employees will benefit from a selection of menu hierarchies from which to choose. There should be a standard, default, or public menu that's consistent for all employees, especially for the purposes of getting started with the portal desktop, training classes, and reference. Additional menu hierarchies specific for employee roles or departments can be available for individuals to set as their favorite, preferred, or personal menu hierarchy. You need to identify and document how employees are going to use the corporate portal menu to determine how many menu hierarchies to make available. Verify that the corporate portal menu requirements your strategy team identifies are supported by the third-party portal software application(s) being evaluated.

The second taxonomy feature is the creation of secondary menus and hyperlinks based on employee roles, personalization settings, or other self-service application requirements. An instinctive response is to create a directory hierarchy and folder-related data points (i.e, an expandable outline) to present information according to a classification scheme defined by your organization. However, this method significantly reduces the effectiveness of the corporate portal by requiring employees to navigate through several levels of the hierarchy to find the information they are looking for.

A more elegant solution to consider is to create an environment that has established multiple relationships between the data points and information. This approach takes advantage of the employee's roles, responsibilities, and personal needs to present a refined and unique collection of data points for the employee to select from or navigate to. For example, sales managers require data points and information associated by territory to perform their responsibilities. A marketing manager requires information to be categorized and organized in the corporate portal in terms of product lines. If user preferences are stored and maintained they can be accessed through portal pages to maximize the relevance of information presented and minimize the directory searching to locate relevant information. Chapter 8 gives additional information on how to implement these multiple relationships.

The lesson for corporate portal planners is to consider a knowledge-mapping strategy that can grow and support all identified roles of corporate portal employees. At the same time, for the corporate portal to succeed, the information available must reflect the established patterns and familiar context core to your organization. The strategy you create should reflect or be the first step toward knowledge management practices in your organization. The huge benefit that knowledge management brings to the corporate portal is information context. Employees operate in domains of understanding created by interrelated layers of meaning. The knowledge maps created need to support your organization's business by presenting the context in the interface that provides the appropriate level of information to each employee.

Quality and Usability

The corporate portal solution must provide assistance or help to users regardless of how useful the content available is or how intuitive the user interface is. Several user assistance requirements need to be considered in the corporate portal solution. They include online help, printed documentation, tips, status bar information, and wizards. The user assistance model needs to be defined like any other part of the solution and written into the business case. The contents of the user assistance and online help model will continue to expand in complexity as the corporate portal solution evolves.

Online help is the first place users will look for assistance and is considered an important objective of the corporate portal solution. Online help should be provided for every self-service application added to the corporate portal and incorporated as part of the prototype acceptance-testing procedure. When designing online help systems or evaluating third-party applications that build online help solutions, the primary purpose is to anticipate and answer questions that users will have while interacting with the self-service applications and other corporate portal features. The implemented online help system usually includes a tree structure that can be browsed or searched to locate help information. Make sure the online help is designed to be context-sensitive so that the standard F1 key can be used to get help on the current item in the content page being used or referenced. In some cases you may want to include online help as an integrated feature (e.g., within the content page or content window) of the corporate portal solution. An example of this approach can be seen in Figure 5-3.

The help element of the corporate portal solution will be one of the most beneficial and used features if it is well designed. If the

Figure 5-3. Corporate portal search help feature.

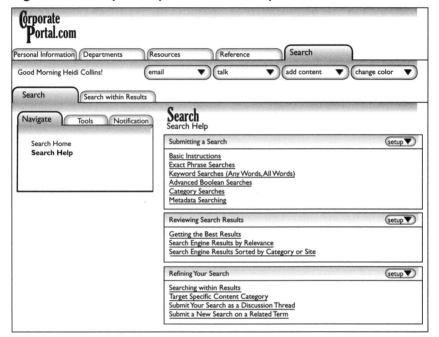

online help system is considered an important benefit of the overall
corporate portal solution, make sure that the business case includes recommendations for online help standards or best practices. When getting started or while working in the corporate
portal, all users occasionally need assistance. A variety of help solutions should be available to explain topics or show users what to
do. There are two primary help solutions to consider:

1. *Guided Help* (i.e., an online help system that directs users
   to the topic they are interested in)
2. *Topic Help* (i.e., a content hierarchy of help subjects or topics designed to lead users to information they might not
   know was available)

The online help system implemented inside the corporate portal
should include links to related topics, Internet support, and intranet support. Search features may need to be incorporated as part

of the help solution included in the corporate portal solution. The search features will be used to locate a collection of additional information or documents within the help system or throughout your organization that may be useful when looking for assistance. In some cases, application manuals or other conceptual documentation material can be made available as printed manuals or on CD. It is valuable to suggest such additional resources when information needs to be conveyed in more detail than online help. If conceptual documentation is difficult to provide, then "read me" information should be available for the user to review if necessary.

Additional user assistance components that can prove valuable include:

- *Tool Tips*. A tool tip is a small label that is displayed when the mouse pointer is held over a control element for a short period of time. It displays information that describes the control element's function. Tool tips work well in any part of the user interface but are usually associated with toolbars.

- *Status Displays*. A status display provides user assistance in the status bar, giving instructions or messages when the mouse pointer is held over a control element for a short period of time. It displays a short description of the control element's function. A status display works well with any part of the user interface.

- *Wizard*. A wizard is designed to provide a step-by-step procedure for users needing assistance with a task in the corporate portal. Wizards are usually used to provide task-specific assistance when a considerable learning curve would be required for users who are currently inexperienced using the self-service application.

The best way to test the usability of the corporate portal application is to involve the users in the review of the prototype of the self-service applications being added to the corporate portal. This process can be as formal or informal as your organization has identified for the review process. The information you collect about the usability of the corporate portal solution can then be used to improve or enhance the user interface with each new iterative delivery of the corporate portal solution.

Corporate Portal Information Organization Checklist

A generic checklist, such as the one that follows, can be used to record background information of each business function or process incorporated in the self-service application included in the initial phases of your corporate portal solution. For each business function identified, please copy the appropriate section (heading and questions), change the heading to match the name of the business function, and answer the questions contained in that section with the business domain experts in your organization. It is important to get a broad range of perspectives on the reasons each business function exists and what its objectives are. Allow the appropriate business process owner to describe the background of the business function.

GATHERING BACKGROUND INFORMATION: BUSINESS FUNCTION AND SELF-SERVICE APPLICATION

☐ What is the history of the business function?
☐ What is the background of the business function from the perspective of the team members?
☐ What is the current business function? What is the business reason for adopting a new business function? (Be prepared to follow up on any reasons that come up for replacing the existing business function. Your goal here is to understand what the "needs" are and how the existing process or available information does not meet those needs.)
☐ What is the scope of the current business function?
☐ Who are the major users of the existing business function (automated and manual)?
☐ What are the major objectives of this business function?

BUSINESS FUNCTION OVERVIEW

☐ What is (in general) the scope of the new business function?
☐ What is the planned operation of the new business function?
☐ What should the business function do? What should the business function not do?
☐ What will the business function have to do in the future?

☐ Have spreadsheet and charting features and options (or other spreadsheet and charting requirements) been reviewed and considered for each function?

☐ What information is necessary for each decision (e.g., reports, news updates, status, other)?

☐ What actions can each user perform while viewing the information?

☐ What types of what-if analysis does each user need to perform?

☐ How often will the information need to be updated?

☐ How will the user be able to personalize the information?

☐ How should information be summarized and distributed to other levels of the organization? Who should have access to each level of detail?

☐ What information is necessary for tracking the industry and the latest news (e.g., breaking news items, links to industry sites, search, notifications, discussions, other)? What should be the layout of this information?

☐ What information is necessary for tracking a customer, vendor, competitor, or partner (e.g., stock price, web links, news items, order levels, actuals versus plan, transaction history, contact list, other)? What should be the layout of this information?

☐ What key metrics and financial information are necessary? What should be the layout of this information?

PROCESS AND ACTION

☐ What specific collaborative or workflow applications are being considered (examples: job posting with online applications, human resources benefit enrollment, sales force automation)?

☐ Has each stage in the workflow process been defined? Have the requirements and approval cycle for each stage been identified?

DESIGN AND CONSTRUCTION

☐ *Flexibility*. Is the corporate portal system able to adapt to changing requirements?

☐ *Portability*. Is the corporate portal system easily modified for a new environment?

☐ *Reusability*. Have the requirements for all or part of existing or new applications to be used in the corporate portal application been identified?

☐ *Testability.* Have the critical success factors for the corporate portal system, as well as measurements to ensure that these critical success factors are achieved, been identified?

☐ *Usability.* What are the requirements in terms of the corporate portal being easily learned and used?

☐ *Standards.* Is there a particular standard that must be used involving the design or construction of the system? Examples:

　　☐ Design or construction standards
　　☐ Data standards
　　☐ Programming language requirements and standards
　　☐ Development environment standards
　　☐ Documentation and online help standards

☐ *User Interface.* Are there specific user interface standards that must be followed (e.g., graphics on each page)?

☐ *Identifying Marks.* Are there identifying marks such as nameplates, part marking, or serial and lot number marking that need to be included as part of the interface?

☐ *Future Growth.* To what degree does the system have to be flexible or expandable so that it supports future growth in either functionality or changes in technology?

ONLINE HELP REQUIREMENTS

☐ What business functions and corporate portal features require online help for associates?

☐ How will online help be accessed from the corporate portal user interface?

☐ What will the taxonomy (i.e., skeletal structure) of the topic help solution look like?

☐ What source information will be used to populate the online help system?

☐ What will be the standard look and feel for online help documents? How will hyperlinks or related topics be defined?

☐ What additional help features need to be available (e.g., pop-up help, navigation buttons)? Where will these features be included in the corporate portal solution?

CorporatePortal.com Case Study

The business functions being considered for the portal desktop at CorporatePortal.com need to be looked at in more detail. Initial ideas regarding the balance between what is constant in the corporate portal user interface and what is available to be selected and personalized by users has been completed. The static portal desktop features include the portal banner, the portal menu, and personalization options. The preliminary self-service applications to be incorporated into the portal desktop include:

• *Corporate Objectives and Metrics.* This information has been identified to be key financial information, current project (tax and audit) status information, and customer satisfaction metrics. These collections of summarized reports are used to track the success of the organization and will be made available from the portal menu. CorporatePortal.com has determined that they should be accessed through the primary menu option Reference and the secondary menu option Scorecard. The content page contains three content page tabs: Financial Metrics, Project Status Metrics, and Customer Satisfaction Metrics. The content windows available for each page will be unique depending on the employee's role. An example of what this screen might look like is presented in Figure 5-4.

• *Document Repository.* A corporate document repository needs to be accessed from the portal desktop. This information needs to be distributed throughout several content pages in the corporate portal. The scope of documents and material includes information from departments across CorporatePortal.com. Accessing department-specific information is done from the Departments option of the portal menu. Another navigation scheme was used to find information in the portal desktop. Rather than access the secondary menu options from the Navigate tab of content-relevant information, the content page tabs were used. Third-level navigation features were included on the Navigate tab of content-

Figure 5-4. Corporate portal objectives and metrics application.

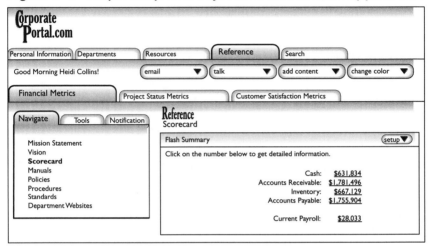

relevant information. An example of how this would be implemented for the Accounting department is shown in Figure 5-5.

• *Collaboration and Discussion Forums.* The portal desktop allows project teams to collaborate and coordinate their activities. Employees have the ability to join discussions and access instant messaging services. CorporatePortal.com has decided that team and corporate collaboration tasks are personal information management (PIM) activities and will be available from the Talk option in the personalization section of the portal desktop. Personalization options are below the portal menu section and can be viewed in Figure 5-5.

• *Expert Locator.* Expert locator features are included in the portal desktop for employees that need to be able to locate knowledge workers to ask questions or recruit their assistance in resolving issues. Listings of employees and their skills are available from the Resources portal menu. CorporatePortal.com also wants this information to be an aspect of the information presented in the content page or content windows. A Contact Expert option is available as an option on a drop-down menu from the Setup button on content pages and content windows. The Setup button is available on the title bar.

• *Personalization.* Employees need the ability to choose and personalize how information is organized and presented in the por-

Figure 5-5. Corporate portal document repository application.

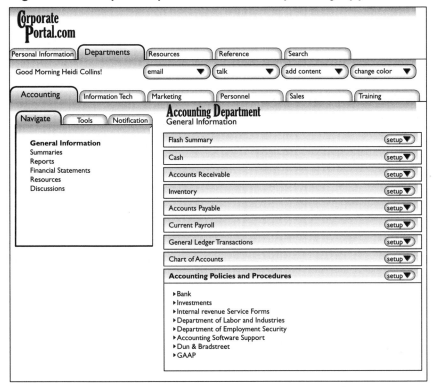

tal desktop. The ability to personalize aspects of the portal desktop is provided through the Add Content and Change Color options in the personalization section of the corporate portal. The portal desktop demonstrates where these buttons might appear in Figure 5-5.

Because help features are an important benefit of the corporate portal solution, CorporatePortal.com is evaluating third-party online help products to include as part of the first phase of the corporate portal. As business functions and self-service applications are identified for inclusion in the portal desktop, their online help requirements as well as their functionality need to be established. Help features will be included as part of the corporate portal development, deployment, and maintenance activities. CorporatePortal.com wants to integrate guided help and topic help into the portal desktop. Several online help software products need to be researched to determine what features should be included. A useful online listing of several possible solutions to consider can be found at http://members.aol.com/LindaMoore/helpauth.html. Figure 5-6 shows a topic help format based on the Help & Manual solution by EasyCash Software; this kind of help feature needs to be created and integrated into each self-service application of the portal desktop.

The main portal menu gives direct access to the identified business functions and self-service applications as well as help and search. CorporatePortal.com has identified five primary menu hierarchy selections with several secondary or drop-down menu options to implement in the first phase of the corporate portal solution. The associated content pages that are presented to the user can then be customized based on the employee's role in the organization. The main portal menu options and financial reports CorporatePortal.com makes available for its sales staff are outlined in Figure 5-7.

Figure 5-6. Topic help example.

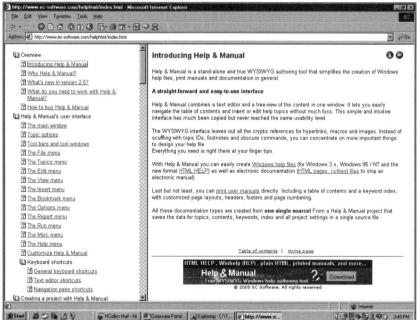

Figure 5-7. CorporatePortal.com's main portal menu hierarchy.

Primary Menu	Secondary Menu
Personal Information	• Daily Planner • E-Mail • Discussions • Chats (Instant Messaging) • Interests

Departments	• Accounting
	   o Financial Statements
	     ▪ Flash Summary
	     ▪ Current Run Rate
	     ▪ Financial Statement Library
	     ▪ Trend Analysis
	   o Exception Reports
	     ▪ Overtime, Bonuses, and Commissions Pay
	     ▪ Past Due Accounts Receivable
	• Information Technology
	• Marketing
	• Personnel
	• Sales
	• Training

Resources	• Company News • Events Calendar • Discussions • What's New • Support • Site Map • Help

Reference	• Mission Statement
	• Vision
	• Scorecard
	   o Scorecard
	     ▪ Flash Summary
	     ▪ Today's Sales
	     ▪ Sales Compared to Budget
	     ▪ Variance Reports
	• Manuals
	• Policies
	• Procedures
	• Standards
	• Department Websites

Search	• Search Home • Search Help

CORPORATE PORTAL SEARCH FUNCTIONALITY

Your organization will want to include several common search features in the search software function of its corporate portal solution. The standard search features that are available from Internet sites include:

- *Exact Phrase Search.* The query returns results that contain at least one occurrence of the string of words entered in the search box.
- *Keyword Search.* The query returns results that contain at least one occurrence of at least one of the words entered in the search box.
- *Boolean Search.* The query returns results that use Boolean operators and syntax to perform advanced searches.
- *Category Search.* The query returns results that are associated with the type of information the user is interested in.

There are currently several types of search functionality available from third-party search products that should be evaluated and considered to be implemented in a corporate portal solution. These include:

- *Standard Search Features.* Guided approaches (e.g., exact phrase, keyword, Boolean, and category searches) locate the occurrences of a specific target string.
- *Concept-Based Search.* Statistical and other guided approaches locate small clusters or networks of related word occurrences.
- *Metadata Search.* Stored relationships of structured and unstructured information sources locate data points that are directly and indirectly related to the specific channel or context in focus.

The results or presentation of search elements in the corporate portal solution can be in the form of ad hoc requested searches and predefined searches. Query screens and search options available to employees for ad hoc searches should be incorporated into the presentation layer or interface of the corporate portal. Predefined search features and results can appear in many different forms in the corporate portal interface, including as:

- Predefined reports containing search results
- Hyperlinks to related information

It is likely that third-party search tools need to be incorporated into the corporate portal solution. There are advantages to using third-party products to add search functionality to your corporate portal solution. Third-party software products may provide consistent results and services to all corporate portal users, equivalent search features and services for all data sources available in your organization, and administration and wizard tools to simplify and accelerate query creation and management. The search requirements of the corporate portal solution should be researched and included as part of the corporate portal business case document.

The corporate portal can easily be leveraged to present the results of predefined or on-request queries that search data sources inside and outside your organization. The ability to have access to information that is necessary or advantageous to making better decisions or obtaining additional knowledge about an employee's responsibilities can give your organization the edge it needs to stay ahead of competitors. Employees should be able to access any kind of information without taking the time to research or locate unknown data points and sources. The corporate portal solution provides the knowledge desktop that continuously grabs data and extends and expands the experience and expertise of your employees by accessing data points and related information that is relevant to their job requirements and their interests.

Your primary goal is to determine what information required by the proposed corporate portal system is needed by employees throughout your organization and make this information easily available such that employees can find information they need without even knowing it existed. To accomplish this, you need to build a query system for your corporate portal users. The importance of search software is to find and filter the information available to users in your organization and, in effect, turn large quantities of documents and data sources into knowledge by focusing and categorizing exactly what users need to know into a single location. Query results should be presented in the best time frame possible. Some queries can be predefined and scheduled to run automatically presenting updated information to portal users. Other queries can be predefined and only run when executed by a portal user. The results are returned to the portal desktop for immediate review. An additional query feature is to allow portal users to define their own queries and review the results from the portal desktop. Working with your employees, review the search requirements for the corporate portal solution. The results of this research can be used to evaluate the best third-party search application to be included as part of the corporate portal solution.

Third-party search engines provide services to execute predefined queries that return the data points or information from multiple or identified sources that match the criteria in the query. These matches are stored in an index or catalog by the search application. The index or catalog is used to provide reports or information in content page windows presented to the user. The data points and information returned to the corporate portal from the search catalog can be presented in several formats. Some of these formats include:

- A link to an Internet website
- A link to a report inside your organization
- A listing of available reports within your organization for review or research purposes
- A collection of hyperlinks that might provide relevant information related to the content page

There is a broad set of requirements that organizations must implement to provide the searching features needed to quickly find information within your organization and on the Internet. When users create and submit their own search requests, these features fall into three basic categories:

- Standard search features
- Concept-based search
- Metadata search

Portal software vendors support search features and several third-party search engines. As your search requirements become clear and you begin evaluating portal software solutions for your corporate portal solution, review the search capabilities supported or integrated into the different products. The InfoImage freedom product supports Microsoft Site Server and the Verity K2 search engine. An example of searching Exchange Public Folders using Site Server and displaying the result set in the portal desktop can be seen in Figure 5-8.

Standard Search Features

Search engines have a variety of standard ways to control the results returned by the query agent. Searching commands available for basic search requirements that you need for your corporate portal include the following:

- *Match Any.* Locates any of the keywords or phrases in the search query.

Figure 5-8. InfoImage freedom search feature.

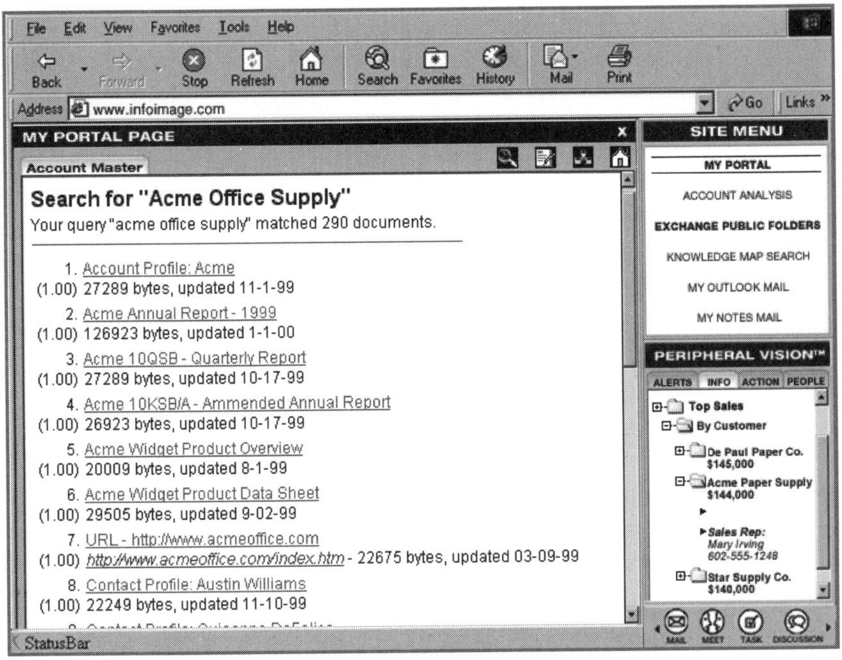

- *Match All.* Locates all of the keywords or phrases in the search query.
- *Exclude.* Submits a keyword or phrase that will be used to narrow a search result set.
- *Title Search.* Allows a search request to be submitted against the HTML title of a web page.
- *Site Search.* Provides the ability to control what websites are included or excluded from a search query.
- *URL Search.* Provides the ability to search the text contents of a URL.
- *Link Search.* Offers the ability to search for all the pages linking to a particular page or domain.
- *Wildcards.* Allow a search for plurals or variations of words by using a wildcard character such as an asterisk (*).
- *Proximity.* Allows the search query to include information about how close words should appear to each other to be included in the results set.

These types of searches return the largest number of document and articles. These standard approaches can be effective for basic searches across several types of data sources that a user may need to complete an online query (see Figure 5-9).

To provide much more accurate and complete search results to users from data sources within your organization, more sophisticated search features may be incorporated into the corporate portal solution. In most cases the results of a search query are predefined and executed to present the results to the user when the content page is opened. These predefined search agents cross-reference data throughout your organization to push information to the user based on these cross-references and relationships about employees and data included in the corporate portal. There are several different approaches or technologies used to establish these relationships. Your IT department needs to be able to support the third-party search engine and the relationships throughout your organization that are required to implement search requirements for the portal solution.

Concept-Based Search

A topic or idea can be described using different words or phrases. For this reason, standard search features may be too limiting when

Figure 5-9. Corporate portal search features.

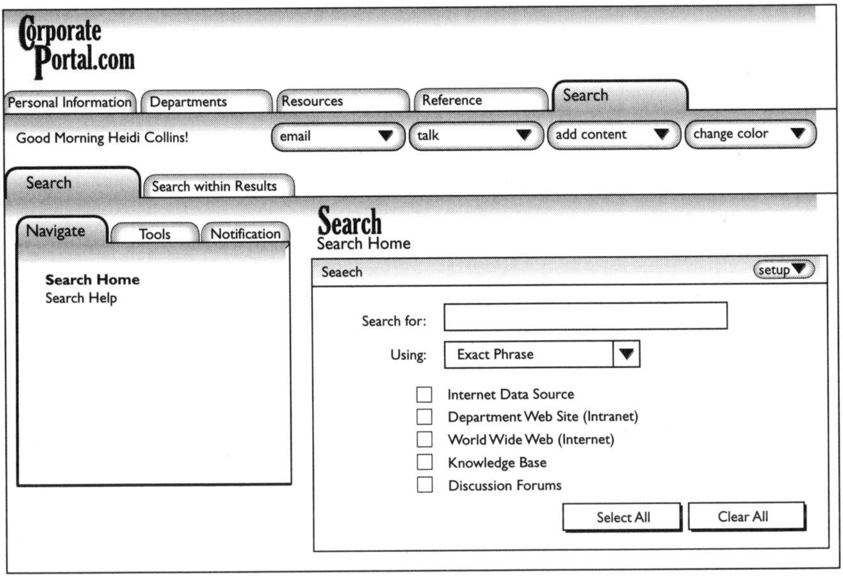

you are required to research a topic or subject area. Concept-based searching allows information to be collected by relationship or relevance rather than by exact phrases or keywords. For example, with a concept-based search query of the phrase "project management," the search software returns two types of results: a first set that explicitly mentions "project management" in the text and a second set about project management that references "systems development life cycle" or "software engagements." Concept-based searching can retrieve documents and articles on the systems development life cycle and software engagements even if these documents or articles contain none of the original query words of *project* or *management*.

Two approaches for implementing concept-based searching are available:

1. *Thesaurus Approach.* You need to have a knowledge base in your organization to use this approach. This knowledge base is a dictionary of terms and additional details about grammar and punctuation. The search software reads the submitted text, transforming or enhancing the original query with the information con-

tained in the knowledge base. This creates a cross-referenced collection of related phrases that are submitted to the search software to generate the results set.

2. *Statistical Approach*. The search software begins the process by accepting the submitted text and generating a list of terms that are related statistically to the words in the original query. The added terms are known to have a significant degree of co-occurrence and are selected to be cross-referenced with the original terms requested. The concept-based search request is complete and all the results are returned to the user. You will find that many of the documents and articles in the results set do not contain occurrences of the original query words but should contain information relevant to the requested search.

If information in your organization is dispersed through multiple systems and data sources with multiple indexing or naming patterns, then concept-based search features may be very useful to cross-reference or establish relationships between data sources, data points, and employees. Corporate portal users who are searching for information throughout the organization do not need to be familiar with all the naming and categorizing patterns to locate the information they are looking for. To implement the thesaurus approach, the knowledge base has to be developed. The knowledge base design and creation can be a time-consuming task that requires continued maintenance. Implementing the statistical approach does not require additional planning, but it will not be as accurate or relevant as the thesaurus approach in most cases.

Metadata Search

Metadata describes a data point or helps provide access to the data point. These collections of metadata items or elements are used to describe one or many information resources in your organization. There must be an association between the data point and the metadata element to be able to use this type of search to locate information. With respect to the Internet, this metadata relationship exists between the information stored in the "META" tag and the HTML web page it is stored in. The purpose of a metadata search is to improve the recall (identifying all the information available on the topic) and precision (quality of accuracy of the information returned) of information retrieval.

Search software often returns irrelevant information because the query agent cannot distinguish between important and insignificant words in documents and articles. The goal of a metadata search is to target the words that are significant terms in the document or article to achieve precision in the results that are returned by the query agent. Metadata achieves this precision by classifying the information resource characteristics. For example, you need to locate data points or resources where the word *crest* refers to a family coat of arms and avoids resources about a mountain crest or toothpaste. Retrieving or recalling as many of the appropriate resources as possible can be critical for the corporate portal to be completely effective. This is difficult when the relevant information is stored in databases, images, or PDF documents and can be easily missed by standard search queries. Metadata searches can support retrieval of these resources by identifying them through the metadata tags and not the content of the documents or articles.

In larger and more complex sites, indexing or cataloging information is limited to only the top levels of the site's hierarchy. If a metadata repository of the information available about the site existed, then the query agent could create an index or catalog for a much larger collection of resources. A variety of metadata standards are available to (1) access specific types of data sources and (2) provide a standard way of describing different information resources and data sources that can be returned from a single query agent or search process.

Corporate Portal Search Functionality Checklist

For the collection of business functions you've identified to be included in the initial phases of the corporate portal solution, please copy the appropriate (heading and questions) section of the following checklist and answer the questions with business domain experts in your organization.

DEFINING SEARCH REQUIREMENTS

☐ What data sources does the user need to search?
☐ What operators can be used during a search (e.g., and, or, not)?

☐ What will be the layout of the search interface?

☐ Will the search be based on a full-text search, on metadata and values in key fields, or other parameters?

☐ Will the user need to perform advanced searches where keywords are selected from drop-down lists?

☐ Will the user need to limit the number of matches that are returned?

☐ How should the search results be displayed? What information should be included? How is the information sorted?

☐ What actions can a user take on a given item in the search results?

☐ Will the user need to save search queries? How will this function be performed?

☐ Will the user need to save search results? How will this function be performed?

☐ How will the user search the Web?

☐ Can the user specify a limited set of websites to search? How will this be performed? How will users add, delete, or update their limited set of sites?

☐ Will the user need to establish predefined criteria and then receive notification when an item is found that meets the criteria?

CorporatePortal.com Case Study

A listing of several available search tools to review can be found on the Internet at http://www.searchtools.com/tools/tools.html. CorporatePortal.com is interested in integrating search engines and tools that can provide the following services:

- The ability to create indexes specific to the organization, with the IT department maintaining control over the indexing process
- The ability to integrate internal databases and enterprise systems with the index
- The ability to create Internet websites as links in the organization's index
- The ability to control the accessibility and response time of the search engine

CorporatePortal.com is integrating a third-party search engine as part of its corporate portal solution. The data sources that need to be integrated with the search engine software include external websites, enterprise systems, and data sources. A collection of catalogs and indexes contain information to access this collection of external and enterprise data sources. The preliminary self-service applications incorporated into the company's portal desktop are fed information from a variety of data sources, as indicated:

- *Corporate Objectives and Metrics.* There are two enterprise systems that provide the financial information, project information, and customer satisfaction metrics for this application. The data sources are the Oracle Financials system and Oracle databases. Portal users are interested in drilling into additional records or detail when they review these summarized reports. CorporatePortal.com therefore wants to allow the search engine to run queries and return results from Oracle Financials and Oracle databases.

- *Document Repository.* A content management third-party solution is being used to catalog the collection of documents contained in the document repository. This content management application must integrate with the search engine. CorporatePortal.com is interested in implementing metadata information into the content management data storage to provide relevant and precise results to portal users' search requests.

- *Collaboration and Discussion Forums.* The portal desktop must provide access to discussion forums and team project collaborative systems. CorporatePortal.com is evaluating a team project collaboration application to manage documents and material for the portal desktop. Microsoft Exchange public folders manage discussions for CorporatePortal.com. These two applications need to be accessed by the search engine to provide information and documentation to portal users.

- *Expert Locator.* Expert locator data is available in an Oracle database and needs to be accessed by the search engine to identify knowledge workers from the portal desktop.

- *Extranet and Internet.* Employees need the ability to search websites from the search functions available in the portal desktop. A defined set of search catalogs and indexes for external websites must be created and maintained for use by corporate portal users to provide quick and accurate results. Employees can then submit queries that will search the Internet when more extensive results are needed.

FURTHER READING

Fleming, Jennifer. *Web Navigation: Designing the User Experience.* Sebastopol, Calif.: O'Reilly and Associates, 1998.
Lynch, Patrick J., and Sarah Horton. *Web Style Guide: Basic Design Principles for Creating Web Sites.* New Haven, Conn.: Yale University Press, 1999.
Szuprowicz, Bohdan O. *Search Engine Technologies for the World Wide Web and Intranets.* Charleston, S.C.: Computer Technology Research Corporation, 1997.

KEY POINTS

These recommendations regarding information organization and search capabilities are critical when preparing your corporate portal strategy:

• Adopt a consistent look and feel throughout the corporate portal solution to facilitate and optimize the user experience while using the knowledge desktop.

• Include the most appropriate information in the most appropriate format, with hyperlinks and other navigation features to easily locate features, functions, and data for employees.

• Facilitate feedback avenues and online assistance features for employees. User feedback can be used to continually improve the quality and usability of the corporate portal solution during new iterations or deployments of the corporate portal.

• Incorporate standard search features, concept-based search features, metadata search features, and other search features into the corporate portal solution on the basis of how the employees in your organization need to find information. An analysis of user requirements and third-party search applications that can meet the identified requirements should be included as part of the corporate portal business case.

- Present predefined search results in content pages, content page windows, and relevant information sections of the corporate portal. Ad hoc search features and query screens can be included in the corporate portal as well for employees to use and should be easily accessible.

Use the following checklist to review or analyze how information is organized and what search capabilities are required for your organization's corporate portal solution.

ANALYZING YOUR CORPORATE PORTAL'S INFORMATION ORGANIZATION AND SEARCH CAPABILITIES

☐ Are business domain experts directly responsible for creating, publishing, and distributing knowledge to your organization? If yes, is the information current?

☐ How do employees learn about and become familiar with important information in your organization? Is this solution working?

☐ Is important information made available to employees through e-mail or bulletin boards? Are employees overwhelmed with too much e-mail?

☐ Are the correct employees or the most knowledgeable employees of the topic or issues responding to discussion forums?

☐ Are employees able to search through data sources in your organization to find information they are interested in?

☐ Are employees made aware of reports or able to request reports in the organization that are useful to them? Does this process work expediently?

☐ Are employees allowed to search the Internet for relevant information? Do you subscribe to any online services that provide information to employees?

☐ Are employees able to locate all the information necessary to perform their assigned responsibilities from a variety of disparate sources in a central location or desktop?

6

Direct Access to Corporate Knowledge and Resources

For employees to work from a central location, they need information about the activities and information available from other workgroups in the organization. Allowing business domain experts to publish and maintain relevant information is a way to distribute content management activities and responsibilities throughout your organization. This is a difficult task, however. Business domain experts need to streamline their various business processes that affect other employees. There are some guidelines to follow when trying to determine the information that's important. These guidelines include:

- Identifying the roles in your organization that will use the information published.
- Streamlining the information from the perspective of the roles identified.
- Streamlining the information to your organization's mission and objectives.
- Improving continuously the published information based on feedback.
- Providing each targeted role with a perspective of the information available.

The publishing and distribution features can be implemented using a content management application that supports content creation, authorization of content, inclusion or exclusion in corporate portal content collections, and distribution in multiple online or hard-copy formats.

The central knowledge desktop allows employees to communicate, collaborate, and coordinate projects with each other using the information in the corporate portal. Employees are able to easily identify and contact a knowledge worker for additional help or information to complete an activity. The collaboration and communication element facilitates discussion, locating innovative ideas, and recognizing resourceful solutions. This portal element gives employees the ability to work together in a qualitatively better way. Creating a portal desktop to meet this objective is a risk management issue. Additional efforts are needed as well to build the corporate portal community and encourage employees to work together using the portal desktop.

CORPORATE PORTAL CONTENT MANAGEMENT

The corporate portal is the central location for shared company reference material. The impact of pushing important company information to the knowledge desktop of your employees can be substantial. Very few employees actively search for updates within their own organization on a regular basis. When employees' awareness of knowledge in the organization improves, as it does when a corporate portal is implemented, employees can build a corporate community. Business domain experts more than likely have several objectives within their individual workgroups or department and can share information throughout the organization. Employees should be able to author or publish information and submit the approved or final version to the corporate portal desktop for other employees to access.

A content management system for approving and widely disseminating documents is essential to broadcasting accumulated knowledge of past and current experiences throughout your organization. The type of information that your organization may want to publish includes competitive reports, forecasts and reviews, policies and procedures, training materials, newsletters, and periodicals. The problem to overcome is that large quantities of public or corporate information can very quickly become available in the corporate portal for all employees in your organization. The company must develop a plan that makes it easy to reference the information. This plan must incorporate a logical storage and navigation system for employees to logically find information when they need it. In addition, you want to consider implementing notification or messaging support for this type of accumulated knowledge information to push important information to employees when necessary. This automatic notification feature has been overused in some organizations, so you need to make sure that employees are not overwhelmed by the amount of information pushed to them.

Your content management challenges are to determine:

- What material and documentation needs to be published to the corporate portal
- How and when this information is published
- Where this information is located in the corporate portal
- Who is responsible for implementing and maintaining the published information
- How employees throughout the organization are informed of or locate the published material

To make these decisions, you need to take advantage of an existing process for publishing and distributing information within your organization—or you must consider establishing such a process. To complete the delivery process, research the data points that need to be made available to corporate portal users and determine what portion of this content is expected to be implemented and maintained through your organization's publishing and distribution process.

One solution is to incorporate a content management product that easily supports the timely creation and flow of information in your organization. The corporate portal strategy team needs to identify your organization's authoring and publishing process, including the infrastructure and administration requirements. There are three areas for corporate portal strategists to focus on:

1. *Publishing Process (Authoring).* The corporate portal must be insightful, accurate, and interesting in the way it presents information. It must support whatever transparent operation and content flow the company requires. Intranet deployments (i.e., company information available to employees using a browser such as Microsoft Internet Explorer and Netscape Communicator from web servers inside your organization) require transactional business data as well as static content. Employees need access to format-conversion services for structured documents, common desktop authoring environments (e.g., Microsoft Word and Microsoft Excel), and collaborative tools depending on how documents are published. When creating the corporate portal strategy it is important to identify all the applications and services that feed data points and information to the corporate portal desktop. An identified document hierarchy or taxonomy is also critical for documents and material included in the content management solution so that employees can easily recognize, understand, and use the content.

2. *Approvals and Posting Process.* Corporate portal strategists need to evaluate whether the development of a corporate portal solution creates new management challenges in your organization. At some point the corporate portal user community will wish to contribute content into the corporate portal. An approval process helps ensure that information presented in the corporate portal is accurate and timely. If your organization already has a process for creating, approving, and publishing new web pages and content, then this existing process can be adapted for adding new content to the corporate portal solution. If not, then a distributed administrative function to provide these services needs to be recommended or suggested. During the approval process the document hierarchy originally set can be validated or modified if necessary.

3. *Maintenance.* Corporate portal content configurations must be managed. Content management administration that includes an established life cycle management approach is a prerequisite to control corporate portal content that employees expect to be available. The actions taken and procedures considered need to avoid complex infrastructure and administration requirements.

The corporate portal is an ideal distribution channel. It has low maintenance costs in terms of distributing the software and broad availability in terms of the number of employees in an organization with access to a browser. Whereas you have systems and applications to manage most of the formal procedures and processes in your organization, the content management application is used to catalog and coordinate unstructured information in your organization. There are many documents and material that have grown from information processes that need to be shared with employees in other departments. The content management solution is about cataloging and adding structure to these collections of documents. The corporate portal solution's knowledge desktop combines the structured and unstructured information together in a single environment. As well as working with enterprise systems, employees can access dynamic data formats (e.g., graphs, spreadsheets, reports, and simulations) and interact with this information using the features and functions available from the portal desktop.

Your challenges include selecting business domain experts to champion the application. They are responsible for establishing and maintaining the content management documents for their department or workgroup, organizing and refining these documents for specific roles in your organization, and streamlining access to the content management documents from the portal desktop. For example, a corporate customer satisfaction goal is for any employee to be able to respond to customer account status questions without having to escalate these issues to specific departments. Each department in your organization needs to research and identify the information it needs to provide to meet this objective. The sales department determines that proposals and contracts need to be made available for certain types of customer questions. The business domain expert responsible for making proposals and contracts accessible determines that this information is accessed primarily by two roles: customer services representatives and sales representatives. The decision is made for proposals and contracts to be added to the content management system and cataloged or indexed for both customer service representatives and sales representatives.

Business domain experts must also interview employees in the identified roles to determine how they work so that the appropriate information can be logically made available to them. The results of these interviews provide the logical process or procedure used by employees in your organization. The corporate portal strategists should document this information as a collection of scenarios. These scenarios outline how each role functions from the point of view of someone in that role or job. The business domain experts can then establish or create the material for the content management application. The corporate portal solution requires the content management material in conjunction with other enterprise systems to implement the identified scenarios from the portal desktop. Use these documented scenarios as part of acceptance and usability testing when implementing the corporate portal solution.

There is an additional benefit received by incorporating these business processes into the portal desktop. Employees across your organization are able to recognize their contribution to processes. Each step of the process becomes obvious to everyone in the organization. This can be an important benefit and transform the way employees view processes. One concern of the corporate portal strategy team is that the process of deciding how funding is allocated for internal projects be fair, impartial, and visible to employees who want to closely examine the decisions. A consequence of making processes transparent is the number of employees you'll discover who are interested in the information. For example, the projects selected directly affect the responsibilities of information technology (IT) system administrators, application developers, and project managers. These users wanted to be able to submit comments and establish risk factors that may have been overlooked as part of the decision-making process. Success is measured by the increased communication around decisions made and employees gaining confidence in your organization by being involved and included in these decisions.

Business domain experts, system administrators, and web developers are the employees responsible for designing, improving, and maintaining your organization's corporate portal. The portal desktop implemented becomes their best attempt to anticipate employees' needs and interests. The corporate portal development team needs to analyze the feedback and actual usage patterns to look for ways to improve the navigation, content, and usability of the portal desktop. Improving the corporate portal solution is an inexact procedure, so your design and development team must collect feedback in as many creative ways as possible. If you pay attention to the results collected, the redesign efforts of the corporate portal solution will be easy to determine and implement in the next development and deployment phase.

Web Publishing

In many cases you want to deliver to a web browser static information or information that remains unchanged or current for a defined amount of time. Each business domain expert that is responsible for distributing information into the corporate portal must update or replace this published information on the appropriate scheduled basis. These static web pages work very well for information that needs wide dissemination. This format provides content creation with graphics files, white space, color, and varied font styles to enhance web pages. With the use of hypertext links that allow a web page reader to click to other parts of the same page or other web pages, you can give employees in your organization several options to get to as much (or as little) of the information published as appropriate. Some guidelines for web publishing follow:

- The frequency with which information is published to the corporate portal should match the expectations of the employee roles in your organization.
- If you are unsure of which employees will be using a specific web page, you should include a feedback option, such as a "Mail To" link that lets users of the page tell you what they liked or disliked about the content.
- A well-defined set of standard or best practices is required for hyperlinks and other navigational controls so that employees can easily recognize where they are in the corporate portal desktop.

These web pages contain several types of material. There's background information about the documents and material available and how different employees in different roles use them. This textual material contained on web pages is to supplement the variety of documents indexed in the content management system and easily accessed from the portal desktop. Depending on the business processes, you should consider simulations, audio, graphics, and e-mail correspondence as appropriate material to incorporate. You must decide how to best present the subject matter to meet the diverse requirements of the employee roles supported.

The content available may work specifically with internal links, where one hypertext link leads to additional information about the process. For example, you might access related documents from a table of contents. However these links are created, the objective is to allow employees to move from basic information to more specific information. External links should be included to other departments or other websites to help employees find information about related topics.

A set of guidelines is also needed for creating internal and external links. Hypertext links use a word or phrase to link employees to individual pages of information. It is helpful to employees if the textual link changes color once the link has been accessed (the link can continue to be reused). Because employees can select the information in any order, the color reference helps employees remember which links have been used. Another advantage to specifying links to change color is that employees are able to chart their progress through the available materials. You want to consider creating links that perform actions. An example is to create an e-mail notification or feedback link that allows employees to send comments or ask questions. This is a useful feature if it is important for employees to be able to send their questions or comments to other knowledge workers while working with the current content page. For navigational links that are frequently accessed, you may want to create a duplicated set of links on a pull-down, pull-over, or pop-up menu. Another option is a set of buttons placed along a margin or within a graphic. These frequently used links should include a link to the home page or other key pieces of information.

Dynamic Content Creation

Some subjects and material change very little, so you may be able to refer employees to the same core documents for a long time.

However, to keep the material current and to meet the needs of different employees over time, you must update or alter the material periodically. You may need to redesign the subject matter, add new examples, include more graphics, or make online activities more interactive. Some subject matter changes frequently within a short time. If the information or material will change or be updated at specific intervals, then the page should announce to employees the date and time the current information was created and when new information will be available.

Application Distribution

A benefit of the corporate portal desktop is that the types of information that can be centralized in a single location are almost limitless. Because the information is stored in the content management system and easily located, employees with access to the portal desktop can download or use the documents and material online. The corporate portal allows employees to work at their own pace and visit the material in the content management system as often as they need to. Business domain experts provide background information, unstructured documents, and simulations. Multimedia demonstrations and samples are two types of training documentation that can be used to present basic assistance and information on how to use the content available in the portal desktop.

Employees who are responsible for the business processes covered in these content pages need access to all the information. Corporate portal administrators, business domain experts, and application developers require complete access to the content as well. However, these identified employee roles may be the only users that need complete access to this material. If this is the case, then some links can be designed so employee roles are assigned designated access to content materials. In the event that access is limited to identified roles, you should design the content pages carefully so that each role sees only the material and links that they are allowed to interact with.

Additional administrative content pages should be considered to manage daily interaction with content available in the corporate portal. You may need to create request or subscription screens explaining how interested employees can be granted access to the content pages or find more information about the material in question. When content pages are unavailable for upgrades, maintenance, or other reasons, you want to warn employees in advance of the dates and times information will be inaccessible. As content pages change, you want to make employees aware of exactly what information will be constantly or periodically available. Consider warning employees that material or processes are changing with details on how and when information and access to information will be updated.

Corporate Portal Content Management Checklist

Based on the results of your previous interviews with employees, you have a good idea about the ways users prefer or are required to use the material available. The more interactive you can make the content, the better employees will understand the information presented. Employees can respond to the information by asking questions, making decisions, participating in discussion groups, or completing a task. To help you get started in designing the content that needs to be made available from the portal desktop, the checklists that follow outline key issues to consider regarding each page and the links contained within it.

PURPOSE OF THE CONTENT

- [ ] Why will employees visit this website and content?
- [ ] When will employees visit this website and content?
- [ ] What do they need to know first?

PURPOSE OF THE CONTENT PAGE

- [ ] Why will employees visit this content page?
- [ ] When will employees visit this content page?
- [ ] What do they need to know before accessing this content page?

CONTENT (SUBSTANCE AND FORMAT)

- [ ] How much information will be provided about the subject matter?

☐ How much information will be links or navigation features?
☐ How much information will be instructive?
☐ How much information must be available in the content management system to complete the business process identified?
☐ Should the information be accessible only as text?
☐ Should the information include documents, graphics, or other material?
☐ How should the information be organized for clarity of meaning?

Frequency of Updates

☐ How quickly will the information be outdated?
☐ How much information will become outdated?
☐ How much information will remain constant?
☐ How often should the information be updated?
☐ How easy is it to update this information?

Links

☐ To what addresses or other content areas should this information be linked?
☐ How will employees find this information?
☐ How much information should be linked within this content page to corporate information?
☐ How much information should be linked within this content page to external information?
☐ What types of links (e.g., hypertext, graphics, buttons) are appropriate?
☐ How can links be made intuitive so that employees understand how to use them?
☐ Do the links work?
☐ How often should the links be checked to verify their accuracy?

Design

☐ How much information must appear on the screen at one time?
☐ Is the overall design functional and attractive?

☐ Is the overall design well suited for the corporate portal desktop?

☐ How often should the design be updated?

CorporatePortal.com Case Study

CorporatePortal.com is concerned about publishing accurate company information. As company policies and other online information changes, the updates need to be available in the portal desktop. In developing its content management solution, CorporatePortal.com has chosen Documentum, a third-party product, to provide the tools and processes necessary to facilitate the electronic publishing process. Different employee roles within the company remain responsible for the accuracy and authenticity of the material being released to employees. A sample input screen employees use to submit documents and other material into the Documentum application is shown in Figure 6-1.

Figure 6-1. Content management example.

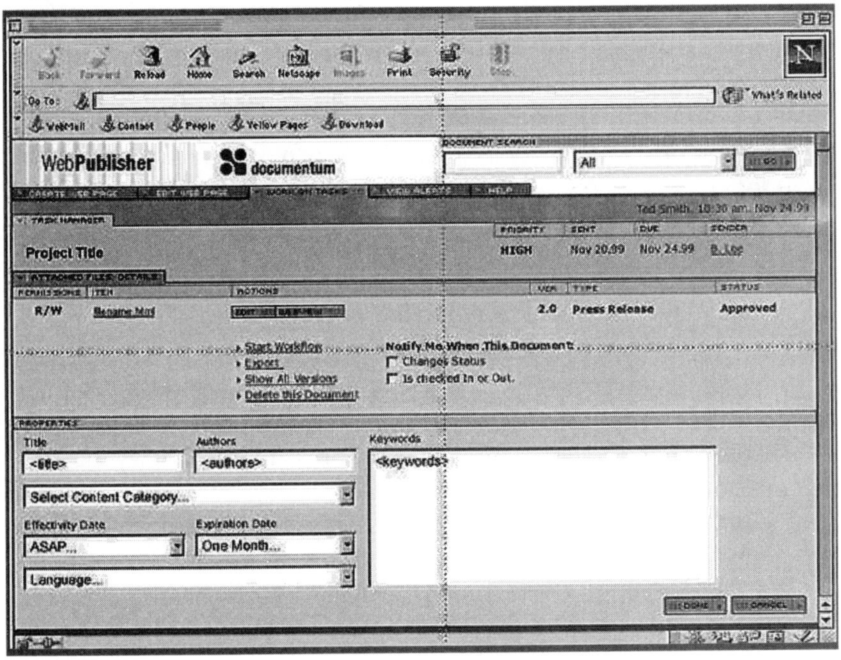

The published material is to be supplemented with database or index fields of parameters and attributes that allow employees to find information they are looking for. For example, an employee needs to find the actual expenses incurred for computer hardware on enterprise projects over the past three years, then all these attributes need to be available as search criteria. All the customer and employee roles that will likely be interested in reviewing and searching information when the attributes are established also have to be taken into consideration. Each constituency will have different search requirements and expectations on where to find published material. The metadata information to be added to data sources must be compiled during the architecture and design phase of the corporate portal development project.

CorporatePortal.com has established several business-to-employee initiatives for the portal desktop to implement. The goal is to do more than just make it easy for employees to get information, review corporate policies, check on the status of tax and audit projects, and get help. These are all prerequisites. To achieve the company's knowledge management initiatives, it is necessary to understand exactly how information fits in each employee's daily activities. CorporatePortal.com needs to understand how this information is used and how the corporate portal will make it easier for employees to achieve their assigned tasks and quarterly objectives. The content management material needs to be created, organized, and maintained with the clear benefits in mind. These objectives include:

- Developing a solid understanding of how employees do their jobs.
- Refining business processes and self-service applications continuously to make it easier for employees to do their jobs.
- Giving employees direct access to the information they use frequently.
- Giving employees the information and tools they need to make decisions.
- Making it easy for employees to meet their quarterly objectives.

The preliminary self-service applications chosen to be incorporated into the portal desktop include:

- Corporate objectives and metrics
- Document repository
- Collaboration and discussion forums
- Expert locator
- Personalization

Each self-service application needs to be reviewed from the perspective of the following employee roles:

- Accounting
- Information technology
- Marketing
- Personnel
- Sales
- Training

The content checklists (outlined previously in this chapter) can be applied to the process identified to determine the material and documents that need to be incorporated into the Documentum application. Consider an example where the application is the corporate objectives and metrics process used by employees in the sales role. Sales employees are interested in keeping the high-level or summary information in a single content page of the corporate portal. The company has designed the solution to have three sections or content page tabs, one for each type of objective being measured. These sections include:

- *Financial Metrics.* The financial metrics include several reports that originate from the Oracle Financials system. Supporting documentation is also required that describes the corporate and sales objectives these reports reflect and procedures about how these reports should be used and analyzed.
- *Project Status Metrics.* The project status metrics provide a pivot table with customer, time, and project dimensions (see Figure 6-2). The content-relevant information section includes Navigate, Project Information, and Notification options. The Project Information tab (shown in Figure 6-3) contains links to the content management application (i.e., Documentum), where service agreements, statements of work, published reports, research information, white

Figure 6-2. Corporate portal with a multidimensional table (content window).

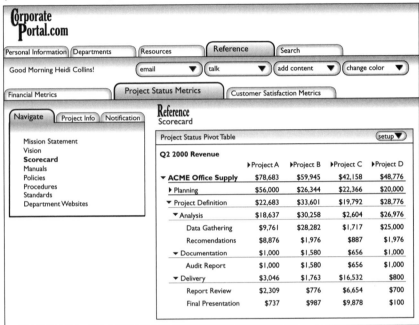

papers, forms, and procedures about how tax and audit projects are executed and managed can be found. For example, there's a link to Internal Revenue Service (IRS) forms from the content window on the Project Status Metrics content page (see also Figure 6-3).

• *Customer Satisfaction Metrics.* The final set of metrics is used to measure customer satisfaction. Supporting documentation on how to interpret the reports presented on the content page needs to be available. If there are satisfaction issues identified, the risks must be analyzed and a strategy implemented to improve the situation. The strategy document and any related activities or action items need to be created, approved, and completed from the content management system.

CORPORATE PORTAL COMMUNICATION, COLLABORATION, AND COORDINATION

Communication is the sharing of your organization's information. This is most commonly supported through electronic mail. E-mail

Figure 6-3. Corporate portal with content management (content window).

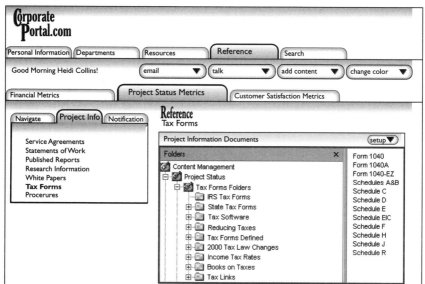

should only be part of the communication answer. It has built-in limitations due to the fact that it is an unmanageable data store and only supports one-to-one and one-to-many communication. The volumes of information available in e-mail files are available to only a single or small number of employees that received the e-mail message. Often information that would be valuable to the entire organization exists in the form of a message in an employee's e-mail file. It is unlikely that this information will ever make the transition from the e-mail file into a format that can be made widely available to users throughout the company. The goals of corporate portal communication features are to establish an information management model that can support the unstructured and many-to-many communication requirements of your organization.

It is important that information presented in the corporate portal is actually created in other systems throughout your organization. The business processes that are supported from the portal desktop rely on data that exists in other data stores external from the portal application. These data stores maintain the integrity of the data for your organization. The corporate portal infrastructure and architecture should seamlessly import, share, and leverage structured data sources, desktop applications, document management systems, and public information services. The communication and collaboration extensions from these existing applications and systems include an ability to discuss and research data points or business processes outside the context of the applications or systems that manage these business functions. Examples might be using discussion forums, messaging services, and other resources available throughout your organization that facilitate collaboration and communication services that are easily accessed by users from the corporate portal.

The corporate portal solution combines the structured and unstructured information from back- and front-office systems with existing collaboration systems in order to speed up the decision-making cycle. With collaborative systems integrated into the corporate portal solution, information can be easily shared to stimulate opinion and insight. This type of collaboration is difficult or even impossible in existing enterprise solutions when each purpose and function of the organization is deployed throughout many different and often unrelated applications and modules.

Employees frequently need to submit a change in procedure, schedule time off, or make another type of request that requires approval. Process and action automation functions are designed to route documents, records, and forms; receive and respond to the activities required in a business process (e.g., credit approval messages from authorization systems); and generally interact and respond to predefined process flows. Adaptation to the corporate portal from the appropriate data sources and legacy environments may not succeed in being fully transparent to the employee. Self-service applications that include process and action (i.e., workflow) activities rarely exist in isolation. These process and action systems have front-office components linked to specific back-office systems that are fully automated. In many cases, the corporate portal self-service application can be used to enhance the classic transaction processing systems in your organization. For example, a typical purchasing system begins with an approved purchase order requisition and concludes successfully with a purchase order. When the back-office system rejects the purchase order requisition, an employee needs to research the problem and resubmit the purchase order requisition. Because exceptions make it difficult to determine what the best solution is, an employee might request approval on a decision before taking action. Creating an ad hoc approval process to quickly evaluate how to correct the problem and resubmit the purchase order requisition to the back-office application can be implemented as a process in the portal desktop. Once the corrective action has been decided and approved, the requisition is corrected in the back-office application and reprocessed to become an approved or rejected purchase order.

Process and action support is a critical element for the portal desktop if the self-service application being included in the corporate portal solution is expected to have interactive or workflow features. You need to verify with your IT department how difficult it will be to submit changes or create new documents in the enterprise systems affected by the process and action activities completed from the corporate portal. The implications of the presentation layer (i.e., the desktop interface) automatically submitting changes may be significant, and the appropriate infrastructure for process support must be incorporated in the design of the self-service applications. Integrating a web application with legacy systems and enterprise applications that currently manage most of the transactions in an organization is difficult because there are:

1. Data and application security requirements with a limited number of users being allowed to access the information
2. Infrastructure limitations to support robust transaction services

The corporate portal strategy must address process and action support issues that exist in your organization and define the available solutions that can be considered in the corporate portal outlining the benefits and drawbacks and when each solution would be appropriate.

Collaboration can be between two employees or involve a group of employees sharing information. Activities such as problem solving, brainstorming, and identifying and locating data sources are all collaboration tasks. Collaboration requires that the participants share their knowledge so that the context of the issue becomes clear or understood by the group at large. Collaboration often involves meetings, telephone calls, and conferences where people are together at the same time in the same place. The corporate portal solution focuses on asynchronous collaboration where participants can contribute to the process at different times and from different places.

In developing the business case for a flexible and customizable corporate portal for collaboration, it is important to separate or make the distinction between the technology and applications implemented with the technology. A shared forum provides the platform for a wide range of self-service applications. These self-service applications range from discussion forums to sales force automation systems. These types of applications are a good choice for the corporate portal since they are essential for common work and shared reports and for clarifying information in organizational knowledge.

Self-service applications that require process and action activities are often referred to as workflow applications. These applications require that the processes or activities and actions complete an identified task. These tasks can be structured and defined or they may be fuzzy, where the rules, routes, and roles are dynamically defined as the tasks are being completed. The portal provides an avenue for bringing a sequence of structured tasks and designated employees into and out of a process as needed, passing knowledge that is essential to the completion of a process, and allowing for information exchanges (through e-mail, discussion forums, and published reference material). As an example, Figure 6-4 illustrates how InfoImage freedom software is used to create a discussion document that incorporates information from an ACME Office Supply content window. Notice that there are additional navigation features called Alerts that deliver to employees important information related to recent activities on the ACME Office Supply account.

Virtual Team Collaboration Requirements

A well-implemented and controlled collaboration environment allows your organization to be responsive to market conditions. There are several reasons for the expansion or explosion of information and data sources in day-to-day business operations. Some of these include:

- Geographically dispersed corporate intranets
- Customer resource management (CRM) systems

Figure 6-4. InfoImage freedom collaboration feature.

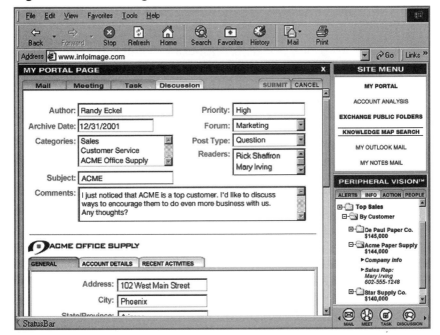

- Sales force automation (SFA) systems
- Supply chain management (SCM) systems
- E-commerce applications and activities

These global solutions lead to the need for an optimized collaborative solution with integrated information sources and the appropriate tools to disseminate the knowledge gained in a rapid and meaningful format. Employees throughout your organization have an increasing need to identify all pertinent information on a subject. A few additional requirements need also be considered for inclusion in the collaborative solution. They are:

• *Enterprise Scalable Messaging.* This is the e-mail or Internet mail systems used to send notifications and provide one-to-one or one-to-many communication.

• *Asynchronous Collaboration Tools.* Such tools include public bulletin boards or discussion forums for many-to-many communication.

- *Search Features.* These are services available from the messaging and collaboration applications to help users find messages, discussion threads, documents, and other material.

- *Filtering Agents.* These are functions that allow the user to create rules and actions to organize, categorize, index, and delete material and information automatically when the appropriate condition is identified.

- *Secure Information Access and Storage.* There are two different security features identified here. The first is being able to use the messaging or collaboration systems. The second is the assigned ability to read, edit, or delete material in the messaging and collaboration systems.

Organizations are required to make decisions using virtual team members that are unique individuals who are geographically dispersed and working at different times, with different responsibilities and job requirements. It is important that each user can access information in a way that meets individual expectations and needs. Employees have different work modes depending on the task at hand (see Figure 6-5). The complete communication and collaboration solution provided by your organization should allow for different means of accessing, manipulating, and disseminating information. The corporate portal provides a central location to access communication and collaborative technologies throughout your organization. To provide the appropriate level of coordination between employee roles, collaboration solutions need to be integrated into the existing applications and processes so that your corporate portal solution can take the greatest advantage of the services provided.

Corporate Portal Collaborative Services

Human and computer interfaces continue to evolve. The corporate portal solution is designed to enhance the collaboration experience with improved integration and interoperation of applications and information sources in your organization. Your goal is to identify the communication and collaboration activities your employees engage in and add any coordination (i.e., process and action) activities. These additions are designed to help employees make more

Figure 6-5. Work modes based on the task-at-hand.

Function	Corporate Portal Feature
Content Access	• Corporate Intranets • Database/Data Warehouse • Directories • Document Repositories • EDI • E-Mail Repositories • File Servers • Image and Fax Repositories • Mainframe Reports
Applications	• Access to ERP Transaction Processing • Decision Support Tools • Document Management • Data Search and Federated Text • Forms Processing • Groupware Applications • Personal Productivity Tools • Process and Action/Workflow Routing
Specific Corporate Portal	• Pushing Information to the Desktop • Administration • User Profiling • Expertise Networking • Load Balancing • Metadata Management • Single Login • Taxonomy and Categorization Management

consistent and informed decisions. Try to identify patterns or recurring requirements in order to establish a generalized solution for the corporate portal business case. Consider, for example, the actions you would take to find answers to the following strategic questions:

1. You collect data about production processes used in your organization. You have information on the raw materials used in the process and on the quality of the final product produced. How can you relate the two collections of data points to the efficiency and effectiveness of your production processes?

2. You have warranty claim data available from your customer service department. You wish to identify if there is a correlation between this set of data and the data available regarding the quality of the final product produced. The warranty claim data consists of one set of attributes and the product quality data a different set of attributes. There is data available from the fulfillment department that can establish a relationship between these two sets of data. How do you combine and analyze these collections of data to improve production processes that will reduce warranty claims?

3. You have multiple warehouses that fulfill orders using separate systems. There are established guidelines that define how these fulfillment processes are to be implemented, yet each warehouse has evolved differently. These differences and separate systems make it difficult to evaluate fulfillment data consistently. How can these data sources be combined so they can be evaluated for variations in fulfillment processes?

In some organizations, these actions or steps that would need to be completed and possibly repeated before the final decision is arrived at:

1. Submit a request to the IT department for the data needed to analyze or evaluate these business processes. This data could come from several different sources, including:

- Legacy systems
- Enterprise data warehouse
- Relational databases
- Proprietary data sources
- Electronic spreadsheets
- Paper documents

2. Establish the data attributes required from all of the individual data sources. Identify problems or inaccuracies in the data and clean or refine the data collections. This step could entail converting to the same units of measure, removing inconsistent data, or standardizing identifiers between different data sources.

3. Submit a request to an IT programming resource, requesting the programming department to write an application that will

transform the data sources and create the data collection needed to complete the analysis.

4. Use the appropriate applications and tools to analyze the data collection and make a strategic decision about the effectiveness of your production and fulfillment processes.

5. Publish and distribute the results of your analysis.

Consider the actions you would take to find answers to the following operational questions:

1. You are responsible for creating new sales opportunities. You have guidelines and best practices that are used to enter the information required in the sales force automation (SFA) system. How can you easily verify that the information being collected and submitted for new sales opportunities is being completed correctly?

2. You have the responsibility of qualifying the sales opportunities submitted in the SFA system. You wish to verify that the extensive list of recommended products proposed in a sales opportunity is correct. The sales opportunity could be split into multiple opportunities, each with a unique qualifier, or the products recommended could remain in one opportunity with a lower chance of closing. Is there a process that already exists to follow in this situation, or do you need to speak to the sales representative or a collection of employees to ensure that the sales opportunity has the best chance of being accepted by the customer?

3. You have an enterprise resource planning (ERP) system that assigns purchase order numbers to sales opportunities that are sold. There are synchronization programs that exchange data between the SFA system and the ERP system. You are responsible for submitting transactions to either the SFA system or the ERP system when the synchronization cannot be automatically completed due to a data exception or process exception. There are established guidelines and recommendations to define how these transactions are supposed to be handled. How can you collaborate with other employees in similar positions or employees involved in the process to confirm that an unusual exception is being handled the best way?

In some organizations the following actions or steps would need to be completed and possibly repeated before the final decision is arrived at:

1. Submit the question to a help desk or a discussion forum, send an e-mail message, or start making phone calls to find the appropriate answer.
2. Establish the best course of action to take by reviewing and evaluating previous actions taken or recommendations of several employees.
3. Submit a request for approval (if required) to follow the course of action selected.
4. Use the appropriate applications and tools to document the decision made and the operational processes that did not support the standard procedure.
5. Publish and distribute the results of your research.

Understanding how employees make organizational and strategic decisions will help you evaluate what types of collaboration features best facilitate their requirements for ad hoc workflow, messaging, forwarding content, and discussion forums in the corporate portal solution. If you do not have a standard course of action for collecting the decisions made outside the structure provided in the applications and systems in your organization, the corporate portal represents an excellent opportunity to begin to capture this knowledge and share it.

Corporate Portal Communication, Collaboration, and Coordination Checklist

Usually several combined business functions are selected for the initial phases of the corporate portal solution. In the following checklist, please copy the appropriate section (heading and questions) addressing the business functions incorporated in your portal application and answer the questions with business domain experts in your organization.

COLLABORATION TOOLS

☐ What e-mail and collaboration tools should be included in the portal (e.g., Outlook Web access, Outlook 2000, Domino Web applications)?

☐ What navigation and tools (related to e-mail, message forwarding, tasks, calendaring, and discussion) should be included in personalization of the corporate portal?

☐ Will the collaborative tools (e.g., e-mail, calendar, tasks) need to synchronize with any other data source or device (e.g., Palm Personal Data Assistants, scheduling systems)?

E-MAIL

☐ What e-mail functionality will be included (e.g., inbox, view, edit, delete, forward, reply, reply to all, reply with history, save as draft)?

☐ Will the user need to view a log of sent e-mail?

☐ Will the user need to sort messages by recipient or date?

☐ Will search capability of e-mail exist?

☐ Will the user need to create, sort, delete, rename, and organize mail using folders?

☐ Will the user need to filter mail by sender, action required, date, or other criteria?

☐ Will users need to have access to their contact list (with the ability to add, delete, update, group, or send e-mail to a group, address book lookups, etc.)?

☐ Will users need to have search capability for their contact list?

☐ Will the user need to archive e-mail? How will this be performed?

☐ Can users assign access to their e-mail to another user?

SELECT AND FORWARD

☐ Will the user need to select a document and forward it to another user (with comments attached)?

☐ Will the user need to select a web component and forward it to another user (with comments attached)?

TASKS

☐ Will the user need to add, view, delete, and update tasks to a personal to-do list?

☐ What are the states (new, open, closed, past due, on hold, other) available for a task?

☐ Will the to-do list have any time-sensitive alarms?

☐ Can a person assign a task to another person and have it appear in the new user's to-do list?

☐ Can users assign access to their task list to another user?

CALENDAR

☐ What calendar functionality will be included (e.g., view, edit, delete, forward, schedule a meeting, invite participants, find free time, send invitation to groups, accept or decline, counter-propose, track responses)?

☐ Will the calendaring functionality integrate with resource reservations? Where is this information maintained?

☐ Can a person view the calendar of another user?

☐ Can users assign access to their calendar to another user?

DISCUSSION

☐ What discussion functionality will be included (e.g., view, post, respond, vote, respond to a response, categorize)?

☐ Will the discussion functionality integrate with the messaging capabilities (e.g., e-mail of discussion threads, e-mail notification of an available discussion)?

☐ How will discussion items be categorized?

☐ How will discussion items be moderated?

☐ Will the user need to be able to create a private dialog (or discussion for small groups)?

CorporatePortal.com Case Study

CorporatePortal.com wants to take advantage of the process and action (or workflow) features from the portal desktop. The document repository self-service application that is being considered for implementation in the first phase of the corporate portal includes process and action features. Since the Documentum content management application has been selected to coordinate and manage these requirements, the process and action functions of the product are being used to implement the approval and publication of submitted documents. The process and action features allow different employee roles to own the content, working with business domain (i.e., department) experts to approve the information before it is published. Each user group can define a unique approval process. The different approval processes can each be implemented and controlled through the Documentum administration and configuration features. A sample approval screen is shown in Figure 6-6.

The corporate portal is a natural venue for building and sustaining communities. The discussion forums and team interaction features can be subdivided into separate areas designed to appeal to employees with different responsibilities or interests. One common area for all employees is a support forum. Employees are often willing to assist each other solving problems, resolving issues, and sharing tips and techniques.

CorporatePortal.com also wants to consider new team collaboration activities that are supported by the current Microsoft Outlook mail and Exchange discussion features. The goal is to blend the

Figure 6-6. Process and action example.

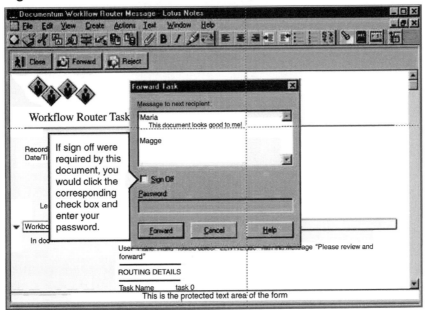

flexibility of public folders with the single-point-of-access features of the portal desktop. Any employee can create a location for shared information that includes:

- *Team Calendar Sharing* (e.g., to schedule events and meetings at times when everyone is available)
- *Contact Lists* (e.g., to create a common, centralized contact list for the employees working on the same tax and audit project)
- *Threaded Discussions* (e.g., to contribute to online discussions)
- *Team Workspace* (e.g., to locate all tax or audit project–related information and documentation from a single location)
- *Team Task Lists* (e.g., to post and assign tasks for team members in a single location that is accessible to everyone through the web)

CorporatePortal.com must identify areas of interest for each employee role that will reinforce common semantics and terms. Moderators facilitate these communities of interest to maintain a set of values, guidelines, and best practices for the group. They create abstracts and activities to encourage all employees to contribute and share their experiences and expertise. The goal is to encourage members of the community of interest to share their opinions about directions and policies that affect the group and organization. CorporatePortal.com believes that fostering communities of interest will be good for business. Some of the benefits and/or goals that should be achieved are as follows:

- The solution cost-effectively supports highly technical or complex issues by recruiting employees to serve in adjunct with the IT support department and other service representatives.
- Employees in each role of the organization can easily make difficult decisions or resolve issues through reports and knowledge stores that streamline business processes.

The development of employee role profiles by administrators means enterprise information can be targeted to the right community of interest. Individual members of the community can also supplement their employee role profile with personal settings that are added to their personal employee profile to customize the content presented to them. For example, information can be targeted to all members of the Java programming community, with each employee able to select preferences for how documents and messages are organized, sorted, or included in personal folders.

• A future collaborative goal is to establish cross-community collaboration for issues that need to be addressed by virtual teams.

• For CorporatePortal.com to manage these collaboration communities it needs several tools and features to provide this full range of functionality. It is developing a collection of question-and-answer forums for employees to look for information and post questions at any time. For example, employees can post a feedback document or comment through a section called Feedback Central or from the Talk option in the portal desktop. Scheduled webcast presentations with subject matter experts that include question-and-answer sessions for employees to participate in will also be available. Employees can formally join a community user group that is closely tied to their role in the organization or their job responsibilities. By officially joining the user group, the employee will receive notifications and invitations to events and other material. This feature is designed to ensure that employees are familiar with the most recent information in the organization without having to search or remember to look for updates and information.

FURTHER READING

Cunningham, Ann M., and Wendy Wicks. *Changing Roles in Information Distribution (Report Series, 1994)*. Philadelphia: National Federation of Abstracting and Information Services, 1993.

Altbach, Philip G. *Knowledge Context: Comparative Perspectives on the Distribution of Knowledge*. Albany, N.Y.: State University of New York Press, 1987.

Coleman, David. *Groupware: Collaborative Strategies for Corporate LANs and Intranets*. Englewood Cliffs, N.J.: Prentice Hall, 1996.

Leymann, Frank, and Dieter Roller. *Production Workflow Concepts and Techniques*. Englewood Cliffs, N.J.: Prentice Hall, 1999.

KEY POINTS

These recommendations regarding direct access to corporate knowledge and resources are critical when preparing your corporate portal strategy:

• Making corporate information available through a browser gives virtually every employee in your organization access to the information. It is important that the published material that comes from both structured and unstructured sources be accurate, organized in a logical and easily understood format, and easy to navigate through.

• Before adding a self-service application into the corporate portal, research that the most relevant content is being published, business processes are automated, web publishing and distribution or content management services are supported, and all infrastructure and configuration issues are resolved.

• Ensure that e-mail and messaging services are supported from the corporate portal solution.

• Ensure that services such as discussion forums, chat features, bulletin boards, feedback, and other employees' requirements for collaboration are available.

Use the following checklist to review or analyze the importance of direct access to corporate knowledge and resources for your organization's corporate portal solution.

ANALYZING YOUR CORPORATE PORTAL'S DIRECT ACCESS TO CORPORATE KNOWLEDGE AND RESOURCES

☐ Is corporate information in the most current version available for employees?

☐ Are departments able to share important information with each other? Is the information current and useful?

☐ Do all employees know the mission of your organization?

☐ Can employees quickly locate data or information specific to their responsibilities and activities? Can they locate information that is relevant to their responsibilities and activities?

☐ Can employees communicate electronically with all employees in the organization?

☐ Are collaboration tools available for all employees to take advantage of? Do they find them easy to locate and use?

☐ Can employees coordinate ad hoc workflow or work processes when a difficult decision or exception needs to be handled or accommodated outside the normal or defined procedure?

7

Direct Links to Reports, Analysis, and Queries

To facilitate the concept of the knowledge desktop that promotes better decisions, you need to present information directly related to each employee's assigned responsibilities. Information specific to each employee needs to be logically organized in the portal desktop. Your task is to identify the reports, sections, or slices of information that are the most useful for each role or related group of corporate portal users. The exercise to categorize comparable responsibilities and define the roles of employees in your organization can be extremely informative. Identification of the roles furnishes a list of primary responsibilities for each group of users, how the identified roles interact, and what information is exchanged between them. Employees in each role throughout your organization often know what sections and slices of information would be the most valuable to them as they perform their daily tasks.

A success factor of the corporate portal solution is the strength of the integration capabilities in the delivered self-service applications. The challenge of the integration effort is to identify and incorporate a network of information sources to support the specific knowledge requirements of day-to-day work for each type of employee role in your organization. Three major categories of information, shown in Figure 7-1, need to be considered, identified, and documented in the corporate portal business case.

Many of the portal content windows display information from structured and unstructured data sources. Some of the content windows display information from multiple data sources at the same time. When employees make selections or choices in one content window, other content windows can be designed, which will reflect new information. You must define the relationships to define content-window-to-content-window business requirements. Interview employees in different roles throughout your organization to gain their perspective of what information would be the most beneficial. Compile the results of these interviews and, equally important, review whether the information technology (IT) department can reproduce or compile with accurate and timely results what employees are requesting. The final result most likely will be a compromise between what is available and what users would like to have available. Any reports or information that cannot be created or compiled by the IT department should be identified as an enhancement for a future implementation phase of the corporate portal solution.

The user perspective of reports and information that they need available to complete their jobs is useful to include in the business case as well. You should also include a summary of what reports and information can be implemented immediately and what would need to be developed at a later stage.

The user interaction and functionality available from each portal content window must be identified. If employees wish to undertake any activity beyond reading information from the corporate portal content pages, then additional interaction with the original data source or other software applications is required. There may also be collaboration, notification, and navigation requirements.

Figure 7-1. Categories of information.

Structured Information	Unstructured Information	Collaborative
• Enterprise Applications	• Document Collections	• Notification
• Legacy Systems	• Groupware Applications	• Collaboration
• Data Warehouses	• Messaging System	• Workflow/Actions
• Data Marts	• Web Pages and Links	• Navigation
• Business Intelligence	• Online Information Feeds	• Other

These requirements are not only associated with the portal content pages and content page windows, but with the personalization features or functions that are persistent throughout the corporate portal solution. Your business case will be more complete if these types of requirements are documented and considered by the corporate portal strategy team.

Remember that there must be a balance between material and reports that are accessed through the portal desktop and when employees need to work directly with the source system or application. If the employees must use all aspects of the related data source or external application, they should be able to bring the related or external application into the corporate portal interface or launch the external application in a separate application window from the corporate portal. Your goal is to create an environment that provides valuable services and that information employees will be drawn to as part of their daily activities.

Summarized information and reports from operational systems and business intelligence systems have to be included in the portal desktop. When designing the corporate portal solution for your organization, the following distinctions between operational systems and business intelligence systems can be referenced:

• *Operational Systems.* These systems process transactional data and are used to automate routine and predictable tasks. An operational system is designed to handle large amounts of transactions used to manage the day-to-day operations of the organization. Examples of operational systems include order processing and invoicing systems, general ledger, and stock control systems.

• *Business Intelligence or Informational Systems.* These systems are used for analysis and reporting of trends found in operational systems. A business intelligence system is designed to process queries used in strategic analysis to create a competitive advantage and affect the profitability of the organization. Examples of business intelligence systems include management information systems and sales control systems. Information used in business intelligence systems consists of three distinct processes:

1. Reviewing the data to discover points of interest.
2. Analyzing these points of interest to discover patterns.

3. Presenting the patterns discovered and how they are interpreted with respect to your organization.

The corporate portal solution is ideal for bringing important "snippets" of information to employees. This subset of information is an abstract or collection of summarized material that employees can use to understand both your organization and their responsibilities better and more thoroughly. This summarized material, called a balanced scorecard, is often used to present how the organization or employee is meeting current defined objectives.

The balanced scorecard is used to measure your organization's performance. The goal is to evaluate the visions and strategies that your organization needs to focus on and convert them into a measurement system. The measurement system used strongly affects the behavior and activities of employees throughout your organization. Traditional financial accounting measures have been used to track performance in the past, but these methods are often misleading and provide inadequate information for continuous improvement and innovation goals. You need to consider how customer service metrics, quality statistics, product sales mix, rates of illness in the workforce, and other indicators directly relate to your organization's goals and strategies. The balanced scorecard is designed to provide a wider perspective of your organization's performance that includes internal and external indicators and metrics.

Business intelligence systems and balanced scorecard systems require data points and integration elements that use new paradigms and technologies to provide the functionality of extracting information, completing any algorithms or transformations required, and loading the summarized report into a content window on the portal desktop. The final corporate portal should be able to access information from a wide range of internal and external information sources and display them at the single-point-of-access desktop from a browser. The corporate portal strategy team members must use their business analysis skills to determine the requirements of employees in the organization and map them into business intelligence and balanced scorecard features the corporate portal delivers to your employees.

Business Intelligence Systems

Structured information is data that can be organized and represented in tables that consist of rows and columns of information. It is also referred to as the relational model of database management. The relational model allows the physical aspects of data to be separated from the logical representation so that data appears as simple tables that remove the complexity of the storage access mechanisms or application specifics. This allows you (with the help of your IT department) to create a corporate portal business case that includes information about the tables, columns, and row qualifiers to locate any data item you need to represent. The type of relational or structured information that you want to include in a corporate portal content window is often collected from multiple systems or database tables. The scope of data manipulation required to successfully implement the initial phases of the corporate portal solution depends on:

1. How up-to-the-minute the report or data points displayed in the corporate portal content window are
2. How the structured data is stored in the production systems
3. How tailored or derived the information needs to be when presented to the corporate portal

The types of features you should consider for the corporate portal solution are those that provide knowledge workers at various levels throughout your organization the ability to make better business decisions. These solutions can be designed, developed, and deployed by your internal IT department or as online analytical processing (OLAP) and other software systems that contribute to business intelligence systems by creating data models that reflect the complexities of data structures found in your organization. These systems include query and reporting features, an ability to view data from multiple perspectives (or dimensions), data pattern discovery (i.e., data mining), and personal information agents. A business intelligence system (BIS) can model multidimensional scenarios that allow users to move from one view of the issue being presented to another view by switching to another dimension. Examples of dimensions within data include areas of interest such as products, time frames, and orders. Business intelligence systems give decision makers a complete overview of a business situation from several desired strategic perspectives.

The Presentation of Structured Information

As defined previously, IT systems designed to help employees make strategic decisions are referred to as business intelligence systems and are unique from operational systems in several ways. For example:

Operational Systems

- Used to automate routine and predictable tasks.
- Characterized by large volumes of small transactions that are generally limited in scope.
- Designed to get data in.

Business Intelligence Systems

- Built to enable analysis and presentation of information including unpredictable queries.
- Characterized by very few queries that are often wide in scope.
- Designed to get information out.

To support business intelligence systems in the corporate portal, your organization must support a data warehouse or data mart repository. The data warehouse contributes the following features in the corporate portal:

- *Query and Reporting Features.* Query and data analysis features allow employees to formulate queries without writing programs or learning how to write structured query language (SQL) statements. There are point-and-click features or ways for typing in a question in plain English (i.e., natural language queries) to submit a request to the data source. If the request is understood by the data source, then the results are displayed in some understandable form (usually a report) to the employee.

Queries can be predefined and designed to automatically execute with the results presented to the employee in the corporate portal as a report, spreadsheet, bar chart, pie chart, histogram, or other desired format. Other query options include:

1. Making the queries interactive.
2. Allowing the queries and reports to be created and saved by employees and executed on demand.
3. Storing the saved queries and executing on a scheduled basis.

• *Viewing Data from Multiple Perspectives (or Dimensions).* Online analytical processing tools create multidimensional data views of relational database information or other data that can be represented in a row and column table format. This multidimensional access allows your self-service applications to incorporate more sophisticated queries and then look at the results accordingly. The OLAP multidimensional model allows you to visualize data easily. Dimensions typically fall into the categories of factual and descriptive. Factual dimensions represent a measurable aspect of an observed object or event. Facts are normally represented in numeric values such as absolute units. Descriptive values have a smaller range of values that are used to order, group, and summarize the values in factual dimensions. Each dimension has a name and a set of elements or values that can be logically assigned to instances for that dimension. Instead of navigating through multiple tables and rows, you look at data as a multi-worksheet spreadsheet with multiple categories.

For example, a product data store would allow you to access multiple dimensions such as time, region, customer, price, and sales. You can explore the different data dimensions at the same time (e.g., What are our sales by product, by customer, by month?). Figure 7-2 represents a diagram of the same data in a relational data view, a multidimensional data view, and a section or slice of the information available in a corporate portal content window summary report. An example of a report with multiple dimensions displayed in the portal desktop, created using the InfoImage freedom product, is shown in Figure 7-3.

Figure 7-2. Three views of data: relational, multidimensional, and corporate portal content window.

a. Relational Data Model

Year	Month	Geography	Expenses	Amount
2000	01	Northeast	Salaries	$78,683
2000	01	Northeast	Supplies	$26,344
2000	01	Northeast	HW/SW	$59,945
2000	01	Northeast	Other	$30,258
2000	01	Pennsylvania	Salaries	$28,282
2000	01	Pennsylvania	Supplies	$1,976
2000	01	Pennsylvania	HW/SW	$1,580
2000	01	Pennsylvania	Other	$1,580
...	...	...	...	...
1990	12	Northeast	Salaries	$42,789
1990	12	Northeast	Supplies	$21,900
1990	12	Northeast	HW/SW	$28,760
1990	12	Northeast	Other	347

b. Multidimensional Data Model

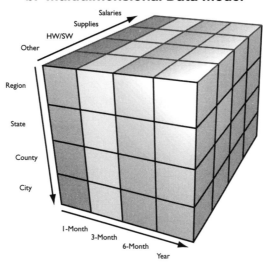

(continues)

Figure 7-2. Continued.

c. Corporate Portal Content Window Report

CorporatePortal.com Report				setup ▼
Q2 2000 Expenses				
	Salaries	Supplies	HW / SW	Other
▼ **Northeast Region**	$78,683	$59,945	$42,158	$48,776
▶ Pennsylvania	$56,000	$26,344	$22,366	$20,000
▼ New Jersey	$22,683	$33,601	$19,792	$28,776
▼ Manmouth County	$18,637	$30,258	$2,604	$26,976
Freehold	$9,761	$28,282	$1,717	$25,000
Colts Neck	$8,876	$1,976	$887	$1,976
▼ Ocean County	$1,000	$1,580	$656	$1,000
Jackson	$1,000	$1,580	$656	$1,000
▼ Middlesex County	$3,046	$1,763	$16,532	$800
New Brunswick	$2,309	$776	$6,654	$700
Somerset	$737	$987	$9,878	$100

• *Data Pattern Discovery (Data Mining).* Data mining tools are designed to sift through vast quantities of information looking for valuable patterns in the data. Data mining tools look for patterns and groupings that you may have overlooked in your own analysis of a set of data. In data mining, the tool does the discovery and tells you something, instead of you asking a question. These are often referred to as "fuzzy" searches. They perform search methods that include:

1. *Associations.* An association looks for patterns where the presence of one data point implies the presence of another data point. For example, customers that purchase luggage sets are good candidates to take family vacations in the next twelve months.
2. *Sequential Patterns.* A sequential pattern looks for chronological occurrences. For example, when the price of Caribbean cruises goes down by 10 percent, the price of resorts in Caribbean locations goes up by 5 percent to 8 percent a month later.

Figure 7-3. InfoImage freedom's multiple dimensions feature.

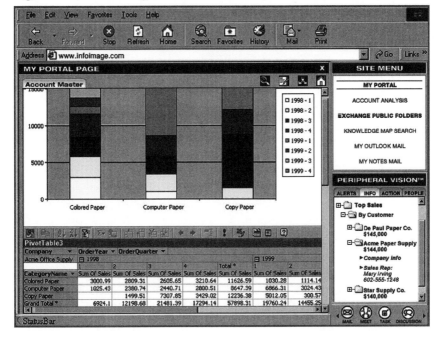

3. *Clusterings.* A clustering looks for groupings and high-level classifications. For example, more than 80 percent of Caribbean cruise vacationers have incomes of less than $40,000 per year, are between ages 20 and 35, and are single or have been married less than five years.

Data mining tools are used in many industries. Banks use them to detect credit card fraud. Attorneys use them to select juries and analyze voting patterns of Supreme Court justices. Stockbrokers use them to identify stock movements and trading patterns. Health researchers use them to discover patterns affecting the success of different types of surgery. Data mining has several important features you'll want to review and consider for your corporate portal solution depending on the types of decisions employees need to make and the relationships that need to be established between data sources and knowledge experts in your organization.

• *Personal Information Agents.* Personal information agents are mobile applications that are launched on demand to perform specific queries or to search for patterns in data sources. Most personal information agents are predefined rules-based programs that are executed when the appropriate trigger or selected event within the corporate portal is activated.

The Decision-Making Process

Knowledge workers go through three distinct phases to make strategic decisions:

• *Discovery*. During the discovery phase the knowledge worker is looking for patterns in the data by identifying comparisons and exceptions. The employee wants to examine the data from many different perspectives and dimensions. For example, knowledge workers are often looking at comparisons across the time dimension (e.g., this year's figures compared to last year's figures for the same product sales). The identification of exceptions and variances could constitute an area of interest suggesting that additional research into the underlying data would be useful.

• *Analysis and Confirmation*. Once an exception or trend has been uncovered, the differences need to be explained. Analysis involves activities such as:

1. Proving that the trend exists.
2. Understanding the factors that are causing the trend.
3. Forecasting the trend over time.
4. Making confident predictions about what the trend means.

The tools and applications that are used for analysis can be launched as a link from the corporate portal solution. It is possible that knowledge workers will need to return to the discovery stage after performing some analysis on the data.

• *Presentation*. Once the analysis of the data is completed and verified, the findings must be presented to employees who are empowered to act on the business intelligence results. Effective presentation of the conclusions reached is required to validate the discovery and analysis activities. The tools and applications available to make the results easy to understand and act on are important. Documentation, reports, tables, charts, and graphics are the most effective formats to relay the business intelligence results. Data visualization and well-written documentation are important aspects of effective presentations.

Business Intelligence Systems Checklist

For each business function selected for the initial phases of your corporate portal solution, please copy the appropriate section (heading and questions) in the checklist that follows and answer the questions with business domain experts in your organization.

IDENTIFYING DATA SOURCES

☐ Have the query, reporting features, and other reporting options been reviewed and considered for each business function?

☐ Have the data sources been identified for each report, content pages, and the content-relevant information section?

☐ Have the data source owners been identified for each data source identified?

☐ Have the data source or data point concerns from the business domain experts been identified?

☐ Have any additional issues or details for each data source been defined?

BUSINESS OBJECTIVES

☐ How do you want to identify problems and exceptions during data access activities?

☐ Are there specific bottlenecks to getting at information?

☐ How much historical information is required?

☐ What opportunities exist to dramatically improve your business based on improved access to information?

EXTERNAL SYSTEM INTERFACES

☐ What external data sources and systems need to feed data to the corporate portal?

☐ How many users are currently using those external systems?

☐ How do you currently get the data?

☐ What do you do with the information once you get it?

☐ Are there potential improvements to your current method or process?

☐ What type of summary reporting and ad hoc analysis do you typically perform?

☐ Who requests summary reports and ad hoc analysis?

☐ What do they do with the reports or analysis?

☐ Which reports do you currently use?

☐ What data on the report is important?

☐ How do you use the information?

☐ If the report were dynamic (real time from the originating data sources), what would the report do differently?

DATA INTEGRATION REQUIREMENTS

For each business function and report that requires information from an external data source, answer the following:

☐ Is the interface real-time, scheduled, batch mode, or other?

☐ What are the required characteristics of the individual data elements that the system must provide, store, send, access, and receive? Considerations include:

  ☐ Data source, keys, tables, relationships, and design logic

  ☐ Data name (e.g., technical name, nontechnical name, natural language name, unique identifier, abbreviations, or standard data element name)

  ☐ Data type (e.g., text, integer, rich text, double, date)

  ☐ Size and data format (e.g., number of characters, punctuation)

  ☐ Units of measure

  ☐ Range or enumeration of possible values

  ☐ Accuracy and precision

  ☐ Constraints (e.g., priority, timing, frequency, volume, sequencing)

  ☐ Security and privacy

☐ Are there any specific requirements for assembling and/or presenting the data?

CorporatePortal.com Case Study

One of the goals identified for the corporate portal solution at CorporatePortal.com is to provide information relevant to each employee that allows them to review metrics of corporate objectives. Oracle Financials is the data source for the financial reports and metrics that employees need to access. The type of information that employees are interested in is depends on the department or workgroup they work in. The departments interviewed for the initial implementation were:

- Accounting
- Information technology
- Marketing
- Personnel
- Sales
- Training

The financial reports and summary information that were identified by employees and need to be accessed from the portal desktop are shown in Figure 7-4. In several cases security issues prevent the financial information from being presented in the portal desktop to all departments. For example, payroll information is only available to Personnel, Accounting, and Sales, provided the employee is allowed access by the Oracle Financials system. In addition, limited levels of detail are accessible from the portal desktop. If more information or detail is needed to complete the task or research the issue, then the Oracle Financials system should be accessed directly. For example, the columns of information and subtotals available for Sales Summary reports would include invoice number, the date, customer name, and sales amount. This is the correct level of detail for most departments. However, the Sales and Marketing departments are interested in seeing the information categorized by customer, product, and geography.

One aspect of the portal desktop that relies heavily on business intelligence, collaboration, and enterprise data that is well defined and easily accessed across the CorporatePortal.com network infrastructure is the Accounting department reports. This collection of reports is accessible from the primary department and secondary

Figure 7-4. CorporatePortal.com's financial reports.

Report Category	Report Name
General Information	• Flash Summary • Cash • Accounts Receivable • Inventory • Accounts Payable • Current Payroll • General Ledger Transactions • Accounting Policies and Procedures
Summaries	• Sales • Today's Sales • Purchases • Payroll • Expenses • Capital Budget
Financial Statements	• Financial Statement Library • General Ledger Transactions • Ratios • Current Run Rate
Exception Reports	• Past Due Receivables (Accounts Receivable Aging) • Employee Overtime

Accounting portal menu options. Business domain experts from across CorporatePortal.com completed a review of how they work and identified a collection of reports that effectively and efficiently present this financial information.

Business domain experts also must provide report formats, descriptions of associated attributes, and documentation of this information. A knowledge expert from the IT department familiar with the Oracle Financials system can review the outlined report formats to verify that these reports can be created and made available to the corporate portal. The IT department can also verify that accurate information is available to generate the reports. The final analysis needs to identify any new report formats that need to be created; new Oracle views required to generate the report; new queries that apply the correct business logic and rules to create the reports; new schedules created to update the reports as necessary; new administration tasks and activities to maintain the report creation process; and any other transformation or distribution issues that must be addressed before making these reports available to the portal desktop. For the business case to be created, only a preliminary awareness, analysis, and estimate of the work required to be completed needs to be identified and documented.

The lists of reports that have been identified by CorporatePortal.com employees for the portal desktop have been organized into several different categories. The categories include General Information, Summaries, Financial Statements, and Reports (Exception). The General Information reports are:

- *Flash Summary* (a report format is shown in Figure 7-5).
- *Cash* (a report format is shown in Figure 7-6).
- *Accounts Receivable (Pivot Table).* This is a dimension table that displays receivables detail by customer ID and can be "piv-

Figure 7-5. Flash summary format.

The following information is as of [current date and time]

Cash	$631,834
Receivables	$1,781,496
Inventory	$667,129
Payables	$1,755,904
Current Payroll	$28,033

Figure 7-6. Cash report format.

The following information is as of [current date and time]

General Ledger Account	Account Description	Amount
000-1100-00	Cash - Operating Account	$407,381.89
000-1101-00	Cash - Bank of America	$9,007.84
000-1102-00	Cash - Bank One	$18,302.17
000-1103-00	Cash - Chase Bank	$6,007.94
000-1104-00	Cash - First National Bank	$7,909.80
000-1105-00	Cash - Wells Fargo Bank (Atlanta)	$12,697.77
000-1106-00	Cash - Wells Fargo Bank (Chicago)	$7,501.90
000-1107-00	Cash - Wells Fargo Bank (Denver)	$6,963.24
000-1110-00	Cash - Payroll	$139,080.67
000-1120-00	Cash - Flexible Benefits Program	$345.32
000-1130-00	Petty Cash	$319.54
000-1140-00	Savings	$16,316.12
Total		$631,834.20

oted" (to lend a different perspective) by customer, date, or document number. The report format for a single customer is shown in Figure 7-7. The Accounts Receivable Pivot Table in the portal desktop allows the customer, date, and document number dimensions to be collapsed and expanded as needed by the employee.

• *Inventory.* A report that allows goods available for sale or back-ordered to be tracked by product line, warehouse location, and date.

• *Accounts Payable (Pivot Table).* This dimension table displays receivables detail, by vendor ID, and can be "pivoted" by vendor, date, or invoice number. The report format for a single vendor is shown in Figure 7-8. The dimensions in the pivot table can be easily collapsed and expanded from the portal desktop.

• *Current Payroll* (a report format is shown in Figure 7-9). This report is a table of the current payroll period information.

• *General Ledger Transactions.* This is a listing of the activity in each chart of accounts that make up the financial statement line

Figure 7-7. Accounts receivable format (vendor: ACME Office Supply).

Customer ID	Document Number	Document Date	Amount
The following information is as of [current date and time]			
ACMEOFFY0001	SVC1000	1/12/00	($2,255.97)
ACMEOFFY0001	SVC11004	1/12/00	$1,859.63
ACMEOFFY0001	PMT11001	1/16/00	$0.00
ACMEOFFY0001	SLS11012	1/16/00	($1,348.71)
ACMEOFFY0001	SLS11014	1/16/00	($3,531.75)
ACMEOFFY0001	SVC11012	1/21/00	$5,872.41
ACMEOFFY0001	SVC11013	1/26/00	$2,356.89
ACMEOFFY0001	SLS11014	1/27/00	$3,531.75
ACMEOFFY0001	SLS11015	1/27/00	$833.33
ACMEOFFY0001	SLS11016	1/30/00	$5,000.00
ACMEOFFY0001	INV1024	2/10/00	$128.35
ACMEOFFY0001	INV1024	2/10/00	($128.35)
ACMEOFFY0001	PYMNT000022	2/10/00	$0.00
ACMEOFFY0001	INV1025	2/15/00	$117.65
ACMEOFFY0001	INV1025	2/15/00	($117.65)
ACMEOFFY0001	PYMNT000023	2/15/00	$0.00
ACMEOFFY0001	SVC1000	3/12/00	$4,322.98
ACMEOFFY0001	SVC1000	3/15/00	($98.31)
ACMEOFFY0001	SVC1000	4/7/00	($1,500.00)
ACMEOFFY0001	SVC1001	4/8/00	$2,155.79
Total			$17,198.04

Figure 7-8. Accounts payable format (vendor: Ace Travel).

The following information is as of [current date and time]

Customer ID	Document Number	Document Date	Amount
ACETRAVL0001	INV11007	1/27/00	$12,849.08
ACETRAVL0001	INV11006	2/28/00	$11,054.39
ACETRAVL0001	INV1003	3/17/00	$10,796.03
ACETRAVL0001	INV1004	4/24/00	$10,605.45
ACETRAVL0001	INV1005	5/24/00	$11,906.44
ACETRAVL0001	INV1006	6/18/00	$12,158.75
Total			$69,370.14

Figure 7-9. Current payroll summary.

The following information is as of [current date and time]

Employee ID	Employee Name	Gross Pay
ALVA0001	Alicia M Alvarza	$2,168.00
NAKU0001	Amanda K Nakumota	$1,849.00
REES0001	Benjamin D Reese	$2,058.00
LEVI0001	Brian C Levin	$2,163.00
ERIC0001	Charles D Erickson	$2,019.00
DUBO0001	Christine L Dubois	$1,891.00
TANN0001	Clarence R Tanner	$1,990.00
BURN0001	David J Burnell	$1,833.00
BANK0001	Katherine A Banks	$2,108.00
YOSH0001	Kenji Y Yoshioka	$1,912.00
GREE0001	Kevin M Greenberg	$1,128.00
LOWE0001	Martin J Lowenstein	$1,354.00
DRAK0001	Robert L Drake	$1,825.00
CARN0001	Rolando M Carnero	$1,191.00
YOUN0001	Russell J Young	$1,288.00
CRAN0001	Ruth M Crane	$1,256.00
Total		$28,033.00

items. This report is available for different time periods and several levels of detail.

• *Chart of Accounts.* This is an explanation of the types of information in each general ledger account and which accounts make up each financial statement line item.

• *Accounting Policies and Procedures.* The Accounting Policies and Procedures content window contains a list of hyperlinks to the content management system, web sites, user-assisted help, and other information sources that allow employees to do their jobs more effectively and make more informed decisions.

These General Information reports are all accessible from a single portal content page to the CorporatePortal.com Accounting department (see Figure 7-10). The Flash Summary has hyperlinks into additional reports. For example, if the Cash amount link is selected, the Cash report (Figure 7-6) is displayed on the content page in another content window. Notice that all the report formats have a limited number of records and attributes displayed so that the report can be easily read from the portal desktop. If a significant number of records or attributes need to be accessed or available for the employee, then the employee would have to leave the portal desktop and access the reporting system or Oracle Financial system.

For strategic decisions or reports that are not currently included in the portal desktop, an employee must submit a report request. The financial report request form is available from the content-rele-

Figure 7-10. Corporate portal general information reports (portal page).

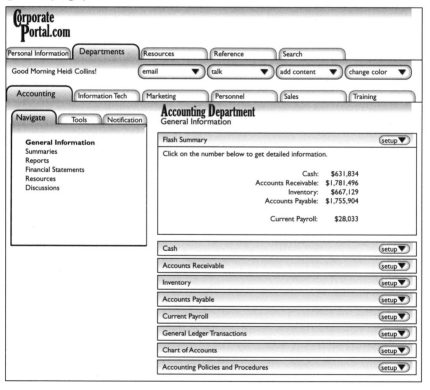

vant information Tools tab. A wizard directs the employee through the creation and submission of the report request. The submitted request and any necessary interactions with the IT department can then be tracked from the Documentum application or collaboration system that CorporatePortal.com also implemented (as discussed in Chapter 6). These strategic report requests are expected to be fairly significant in detail and length. Because of their scope, however, they should be accessed and analyzed in Oracle (or other supported application) outside the portal desktop.

BALANCED SCORECARD SYSTEMS

The corporate portal solution is going to be judged on how useful the content available is and how well the content is managed. The content pages deliver information from multiple sources in dissimilar formats from different domains while maintaining the security schema, business rules, and reuse potential required by employees. Content integration is a critical requirement for the portal's success in your organization. Content about a given issue can span a wide spectrum of information sources including people, e-mail, discussion threads, the Internet, document repositories, and many others.

One issue to be aware of is that structured data sources are not designed to understand unstructured content. During design of the solution, you must tie these requirements together to provide the context relationships. The other major difficulty is the volume of information that exists or needs to be traversed to locate these related pieces of information. All these data sources contain business critical insights that need to be available to employees when they are completing their assigned task and contributing to the organization. Learning how content is used in your organization is the primary method to discover what different information means to different groups of users. Your corporate portal discovery process should identify structured, unstructured, and web pages required to satisfy the critical success factors of the project.

The corporate portal solution needs to remain scalable as the volume of content continues to expand. Scalability needs to be a fully defined process that integrates content into the corporate portal. Each corporate portal user identified must be able to customize the content presented to them. There needs to be corporate portal roles defined and maintained to identify the content pages and content windows for the portal desktop that correspond to the responsibilities of the identified group of employees. This effort yields two benefits. The first allows personalization of the corporate portal environment, and the second is to deliver content relevant to the user that the individual might not otherwise know how to access or locate.

Key areas to concentrate on when researching what information to include in the corporate portal solution and to document in the business case are summarized in the following list:

- *Identification of Relevant Content.* This effort entails (1) locating all the content that is most pertinent to the business activities performed by the individual roles of the corporate portal users, (2) creating personalized views for each workgroup that will improve productivity, and (3) continually synchronizing knowledge workers with changing content and business processes.

- *Automation of Business Processes.* Functionality that automates routing, approval, distribution, notification, and coordination for business processes not supported in other systems should be included in the corporate portal requirements.

- *Web Publishing and Distribution Services (Content Management).* The management of content storage, versioning, security, tracking, and archiving should be automated to ensure content integrity of the corporate portal solution.

- *Infrastructure and Configuration Considerations.* The hardware and software requirements need to be identified and researched to verify that the corporate portal solution can meet the demands of the business requirements. Security and configuration requirements are identified to verify that user roles, static content, dynamic content, and processes can be met by the proposed corporate portal solution.

You should consider balanced scorecard features in the corporate portal solution if your mission includes the ability to articulate, measure, and monitor the behaviors that make your organization successful. Software products are available for automating the creation and maintenance of balanced scorecards. The research and analysis that the corporate portal strategy team completes should provide the details to determine the differentiators between products and establish the most useful solution for your production environment.

The balanced scorecard concept requires that a balanced model of internal and external measures be established to reveal how the entire organization is performing. The specific company goals and strategies of the employees using the corporate portal are critical for determining the performance metrics and goals to be included in the first phase of the corporate portal solution. Along with the performance objectives, some aspects of the outcome metrics that define and describe cause-and-effect relationships should be researched and documented in the business case. Among the several critical success factors to consider and be aware of when planning a balanced scorecard system are the following:

- *Awareness of the Organization's Strategy.* All employees in your organization must understand the mission and goals of your organization. The mission of the organization is outlined as a set of objectives. A measurement is then established for each objective and applied to each responsibility, activity, or department.

- *Personalization Requirements.* The corporate portal is a central location to market and brand the mission and goals of your organization for all employees to understand and comprehend. Using administration and individual personalization features in the corporate portal, each employee is given access to work with only the balanced scorecard measurements applicable to their individual responsibilities, activities, and department.

- *Flexibility to Change Measures.* The environment of business and your organization is under continuous change. As the business and business conditions change, the balanced scorecard system should provide a way to easily enhance existing measures and add new measures.

- *Data Availability.* Once the measurements have been identified, the relevant data and the associated data sources need to be located. In many cases you probably will not be able to locate all the information required, the information will not be in the format required, or the information required will be inaccurate. The corporate portal business case requires that you have some indication of the data requirements and what internal or external activities need to be completed to make the data available for the initial phases of the corporate portal solution.

• *Data Security*. The balanced scorecard system requires a flexible security architecture that is based on user identity and user profiles to access confidential data.

• *Data Analysis*. In some cases employees will need to drill into the summary information to analyze and understand the underlying data. When possible, hyperlinks and other analysis tools should be made available from the corporate portal.

The balanced scorecard is based on a strong focus of your organization's vision and strategy. It consists of a comprehensive and hierarchical view of performance. The steps to designing a balanced scorecard can be summarized as follows:

• *Vision*. Begin with the organization's mission or vision.
• *Strategies*. Understand your organization's structure and outline the strategies that will lead to successfully obtaining the mission.
• *Activities*. The strategies identified need to be broken into a collection of activities or tasks.
• *Measurements*. Establish the metrics for each activity.

Analyzing Balanced Scorecard Requirements

To analyze balanced scorecard requirements, consider the goals and responsibilities of the employees using the corporate portal from four different perspectives:

1. *Financial Perspective*. The financial perspective of the balanced scorecard is focused on the bottom line of your organization and measures traditional accounting results such as return on investment (ROI) and earnings per share. The measurements should reflect whether the organization's strategy is being properly implemented and executed.

2. *Internal Perspective*. This is a summary of the internal processes and performance issues driving your organization. Internal performance management determines which products, services, markets, or other internal initiatives (i.e., personnel retention) to focus on.

3. *External Perspective*. The external perspective of the balanced scorecard is a summary of the customer needs, customer satisfaction, and market share metrics in your organization. These measurements should verify that the organization's strategy is being properly implemented and executed.

4. *Knowledge and Learning Perspective*. The knowledge and learning perspective of the balanced scorecard is a summary of the people and organization issues contributing to the future growth and success of your company.

Your design decisions when defining the content pages and corporate portal features must be completed for every self-service application added to the corporate portal solution. During new phases of the corporate portal solution, the design decisions made should be reviewed and updated with enhancements suggested by existing users and requirements needed by new self-service applications.

The design of most corporate portal content pages and content windows is to present summary information to users as overviews of a larger collection of data sources. The summary information may or may not be presented for display to the browser from the originating data source or application. Any transformation or manipulation of information requirements to be completed prior to presenting the summary data in the corporate portal content page or content window should be discovered during your research and interviewing activities. The summary information presented frequently needs to be reviewed by the corporate portal user in more detail. If additional detail is a requirement of your self-service applications, you need to (1) allow these summary reports to be drilled into in more detail or (2) design the solution so that the source application is launched to perform necessary detailed work processes. How these decisions are made in part depends on what operational or strategic decisions need to be made by associates using the corporate portal, how accurate and timely the information presented must be, and what the performance requirements of the content pages are. The corporate portal should collect feedback to establish the advantages perceived by employees and how users believe the portal desktop can be improved.

Balanced Scorecard Systems Checklist

The following checklist walks through the steps for creating a balanced scorecard and is designed to help you assess the critical success factors from each perspective.

EVALUATING VISION

☐ What part of the organization's mission and vision statements are associated with profitability or financial goals?

☐ What part of the organization's mission and vision statements are associated with internal initiatives?

☐ What part of the organization's mission and vision statements are associated with external initiatives?

☐ What part of the organization's mission and vision statements are associated with knowledge and learning initiatives?

EVALUATING STRATEGIES

☐ What are the specific profitability and financial objectives that can be derived from the profitability and financial goals of the organization? How are the profitability and financial objectives distributed or assigned in your organization (i.e., workgroup or department)?

☐ What are the specific objectives associated with internal initiatives that can be derived from the mission or vision of the organization? How are internal initiative objectives distributed or assigned in your organization?

☐ What are the specific objectives associated with external initiatives that can be derived from the mission or vision of the organization? How are external initiative objectives distributed or assigned in your organization?

☐ What are the specific objectives associated with knowledge and learning initiatives that can be derived from the mission or vision of the organization? How are knowledge and learning objectives distributed or assigned in your organization?

EVALUATING ACTIVITIES

☐ For each objective assigned to each workgroup or department, what are the specific activities and tasks to be completed that will meet the assigned objective?

☐ For each assigned activity or task, which role or responsibility is assigned to complete the activity or task?

EVALUATING MEASUREMENTS

☐ For each identified activity or task, what is the actual metric or measure used to define the degree of success or achievement of the activity or task?

☐ How will this metric or measurement be displayed in the corporate portal? Will the metric or measurement be presented differently for individuals with different roles and responsibilities?

☐ How current does the measurement need to be to provide employees with the knowledge they need to make informed decisions?

☐ How accurate does the measurement and information need to be for employees to use effectively?

CorporatePortal.com Case Study

Financial objectives will be unique for each role identified at CorporatePortal.com. An example of how to incorporate the balanced scorecard for financial objectives into the portal desktop is demonstrated for the Sales department. The Sales department consists primarily of sales manager and sales representative roles. The sales manager role is reviewed in more detail for purposes of our example. Financial objectives for sales managers currently include:

- Meeting or exceeding the budgeted sales goals for tax and audit projects each quarter.
- Recruiting, training, and managing the sales staff that will

generate and maintain a pipeline of sales leads and opportunities to meet budgeted sales goals.

The quarterly sales goal needs to be established and well understood by the entire sales department. Sales managers watch financial reports closely to verify if their sales campaigns and strategies are working effectively (e.g., what percentage of sales campaigns end in a contract or project?) and efficiently (e.g., how many days or weeks are there from the initial contact with the customer to having a signed contract?). They use financial reports to determine if they need to modify sales strategies, the number of employees required to meet the sales goal, or processes. The balanced scorecard reports that sales managers need to be represented in the portal desktop to quickly review the status of financial objectives such as:

- The day's sales
- Account receivables (aging report)
- Sales compared to budget
- Variance reports

Sales managers require that the information is updated or current once each day. The IT department has determined that these reports can be updated once or twice each day with the most current information from Oracle Financials. These reports can be presented at the account level with links to look at the same information at the line-item level for each account in the chart of accounts. If the employee requires additional detail, the full collection of financial reports can be found in the Accounting department content pages of the portal desktop.

FURTHER READING

Orfali, Robert, Dan Harkey, and Jeri Edwards. *The Essential Client/ Server Survival Guide (Second Edition)*. New York: John Wiley & Sons, Inc., 1996.

Kimball, Ralph, Laura Reeves, Margy Ross, and Warren Thornthwaite. *The Data Warehouse Lifecycle Toolkit: Expert Methods for Designing, Developing, and Deploying Data Warehouses.* New York: John Wiley & Sons, Inc., 1998.

Missroon, Alan M. "Demystifying the Balanced Scorecard," *DM Review*, May 1999.

KEY POINTS

To prepare the corporate portal strategy, there are several considerations regarding direct access to reports, analysis, and queries to review. Various systems and their features add value to the corporate portal solution. For example:

1. *Operational systems process transactional data and are used to automate routine and predictable tasks.* An operational system is designed to handle large amounts of transactions used to manage the daily operations of the organization.

2. *Business intelligence systems are used for analysis and reporting of trends found in operational systems.* This information is incorporated into the corporate portal in several formats:

- Query and reporting features
- Data viewed from multiple perspectives (or dimensions)
- Data pattern discovery (data mining)
- Personal information agents

3. *Collaborative business intelligence systems add communication, collaboration, process, and action to business intelligence systems available in the corporate portal.* Among the benefits are the availability of:

- Business intelligence tools to generate reports that appear on the Web
- Knowledge management tools to provide the communication, collaboration, and repository features for storing and organizing these reports
- Search benefits that provide full-text searching by topic (pulling information in) and targeted audience (pushing information out)

4. *Balanced scorecard systems are used to measure perfor-mance.* The goal is to evaluate the visions and strategies that your organization needs to focus on and convert them into a measurement system. Of particular interest in the balanced scorecard approach are:

Planning Requirements

- Awareness of the organization's strategy
- Personalization requirements
- Flexibility to change measures
- Data availability
- Data security
- Data analysis

Analysis Perspectives

- Financial
- Internal
- External
- Knowledge and Learning

Use the following checklist to review or analyze the importance of direct access to reports, links to data sources to perform analysis activities, and the ability to submit queries and review result sets from your organization's corporate portal solution.

ANALYZING YOUR CORPORATE PORTAL'S DIRECT LINKS TO REPORTS, ANALYSIS, AND QUERIES

☐ How are scheduled or batch reports distributed to employees? Are they made available to everyone who needs them or is interested in them?

☐ How are ad hoc reports requested and distributed to employees? How are consistently requested ad hoc reports being turned into scheduled or batch reports?

☐ How are parameterized (i.e., prebuilt options) reports requested and distributed to employees? Are they made available to everyone who needs them or is interested in them?

☐ How are sophisticated queries and data mining activities against data sources in your organization requested? Can this sophisticated request, associated dialog, analysis requirements, and other activities be managed more efficiently?

8

Direct Links to Relative Data and Knowledge Experts

Employees must have direct access to the reports, analysis, and queries required to perform the responsibilities assigned to them. They have an equal need to uncover valuable information related to these reports and other tasks or activities each employee has to complete. Within a point-and-click environment from the content-relevant information section of the corporate portal, an employee can identify links to information that have pertinent meaning or a direct relationship to the reports and other information in the content page and content windows. These features provide the information that allows employees to make more informed decisions one link or click away from the current activity they are completing.

There is a natural need when viewing business information to look up related documents and material or to contact employees who are knowledge experts about the task being performed. The knowledge expert may be directly involved or only indirectly associated with the context of the business information and process being reviewed. For example, a product manager reviewing product shipping and packaging requirements may have to identify and contact a shipping clerk for specific information about inventory. This research identifies a shipping and packaging inventory procedure that could be improved. The next step would be to submit the suggestion for improvement to all parties affected by the change for review and approval. Employees often spend many wasted hours trying to identify and locate the right individual or all the individuals they need to get additional information or decisions made.

The effectiveness of relevant information is based on the logical framework used to establish the cross-references between structured (i.e., business intelligence) and unstructured (i.e., knowledge management) data in your organization. It is important to understand that there is not a correct or definitive list of dimensions available to create this logical framework. An understanding of the relationships or cross-references that need to exist and be implemented in the corporate portal should be outlined at a high level. This determination verifies that the data is available to create a relationship between content pages and associated data and knowledge experts in order to implement the content-relevant information section requirements. The task is to identify the metadata and cross-references that need to exist between the reports and other information in the content page and the content-relevant information section information. The cross-references should provide an easy way to map the secondary relationships between data and people that are to be presented in the corporate portal.

DEFINING RELATIVE DATA AND KNOWLEDGE EXPERTS

Your organization is probably engaged in several data conversion projects. These types of projects include data consolidation, data quality improvements, creation of data warehouses and data marts, and migration from legacy systems to packaged applications. You want to coordinate the implementation of corporate portal features and self-service applications around these data conversion projects. Establishing the links or relationships between these different data sources, knowledge experts, and applications allows the corporate portal users access to the additional information and people needed to complete their assigned responsibilities.

When identifying the self-service applications and business features critical to your corporate portal solution, you are, in the simplest definition, selecting the data source requirements for the content-relevant information section of each content page in the corporate portal. In more complex cases, there are several data sources that supply information into the self-service application definition. How you define and create the cross-references between these data sources that are required to establish the content-relevant information section needs to be documented by the corporate portal strategy team. The results of this research will determine if additional data integration activities are required to display the content-relevant information requested by corporate portal users. In the most complex cases, the data source must be modified or additional algorithms created to manipulate the systems (i.e., data sources) to make the information available to employees needing it.

Making the Portal Desktop Intuitive

Employees throughout your organization should be drawn to the corporate portal for the flexible, personalized work experience. If employees can easily complete their responsibilities and find information they are looking for, then the portal desktop will reach beyond providing a central workspace. It serves as a corporate community where employees can share experiences, ask and answer questions, learn new procedures, and get involved in different user groups. These shared knowledge forums and online help procedures mean the portal solution delivers additional benefits that include reduced administrative and training costs when wizards and self-discovery tools are available online. Each iteration or new generation of the corporate portal must continue to provide additional benefits, so related data integration initiatives must be completed in concert with new development phases of the corporate portal solution. When large quantities of data that originate from several different sources need to be consolidated to meet the content requirements of corporate portal users, then the related data transformation issues must be documented and fed into existing or new data integration information technology (IT) projects. Among the issues that may need to be resolved:

- Multiple data sources have to be identified to create the business intelligence information required in the corporate portal.

- The data sources may not be readily known or easily identified.
- Data is highly redundant throughout the organization, creating data integrity problems.
- Data is stored in several data formats and contents (e.g., inconsistent company names).

The corporate portal strategy team should concentrate on identifying the data elements to be displayed in portal content windows, including the dimensions in terms of drilling paths (both up and down) and available report formats. Drilling paths are the ability to access the underlying detail level of data that is consolidated and displayed in the corporate portal. For example, an organization path may include region to district to department and a time path may be from year to quarter to month to week to day. Available report formats refers to knowing the requirements for (1) drilling into information and (2) basic reporting and querying functionality. The goal is to understand the framework in terms of how the data pieces correlate with each other and the pathways that need to be available for different types of users.

Data Profiling

The taxonomy or categorization of information that the corporate portal is designed around is dependent on the data sources and how employees expect to see and use this data. The profiles you create about data sources and business processes establish the flexible foundation that you continue to build on as the corporate portal grows. Developing an accurate data profile of existing data sources is an essential first step if this information is not already available in the common data architecture. If you need to establish a strategy for data profiling as part of the corporate portal solution, consider documenting three dimensions in each data source. These three dimensions are:

- *Column Profiling (Down Columns)*. Column profiling analyzes the values in each column or field of the data source determining the characteristics. The types of characteristics identified include data type and size, range of values, frequency and distribution of values, required values, unique values, null values, and cardinality. Column profiling defines the metadata information for the data source.

• *Dependency Profiling (Across Rows).* Dependency profiling analyzes data across each row of the data source. The relationships between the values in each column are compared to each other. The primary keys (one or more columns whose values uniquely identify each row in the data source) and foreign keys (one or more columns whose values are equivalent to the primary key of another table in the same database) are documented. Dependency profiling defines the integrity of the data in the data source.

• *Redundancy Profiling (Across Tables).* Redundancy profiling compares data between tables in the same data source or from different data sources to identify any columns that contain overlapping or identical values. The results identify the columns containing the same information with different names (synonyms), the columns containing different information with the same names (homonyms), and the columns that are redundant and can be eliminated. Redundancy profiling defines the accuracy of the data in the data source.

For the corporate portal business case, you should create formal data names that are easily understood by employees to describe the information to be presented in the initial phases of the corporate portal. An inventory of the data names and data sources creates an awareness of the data that exists and is available for use. When you are evaluating the extent of the data transformation effort for your corporate portal business case, concentrate on these four areas:

1. *Data Description.* This is the formal naming of data used to establish a comprehensive definition using a standard predefined taxonomy of data elements.

2. *Data Structure.* For each data source, the structure and relationships of the available data have to be established. The formal documentation of the data structure includes a logical data model for your organization and a physical data model for implementation purposes.

3. *Data Fidelity*. This is the integrity, accuracy, and completeness of the data.

4. *Data Documentation*. This is the written information available about the data sources in your organization.

Dimensions and Cross-References Identified

The logical framework you compose for the content-relevant information section of the corporate portal is a collection of dimensions found in multiple data sources, the roles and responsibilities, activities and tasks, and workgroups and departments found in your organization. The goal is to have a logical framework that gives you a perspective of the employee using the data without knowing the exact level of detail required by the employee in advance. The idea is to establish a multidimensional view of the information available that can be exploited in a wider business intelligence context.

Multidimensional views may seem abstract, but they are a useful format to define how employees are thinking. The cross-referencing of the multidimensional views establishes various perspectives on the information available. This is often referred to as "slicing and dicing" information. In reality, several employees with similar responsibilities or interests usually want to view information from a variety of perspectives. The ability for employees to switch from one perspective to another with a simple click of the mouse is key to the effectiveness of the corporate portal solution.

There are only three dimensions in the physical world; the way employees will want to view data throughout their organization will have many more dimensions. In a customer order example, a sales representative may want to see dimensions that include planned sales against actual sales, or variance, and for a separate business activity review this same information by divisions or geographic regions. The facts between these data sources need to be linked in some way. There is no limit to the number of dimensions that can be included in the multidimensional data model created to define relevant information in the corporate portal. An example of cross-referencing employees-to-employees and employees-to-information can be seen in the InfoImage freedom product. The implementation presented in Figure 8-1 demonstrates how a collection of rela-

Figure 8-1. InfoImage freedom dimensions and cross-references feature.

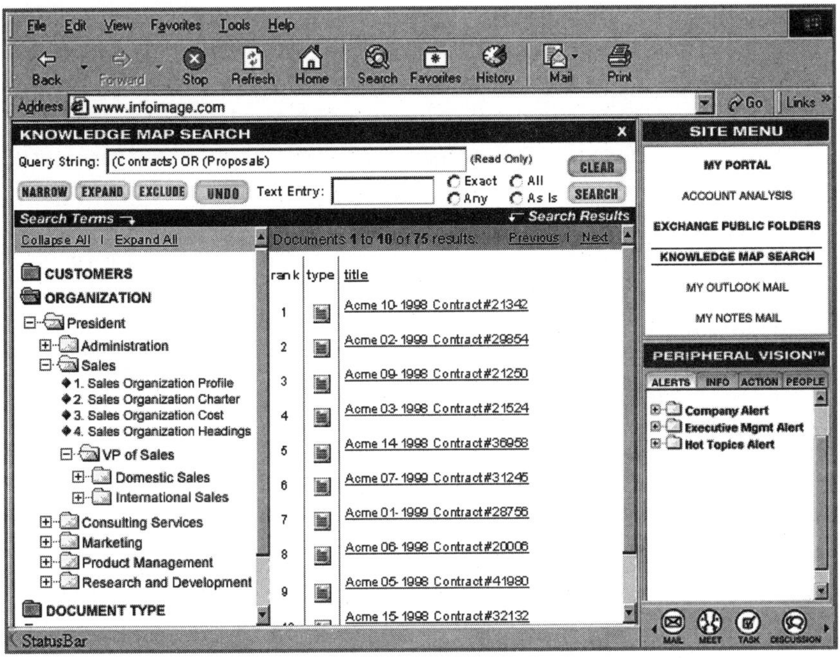

tionships can be defined to search for documents and information. This kind of implementation allows employees to find and use information that was previously unavailable or impossible to locate.

Aggregated Business Intelligence Data Marts

In addition to dimensions, the information that employees investigate or review exists at different levels of detail. Typically an employee will be reviewing detailed information in the content page and content windows of the corporate portal. The employee may wish to check out additional information on a particular point of interest. The ability to move into progressively more detail or access indirectly related information is valuable. The predefined dimensions and cross-referenced material is displayed in the content-relevant information section of the corporate portal so as not to distract from the focus of the context presented in the content page. Employees can locate this information or additional dimensions by clicking on the item they are interested in. All the relevant information that an employee may (or may not) be aware of is nonetheless easily accessed. If additional instruction is required, another report needs to be reviewed, or a discussion thread needs to be started on how to improve a process, then the hyperlink is selected and the content page is reloaded with the requested information or a separate window is opened to display the requested information.

Consider the content-relevant information section of the corporate portal as another navigation menu to quickly locate or navigate to another task or activity. The final self-service application requirements establish how the corporate portal solution completes or handles these additional navigational elements. The corporate portal user assistance or help features should describe how the content-relevant information menu item may require navigation to another content page or launch a third-party application, depending on the complexity of the related task or activity selected.

To support employees' data requirements, a data mart for their specific business needs may be established. Data marts subset enterprisewide data along specific areas of interest such as business functions, departments, and applications. Each self-service application or core business process (e.g., taking customer orders) generates data that is of interest to multiple business functions. These business intelligence data marts bring together relevant sets of data and present the information in a dimensional format that is meaningful.

The IT department must evaluate the dimensions required by the corporate portal users and determine if data staging areas must be created or expanded to accommodate the additional data requirements and transformation processes needed to present information in the formats requested. This knowledge expansion and additional cross-referencing has implications for the data warehouse team in your organization. As the requirements expand and new self-service applications are added into the corporate portal solution, more data marts are often defined and created. The atomic data mart—which holds data at the lowest level of detail defined to meet most of the high-level business intelligence requirements—becomes an enterprise resource that supports all the business intelligence activities and projects throughout the organization. It is important that data marts created in your organization be based on the same standard sources because they need to reference the same dimensions to be consistent with each other. Applying these standards permits the corporate portal to take advantage of the data management and access services supported by the IT department.

The data loaded into the corporate portal using business intelligence data marts follows the same dimensional structure of the data in the atomic data mart. When going through the process of defining the strategy of the corporate portal solution, determine what the basic dimensions of your data sources are. Once you know the basic dimensions that are available, you may use different business rules and establish different derived facts (e.g., gross sales versus net sales). In the content-relevant information section of the corporate portal, some of the dimensions may present different options or not be available at all, depending on the employee's role or function within the organization. The relevant information may also append options to the dimensions based on the role or function of the employee. For example, sales managers may need additional information about budgets and sales territories that sales representatives will not be allowed access to when performing their unique business processes and activities.

Collaborative Business Intelligence Systems

Business intelligence and knowledge management features are being integrated together and then made available as solutions to employees in the front office. Collaborative business intelligence systems add communication, collaboration, process, and action to business intelligence systems available in the corporate portal. This total solution is delivering the results of data analysis to your web browser client. The true value is allowing corporate portal users to act on the information, to make better decisions, to improve processes, and to seize opportunities from a central knowledge desktop. These activities occur in the corporate portal where employees gather information from multiple sources that include structured data sources, web pages, documents, discussion forums, and e-mail.

The corporate portal expands business intelligence, merging employees throughout the organization into the sharing-information equation and allowing everyone to be involved in knowledge creation and collaboration. The corporate portal facilitates the deployment of communication, collaboration, and knowledge sharing of information gathered from multiple sources across the corporate intranet into a single location, where it is then easily distributed back out and stored once again into several disparate data sources. This combination of business intelligence and knowledge management through the corporate portal should have additional benefits, including lower training costs, higher adoption rates, and more consistent, informed business decisions. Figure 8-2 shows how the corporate portal facilitates business intelligence and knowledge management.

Web standards for user interface, delivery, notification, and collaboration fit naturally with current market and technology trends. Business intelligence systems are incorporating intranet standards and enterprise-reporting tools and applications that currently support web interfaces and messaging standards. The corporate portal solution provides:

- Business intelligence tools to generate reports that appear on the Web
- Knowledge management tools to provide the communication, collaboration, coordination, and repositories for storing and organizing these reports (structured information) and documentation (unstructured information)
- Search benefits that provide full-text searching by topic (pulling information in) and targeted audience (pushing information out)

The corporate portal business case should provide a framework for how the organization can deliver dynamically generated reports and information in response to requests for real-time or the most current data by employees. Static content is defined as information that can be updated on a scheduled or as-needed basis. Dynamic content creation is established for immediate viewing requirements and means that content creation and content viewing are synchronously linked processes. The ability to generate reports "on demand" provides ad hoc and heuristic information that can sup-

Figure 8-2. Collaborative business intelligence.

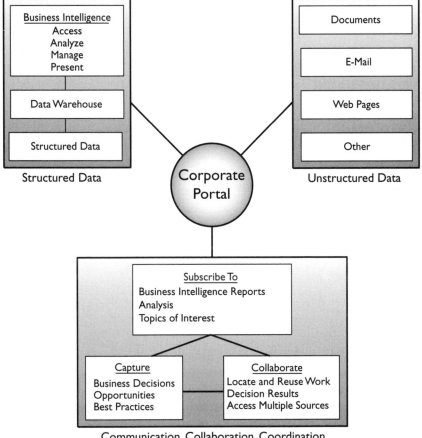

port operational (i.e., routine) tasks with the most recent picture of relevant material. The outcome is usually better customer service, more informed responses to questions, better conclusions, and a more concise view of the company.

The corporate portal self-service applications must be integrated with querying and reporting applications while eliminating direct interaction requirements with data managers and application developers. This means that new or additional reporting requirements can be integrated into the iterative development cycle with new reports and query functions being distributed to a wider audience. Individual report requests and special projects should begin to decline as the corporate portal reporting environment continues to expand.

Beyond making reports available to read, you will want employees to be able to manipulate information in the corporate portal. There should be a balance between the static web pages that can be published and distributed to meet just-in-time requirements and corporate information that is displayed from data repositories to meet real-time requirements. This is primarily decided as users establish how timely the information they need should be and what the most accurate data available is. Following are some key issues to be aware of as you identify the corporate portal business case:

- It is important to match the capacity of the content page or content page window with the capacity of the employee. A several-hundred-line report is best viewed in categories or displayed as an abstract with the complete report available for download, or accessed through a third-party application that can be launched from the corporate portal solution.

- The number of navigation steps or clicks to access a desired report should be kept to a minimum. Too many hierarchies of information reduces the effectiveness of distributed reports by delaying their delivery or making them impossible to locate.

- Employees need to create dynamic report requests from the corporate portal that are submitted for immediate or scheduled processing. Make sure that these requested queries only allow for options that return a reasonable amount of information back to the corporate portal. For large result sets or extensive analysis requirements, third-party applications should be considered and launched from the corporate portal solution.

- Report-generating software must be robust enough to provide maximum flexibility, utility, and design with access to virtually any data source; it must also return the desired report in a wide range of Internet content types.

Defining Relative Data and Knowledge Experts Checklist

For each business function identified and included in the initial phases of the corporate portal solution, please copy the appropriate section (heading and questions) of the following checklist, change the heading to match the name of the business function, and answer the questions contained in that section for each content page. Be sure to have business domain experts in your organization review the information.

RELEVANT INFORMATION IDENTIFIED

☐ Have any queries, report summaries, and other options been reviewed and considered as relevant information based on the context of the content page?

☐ Have the data sources for each additional report summary, predefined query, or knowledge expert been identified as relevant information?

☐ Have all the tools, utilities, and applications that need to be accessed from the content page or content window been identified?

☐ Have the data source owners been identified for each data source identified?

☐ Have the data source or data point concerns from the business domain experts been identified?

☐ Have any additional issues or details for each data source been defined?

☐ Have all relationships between objects in the portal desktop been defined? How are they going to continue to be maintained?

CorporatePortal.com Case Study

CorporatePortal.com wants to make sure that in the initial implementation of the portal desktop, information can be reached from the current content page, main portal menu, or content-relevant information. Employees need only click one or two levels into the portal desktop to find the information they need to do their job effectively. Provided employees have some idea of the information they are looking for, the next logical step is to use the search feature to find the elusive information. If a search is unsuccessful, the third step is to give up, ask another employee, or call the IT department for assistance. The portal desktop is designed to bring to employees information for them to do their job. It needs to have links to reports that are related to the task employees are working on, poli-cies and procedures about the task, knowledge workers or supervi-sors that can answer questions quickly, discussion forums to forward comments, and pervasive desktop features to access per-sonal e-mail files or calendars.

For each content window menu option and content-relevant in-formation link, there is an associated data source being accessed. Taking a closer look at the Accounting department General Informa-tion page (introduced in Chapter 7, Figure 7-10), there are several links and data sources. Notably:

• All Accounting report content windows (e.g., Flash Sum-mary, Cash, Accounts Receivable, Inventory, Accounts Payable, Current Payroll, General Ledger Transactions, and Chart of Ac-counts) are generated from the Oracle Financials system.

• The Accounting Policies and Procedure content window uses information from the Documentum content management ap-plication.

• The Search main portal menu option uses a Verity applica-tion to execute stored or ad hoc searches.

• The Resources main portal menu and content-relevant infor-mation links provide access to employees who create or verify the accuracy of the Accounting reports, experts in Oracle Financials business rules and attribute definitions, IT professionals for assis-tance, and a site map to all information available in the portal desk-top. The data sources include employee locator and customized XML development used by the corporate portal solution.

• Discussion and e-mail features to forward information, schedule meetings, and provide feedback are supported by Micro-soft Outlook and Exchange.

Continuing to evaluate the Accounting department General Infor-mation page in the CorporatePortal.com application, the strategy team works with the IT department to determine if data sources that will be working together in the content page can effectively pass or exchange information between each other. Relationships must be established to provide the requisite functionality. For example:

• If an employee needs help while using an Accounting report, the attribute name, attribute value, or report name, then the item should be highlighted and the F1 key clicked for online help to provide topic help.

• Depending on the employee role and responsibilities, the steps or procedures to follow to complete a task should be linked to reports from the Setup option on the content window to the appropriate content management documents.

• As employees have questions about the Accounting report content, they need access to knowledge experts that produce such reports or manage the Oracle Financials system that stores the business rules to produce the reports. This relationship between employees and the Oracle Financials system must be designed and implemented.

• Different departments in CorporatePortal.com are interested in viewing the same report attributes using unique definitions. For example, the Sales and Accounting departments want to use different definitions of revenue when they are reading Accounting reports. Accounting is interested in seeing this information when GAAP regulations allow revenue to be realized by CorporatePortal.com. The Sales employees want to see revenue when payments are received from the customer. Both user groups refer to this value as revenue, but Accounting reports look very different when one rule or the other is implemented.

• Information or reports in content windows must be included in feedback, discussions, and e-mail forwarding features. Employees need links to the collaboration features of the corporate portal when working with content pages and content windows in the portal desktop.

ORGANIZING CONTENT-RELEVANT INFORMATION

The ability to clearly define the roles and responsibilities, tasks and activities, and workgroups and departments throughout your organization will make the identification of relevant information and the cross-referencing of information and data sources complete. There is a general collection of corporate tools, applications, and information that everyone in your organization needs to access. This includes reference material, corporate resources, department websites, search engines, e-mail, discussions, chat, and training material, among others. However, there is a specific collection of tools, applications, and information for each responsibility, activity, and department. The goal of the content-relevant information section of the corporate portal is to provide a balance between the context of information in the content page and content windows and the collection of general and specific tools, applications, and information that provide the most relevant value to that context information. There is not a specific format or categorization requirement for how the variety of information and material can be made available in the content-relevant information section, and will be defined for each portal page. Consider the general and specific types of tools, applications, and information that need to be made available to employees as they use the corporate portal solution and look for patterns to determine how to logically organize or categorize these collections of relevant information.

For example, when looking at a customer order in the content page, there may be several items that would be relevant or useful for a user to know about in the right circumstances. Therefore there needs to be a paradigm established as to how content-relevant information tabs will be used throughout the portal desktop. In the CorporatePortal.com example, the groups or categories selected for the types of material are Tools, Navigation, Notifications, and Other. Your organization could select another, unique categorization or organization for content-relevant information. The goal is to identify and bring together pertinent information that should be captured and available as hyperlinks through the content-relevant information section of the corporate portal.

CorporatePortal.com Case Study

CorporatePortal.com is using the content-relevant information section of the portal desktop to provide navigation to several services. Business domain experts have reviewed several of the initial business functions and self-service applications selected for the corporate portal. They determine that the portal desktop will be more intuitive for employees if the content-relevant information tabs are consistent throughout the corporate portal solution, although the content-relevant information must remain flexible enough to support an exception when required. The initial paradigm for CorporatePortal.com includes:

1. *Tools.* The Tools category was included in the content-relevant information section and designed to provide access to collaboration and communication applications that are standard in the organization. In the context of a customer order, tools are used to:

- Create feedback or discussion documents related to the customer tax and audit projects.
- Create an ad hoc process and action procedure for a new type of content management document.
- Submit a query to the IT department for a special execution of a financial report.
- Open the team collaboration content page to work on a tax or audit project.
- Open the appropriate accounting reports to work on accounts receivable or payable transactions.

2. *Navigation.* The Navigation category was selected for the content-relevant information section and designed to provide additional navigation options that are related or relevant to the information presented in the content page. Navigational aids would include both data and people (knowledge experts). In the context of a customer order, the following elements were identified:

- Contract information about each customer's tax or audit projects
- Statement of work information about each customer's tax or audit projects
- White papers or discussions specific to a customer's tax or audit projects
- Pricing and invoicing history information about each of the services listed in the customer's tax or audit projects
- Marketing and collateral information about services provided by CorporatePortal.com
- Payment history information about the customer's account
- Sales representative assigned to the customer's account

3. *Notifications.* The Notifications category was selected for the content-relevant information section and was designed to emphasize important messages related to the context of the content page that need to be brought to the attention of the corporate portal user. In the context of a customer order, the following elements were identified:

- Notifications or flags about any aspect of the customer project
- Notifications about new policies and procedures available at CorporatePortal.com
- Notifications about training events or CorporatePortal.com events

4. *Other.* The Other category is included in the content-relevant information section to provide additional features or functionality. In the context of a customer order, an example includes:

- Map to the customer's main address and directions from the airport or the local CorporatePortal.com office

FURTHER READING

Simon, Alan. *90 Days to the Data Mart: Step-by-Step Guide to Planning, Designing, and Building Data Marts.* New York: John Wiley & Sons, Inc., 1998.

Harrington, Jan L. *Relational Database Design: Clearly Explained.* San Diego: AP Professional, 1998.

Shepherd, John B. "Data Migration Strategies," *DM Review*, June 1999.

Olson, Craig. "Know Your Data: Data Profiling Solutions for Today's Hot Projects," *DM Review*, March 2000.

KEY POINTS

To prepare the corporate portal strategy, there are several considerations regarding direct access to related or relevant information. They include:

1. *Defining Related Data and Knowledge Experts.* The selection of the data source requirements and relationships for the content-relevant information section in the corporate portal is mapped to the context of each content page. To determine the scope of work required to build the content-relevant information section of the corporate portal, do your homework and research in the following areas:

• *Reviewing the Common Data Architecture.* To be fully aware of all the data that exists and is available for use in the corporate portal solution, identify the inventory of data names and data sources in your organization.

• *Data Profiling.* A data profile of existing data sources is an essential first step if this information is not already available in the common data architecture. If you need to establish a strategy for data profiling as part of the corporate portal solution, consider documenting three dimensions in each data source. These three dimensions are:

• Column profiling (down columns)
• Dependency profiling (across rows)
• Redundancy profiling (across tables)

• *Identifying Dimensions and Cross-References.* The logical framework you compose for the content-relevant information section of the corporate portal is a collection of dimensions found in multiple data sources, the roles and responsibilities, activities and tasks, and workgroups and departments found in your organization. This process of multidirectional traversing of tables allows documents, employees, roles, and other information to be easily located. The implementation of knowledge links provides for a scalable and maintainable implementation where individual tables of information specific to the organization grow independent of each other.

• *Aggregating Business Intelligence Data Marts.* To support the data requirements of employees using the corporate portal, a data mart may need to be established. Data marts subset enterprisewide data along specific areas of interest such as business functions, departments, and applications.

2. *Identifying Related Data and Knowledge Experts.* The tools, information, and knowledge experts relevant to the context of the portal's content page need to be identified. These types of elements, which typically appear as content-relevant information, must be incorporated and categorized into the corporate portal according to the structure of your organization. One approach is to implement the following items:

• *Tools* (to provide access to collaboration and communication applications that are standard in your organization)

• *Navigation* (additional navigation options to find data and people—that is, knowledge experts—related or relevant to the information presented in the content page)

• *Notifications* (important messages related to the context of the content page that must be brought to the attention of the corporate portal user)

• *Other* (any additional features or functionality in the content-relevant information section of the corporate portal for easy access by users)

Use the following checklist to review or analyze the importance of accessing information throughout the enterprise and being able to locate and work with knowledge experts from your organization's corporate portal solution.

ANALYZING YOUR CORPORATE PORTAL'S DIRECT LINKS TO RELATIVE DATA AND KNOWLEDGE EXPERTS

☐ How are employees made aware of information or reports available in the organization for them to access?

☐ Is this information "pushed" to them as relevant information for all the responsibilities and activities employees perform?

☐ Would employees be able to make better decisions if links to information throughout the organization were made available to them?

☐ How do employees know who the knowledge experts are in the organization and how they can be contacted for process questions, topic questions, or other issues?

9

Individual Identity and Personalized Access to Content

Identity defines what makes each employee a unique individual and what each employee has in common with every other employee in the organization. To effectively distribute and easily locate knowledge throughout your organization and guarantee that each employee has access to only that information they have the appropriate level of authority to review, your corporate portal needs to continually expand employee-to-employee and employee-to-information relationships. How effective your organization is at knowledge sharing depends directly on how much is known about your employees and your data.

Personalization features were previously described as part of the corporate portal universal features (see Chapter 2). These include:

- Comfort and familiarity (user personalization)
- Understanding and knowledge (navigation personalization)
- System intelligence (behavior assistance personalization)

The levels of personalization that can be incorporated into the corporate portal solution are decisions that your organization must establish and revise as the solution evolves over time. The personalization element is a critical component in decision-making enhancement and effective information management, providing context filtered specifically for the working style and content preferences of each corporate portal user.

INDIVIDUAL IDENTITY

To guarantee that security is implemented accurately, each user must have an individual identity as a feature of the corporate portal solution implemented. Most (if not all) of the information about an employee's position in your organization, including skills, activities, roles, and interests, is already available in your organization's data warehouses. The goal is to be able to relate this information to business documents in a systematic fashion to facilitate your knowledge management initiatives and make it possible to deliver the right information to the right people at the right time.

To establish this ability to relate people to people within your organization, your corporate portal solution needs information about each employee, such as:

- Who has knowledge about the information needed (e.g., skills and skill levels)?
- Who currently works directly with or is responsible for understanding the information needed (e.g., roles and responsibilities)?
- What other individuals are interested in the information needed (e.g., activities and interests)?

Individual profiles and metadata are used to compile, organize, and document information about the skills, roles, activities, interests, and responsibilities of employees (people) within your organization.

The Identity Profile

To successfully incorporate identity features into your corporate portal, a substantial amount of knowledge about employees has to be available. This collection of information is compiled for each employee in your organization and is referred to as an identity profile. The identity profile is composed of the following four objects:

1. *User Profile Object.* This object is similar to a network services directory record containing information about the employee. It is needed to manage authentication, access, security, and user interface requirements for the corporate portal. The user profile serves as the hub linking all identity profile objects together.

2. *User Preferences Object.* This object is used to store information about an employee's usability preferences regarding the user interface, application default settings, and other designated employee-manageable information.

3. *Organization Chart Object.* This object defines the structure of your organization in terms of hierarchical levels, employee names, job titles, employee numbers, physical locations, department names, and other information used by applications and systems to uniquely identify each position of your organization.

4. *User Identity Objects.* This object consists of four separate types of objects that capture information about the employee's skills, activities, roles, and interests within your organization. Each of these objects is further qualified by additional attributes related to your organization's structure and data sources, such as:

- Skills (i.e., talents and certifications an employee possesses)
- Activities (i.e., types of tasks and procedures an employee conducts as part of their job)
- Roles (i.e., types of responsibilities usually identified by an employee's position or job description)
- Interests (i.e., topics and issues that appeal to an employee)

The identity profile description is shown in Figure 9-1.

Corporate Portal Identity

Employees can be conceptualized as entities (or objects) that are characterized by attributes that describe (or classify) them. The employee is an entity, the department they work in is an entity, and the activities and tasks they complete are entities. Entities

Figure 9-1. Identity profile description.

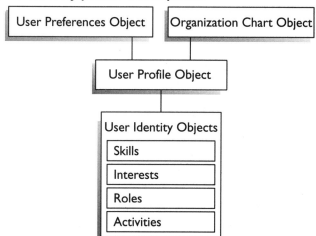

have data that describes them. For example, an employee has the attributes of an employee number, first name, last name, street, city, state, zip code, and phone numbers. Each collection of attributes that define a single occurrence of the entity is an instance of the entity. Each employee that becomes a corporate portal user becomes an instance of the employee entity with the attributes that describe the employee.

You must determine what attributes regarding each employee should be retrieved or used in the corporate portal. These attributes serve three different purposes:

- *Comfort* (i.e., controlling the look, feel, colors, and other user interface preferences of the corporate portal knowledge desktop)
- *Familiarity* (i.e., controlling the organization and categorization of content page tabs, content pages, content windows, and content-relevant information)
- *Configuration* (i.e., controlling the user settings and attributes associated with self-service applications, software functions, and features incorporated in the corporate portal)

The level of detail required to complete the business case should furnish enough information to distinguish one entity from another so you can guarantee that the corporate portal user (i.e., employee) you are authenticating or referencing is unique and can be correctly identified. This is possible by ensuring that each entity has attributes that distinguish each one from another. There may be one attribute (e.g., employee number for the employee) or several attributes (e.g., employee name, Social Security number, start date) that are required to uniquely identify an instance of the entity.

Entity Relationship (ER) Diagrams

Entity relationship diagrams provide a good way to document the results of your research regarding individual identity and the information required for each profile. An ER diagram is designed to document entities along with the attributes that describe them. Different styles can be used when creating ER diagrams. It is not important which style you select as long as everyone reading your documentation can interpret and understand the symbols. For the business case you are only required to document preliminary research regarding the unique identity of employees and verify that the data points or attributes that need to be referenced in the corporate portal solution are already available in your organization or can be made available.

You want to establish the identity entities that describe your employees and your organization. It is important to document the major entities and their attributes for the corporate portal solution. An example identity ER diagram that describes an employee is shown in Figure 9-2. The ER diagram uses one entity for the employee (named "Person") and the following six entities that represent repeating groups of data:

- *Job.* Each instance of the Job entity represents one job the person has held. The date_started identifier—identified by an asterisk (*) in Figure 9-2—is based on the assumption that an employee can only have one job at any one time with your company. The current job will have a null (empty) value in the date_left attribute. All previous jobs will have a date_left value providing you with the job history of each employee (person).

Figure 9-2. Person entity relationship diagram.

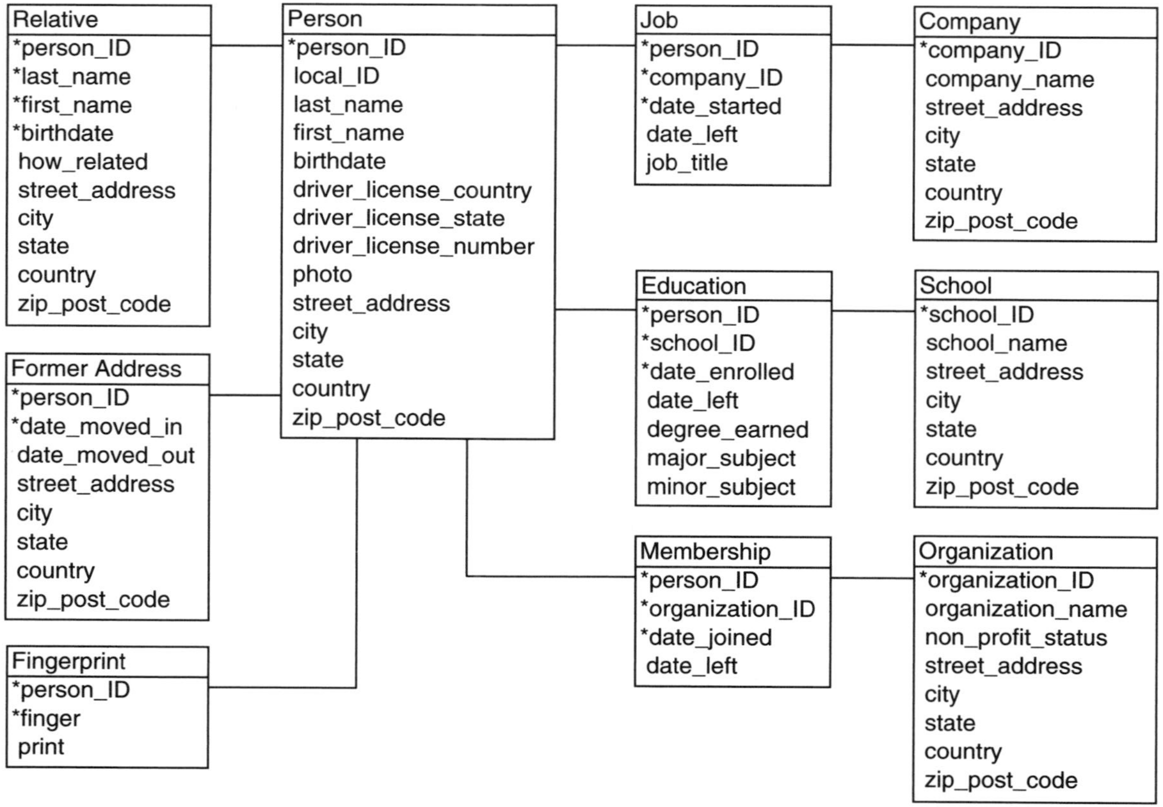

- *Education.* There is one instance of the Education entity for each time an employee enrolls in a school. By including the date entered in the Education entity as an identifier (*), you can track employees who are currently attending school, when they stopped attending the school, and whether they completed their degree.

- *Membership.* Each instance of the Membership entity represents when an individual joined a professional organization on a given date. By distinguishing memberships to professional organizations by date, you can track multiple members of the professional organization over time.

- *Relative.* There is one instance of the Relative entity for each person that is related to the employee. A unique Relative entity is based on the name and birth date of each entity, assuming that no employee has two relatives with exactly the same name born on the same date.

- *Former Address.* Each instance of the Former Address entity represents one place an employee has lived. The assumption is that an employee has only one primary residence at the current time. Each address is unique based on the date the person moved into the location.

- *Fingerprint.* Each instance of the Fingerprint entity represents one finger on one hand. Of all the repeating groups, Fingerprints is the only one where a reasonable estimate of how many there will be can be made. However, there is no way to guarantee that each employee (person) has ten prints each. It is possible there will be fewer.

Software applications are available to create ER diagrams and to document the research completed for the corporate portal business case.

The Identity Schema

The complete ER diagrams and the relationships between the entities represent the logical data model, or logical model, that defines identity for each user of the corporate portal solution. These diagrams are used to create the logical data schema required to support the corporate portal solution. To write the corporate portal

business case you may need to reference identity objects (or entities) when describing how employee-to-employee relationships and
employee-to-data relationships will be defined and used to provide
value to your organization. The logical data schema used to define
individual identity for the corporate portal solution furnishes the
information needed to complete this section of the business case.

The logical data schema and the corporate portal view of the
identity information are all that are needed for the corporate portal business case. The underlying physical storage (also referred to
as the physical data schema) will be created in the architecture
and design phase of the corporate portal project. The important
point is that database designers, application developers, and corporate portal users need not be concerned with the physical data
schema and can continue to define the corporate portal business
case with the ER diagrams from the information available in the
logical data schema. There are three separate representations of
the identity definition used by different employees in your organization. They are as follows:

• The corporate portal strategy team works with the ER diagrams to determine what attributes are currently available in the
organization for them to reference as part of the corporate portal
solution.

• Database designers, database administrators, and application programmers concentrate on the logical data schema of identity to evaluate the data points required to support a corporate
portal solution.

• System programmers and other employees responsible for
maintaining the physical implementation of identity are concerned
with the physical data schema that will be designed after the corporate portal proposal is an approved project.

The Data Dictionary

The data dictionary or catalog is a definition of the properties used
to define the structure of a relational database. Typically you'll find
the following types of information in the data dictionary:

- Definitions of the attributes that comprise each entity
- Integrity constraints placed on the relationships of the entities
- Security information regarding the rights employees have or what operations an employee is allowed to perform on each entity (e.g., read, edit, no access, other)
- Definitions of other structural elements associated with the identity schema

For the purpose of creating the corporate portal strategy you are interested in establishing:

- The type of data that defines each attribute
- Whether the attribute value is required for the corporate portal self-service application and features to function correctly
- If there are upper or lower bounds for the attribute value
- Any other attribute-related information that is identified during the discovery process

The data dictionary is a table in a relational database that documents all the data about the identity entities (tables), the columns (attributes), the keys (unique identifiers), and other details. You want to establish the attribute definitions that describe the entities used to define individual identities in your organization. It is important to document the attribute definitions identified during your research. This information provides details the IT department needs to determine the scope of activities to be completed so that the data required is available for the corporate portal solution.

Individual Identity Checklist

For each business function identified for inclusion in the initial phases of the corporate portal solution, please copy the appropriate section (heading and questions), change the heading to match the name of the business function, and answer the following questions with business domain experts in your organization.

☐ What are the entities (or objects) that best describe your organization and your employees?

☐ What attributes need to be defined for each of these entities?

☐ What enterprise system will be used to store these entities?

☐ How will the user identity attributes be added to data sources in your organization (e.g., adding, renaming, deleting, moving, other)? Who will be responsible for maintaining these attributes?

☐ How will the entity tables initially be created (e.g., extraction, transformation, and load requirements)? Will records need to be created for batches or multiples of users? Will there be defaults established for attributes that are initially unavailable?

☐ Have the administration responsibilities been defined?

☐ Have the user identity security features been defined?

CorporatePortal.com Case Study

CorporatePortal.com has determined for both documentation and implementation purposes that associations must be made between the data sources used in the corporate portal solution. There are seven separate entities directly linked to the employee entity (see Figure 9-3). The User Identity relationship diagram contains additional relationships between entities that are not represented in this diagram. The goal of the diagram is to begin to see the cross-references and relationships that will be established to present several different types of information in the portal desktop. These entities include:

- *CorporatePortal.com Profile (i.e., Company Profile).* There is one instance of the CorporatePortal.com entity for each employee. Each instance of the CorporatePortal.com entity represents the position the employee holds in the company's organization chart. Each CorporatePortal.com Profile record is unique based on the employee_ID of the employee in the organization.

- *Portal Profile.* Each instance of the Portal Profile entity represents the portal desktop configuration attributes that provide parameters to content pages, content windows, and hyperlinks in the corporate portal solution. The assumption is that an employee has only one Portal Profile at the current time. Each Portal Profile record is unique based on the employee_ID of the employee in the organization.

• *Portal Preferences.* Each instance of the Portal Preferences entity represents the portal configuration attributes that employees select. These preferences include colors, fonts, user group memberships, notification preferences, e-mail information, and other settings identified as the business functions. Self-service applications are fully defined. Each Portal Preferences record is unique based on the employee_ID of the employee in the organization.

• *Employee Activities.* Each instance of the Employee Activities entity represents one task or procedure the employee is responsible for as part of their job. The activity_ID identifier (identified by an * in Figure 9-3) is based on the assumption that every activity in the organization has a unique value assigned. The current activities an employee is responsible for have a null (empty) value in the date_ended attribute. All previous activities have a date_ended value providing you with the activities history of each employee.

• *Employee Skills.* Each instance of the Employee Skills entity represents a skill that the employee is capable or certified to perform. Each skill is defined by a unique skill_ID (*) identification attribute. By distinguishing skills and the skill level the employee has achieved by date, CorporatePortal.com can track the skills and skill level acquired by employees over time.

• *Employee Roles.* Each instance of the Employee Roles entity represents one role or job description the person has held. The role_ID identifier (*) is unique. Each employee can be assigned to several roles inside the organization at a single time. The current employee roles have a null (empty) value in the date_ended attribute. All previous employee roles have a date_ended value, providing the company with the history of roles each employee has been assigned in the organization.

• *Employee Interests.* Each instance of the Employee Interests entity represents an area of information that the employee is interested in remaining informed about or actively involved in. Each

Figure 9-3. User identity relationship diagram.

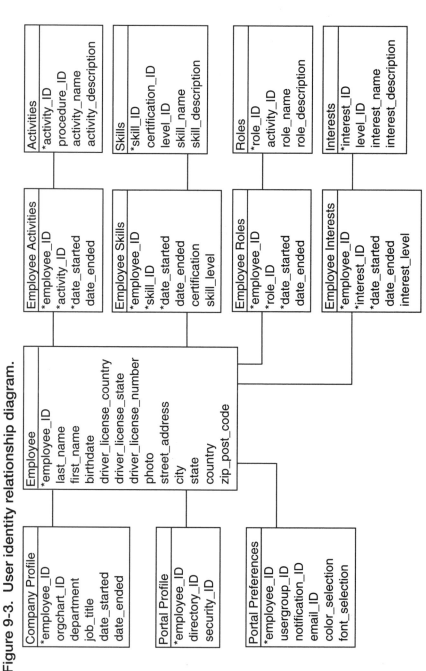

interest is defined by a unique interest_ID (*) identification attribute. By distinguishing interests and the interest level, the employee can track the latest information available on the topics identified.

In Figure 9-3, the attributes with asterisks (*) are used to uniquely identify a record or instance of the record in the table. These attributes—when added or linked to unique instances of records in the company's Oracle Financials system, Oracle databases, Exchange Public Folders, Documentum documents, and other data sources—create the employee-to-information links throughout CorporatePortal.com enterprise systems. Using employee_ID information from the CorporatePortal.com Profile, Portal Profile, and Portal Preferences, the employee-to-employee links can be established for the portal desktop. The IT department must review this information and consider the work required to create and maintain the user identity tables. Additional work will be required to link these user identity associations with data sources throughout CorporatePortal.com. These associations will allow content pages, content windows, portal menu options, and content relevant information to be developed, tested, and deployed in the portal desktop through a standard rapid development environment.

Personalized Access to Content

The ability of the employee to control both the content and the appearance of the portal desktop is one of the biggest benefits the corporate portal solution brings to your organization. Just like Internet e-business solutions must facilitate personalization features to gain acceptance and build community with their customers, the same factors and reasoning applies to employees inside your organization. Most employees already have experience with Internet e-business sites that provide content tailoring and have become the new standard for information interfaces for browser applications. Your organization's corporate portal strategy must address the personalization expectations of employees. The corporate portal solution implemented requires features that can be fully customized, not only with regard to the granularity of content and functionality, but also as to the look-and-feel of the interface.

You need to evaluate the personalization features available in third-party portal software solutions. Employees using the portal desktop also will have ideas about what personalization features they want, so obtain their input. Some features to consider include:

- Selecting a theme that defines colors and fonts in the portal desktop.
- Selecting the layout and location of portal desktop features.
- Creating links to favorite or important information.
- Selecting what content is presented in the portal desktop.
- Organizing where content is located in the portal desktop.
- Creating personal menu items and content pages in the portal desktop.

Information presentation is a science, and employees who are imaginative and visionary should help guide your corporate portal team through the identification and organization of corporate portal content. To start the process, make sure that the goals of the self-service applications and related functions have been established. Try to define patterns in the use and purpose, for example, that will help define a logical procedure or paradigm for grouping content and features together and, in turn, drive the corporate portal design choices made. Proceed to step employees through their daily activities and tasks, identifying what information, in what format, they would use. Establish any other standards or common shared information that employees with similar responsibilities will need. The final step is to put all the pieces (objects) together like a jigsaw puzzle where the final result is yet unknown. This process should be the most fun for employees. Allow the employees to take the common information and explain how they would organize these objects or individual pieces in different content pages, content windows, the main portal menu hierarchy, and content-relevant information sections. For the business case you can compare and contrast the individual results and document the personalization features the corporate portal solution must support.

User Personalization

If you incorporate several business domain experts into your corporate portal planning, you can be assured that employees need and want access to the information being presented. There needs to be a good balance between the amount of content made available and the performance requirements of users. The number of graphics that are used, the amount of information on each content page, the way information is partitioned, and several design and infrastructure issues—all contribute to the amount of time users spend accessing content pages in the corporate portal. The design decisions you make when defining the content pages and corporate portal features is a process that must be completed for every self-service application added to the corporate portal solution. During new phases of the corporate portal solution the design decisions should be reviewed and updated with enhancements suggested by existing users and requirements reflecting the new self-service applications.

These decisions can be detailed and specific. Your objective is to create an intuitive, central, and knowledge desktop, and the effort eventually will lead to a broad understanding of the portal features your employees will use. For example, as employees use the reports from the financial statements library, they may have questions or comments that need to be submitted about any one of these reports. To make this process as simple as possible, each content window should contain the personalization options to create a new discussion topic on the report information or an e-mail message that forwards the report information. Additional personalization features available from the content window include minimizing and maximizing the content window. The minimized content window only displays the title bar, while the maximized content window expands to present the title bar and the report inside the content window frame.

The design of most corporate portal content pages and content windows will be to present summary information to users as overviews of a larger collection of data sources. The summary information may or may not be presented for display to the browser from the originating data source or application. Any personalization requirements that need to be added or incorporated into these reports before presenting the summary data in the corporate portal content page or content window should be discovered during your research and interviewing activities. The summary information often needs to be reviewed by the corporate portal user in

more detail. If additional personalization features are a requirement for your self-service applications, they can be applied to a
specific report or type of business function; some features—such
as colors, fonts, themes, or pervasive tools (e.g., e-mail, feedback,
discussion)—can be applied to the entire corporate portal solution.

Clearly defining and explaining the terminology used in the
self-service application is also imperative. The amount of knowledge each employee has regarding a work process will be different.
Whether the background knowledge that needs to be available for
less experienced users appears in the same content page, in a central help system, or by launching a third-party application is not as
important as knowing that the needs of each employee can be met
logically and timely. The level of assistance or help is very different
for personal information management (PIM) applications compared to job-related responsibilities, for example. Self-service applications that require users to share corporate information and
processes will have fewer personalization options and more built-in
help and process walk-through options.

It is important that the corporate portal team understand the
context in which employees will be using the content pages. As
much as possible you should provide a wide variety of viewing capabilities. Employees generally want to control the colors and organization (order) of the information presented through the corporate
portal. A balance or choice should be made regarding how consistent the information should be for a group of users compared to
how unique or personalized each user is allowed to make each content page. The types of personalization to consider are layout,
choice of corporate portal features, the content windows included
in each content page, and the content presented in each content
window. An example of how users can personalize their portal desktop can be seen in Microsoft's Digital Dashboard Resource Kit (see
Figure 9-4). Microsoft uses the term Web Parts to describe content
windows. The Digital Dashboard (portal desktop) is separated into
five sections called zones. The Web Parts (content windows) can be
dragged and dropped into any of the five zones (sections) on the
content page.

Figure 9-4. Microsoft Digital Dashboard user personalization.

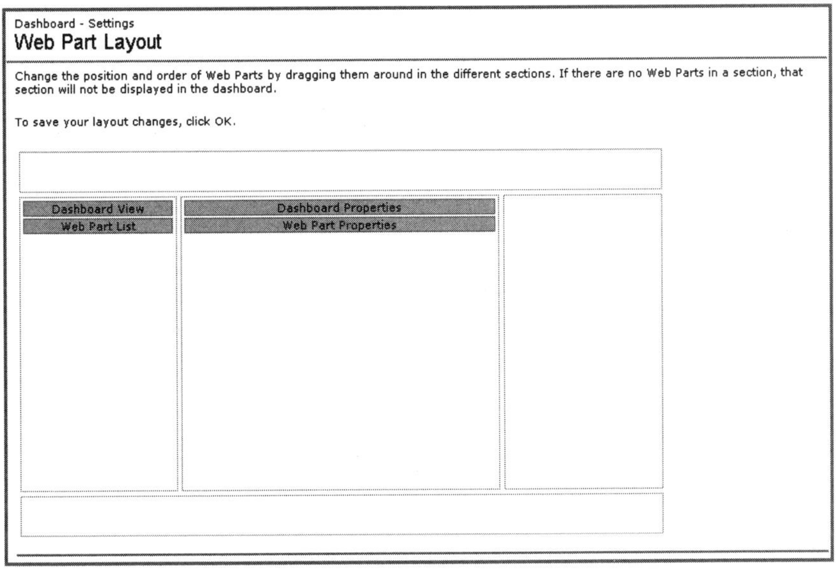

Navigation Personalization

The summary information and additional levels of detail available to employees primarily are presented in content pages and content windows in the corporate portal. The second most common location for information is in the content-relevant information section of the corporate portal. It is beneficial to "flatten" access to information by presenting it to the corporate portal user in the fewest number of navigation clicks or tasks as possible. Given that users can add, move, and remove content windows throughout the corporate portal (provided they are assigned rights to do so) employees can organize their own content pages by creating tabs and assigning individual content windows to the content page tabs. With rich personalization features that allow employees to organize content in a way that makes sense to them, the more likely employees will continue to access and use the corporate portal as a knowledge management tool.

Try to make content windows short and factual and provide links to additional information needed (e.g., background or training knowledge to less-experienced employees). For the corporate portal to be extremely effective, the content windows and content relevant information must be updated frequently and give notification to employees on how current the information is. Some visual clue should indicate to corporate portal users if there is additional content below the information that can be seen on a single screen. Employees may not realize at first glance that more content is available below the edge of the browser window. Scrolling the browser window represents a flow in data content, whereas following a link creates a break in the content flow. Be careful how much information is contained in a content page; users will get lost in the page if it is too long. A page length of one and one-half screens is relatively easy for an employee to scroll and keep track of information on the page. If there are doubts regarding how long content pages should be, ask for feedback from the employees using the corporate portal self-service applications.

For multipart documents, it is important to include document and chapter headings. If content pages are consistently longer than one and one-half screens, then building additional navigation features into the content page (to help quickly focus the key points or sections of the page) is recommended. Suggestions include:

1. *Creating a short list of the distinct sections of the document as links.* Employees will know at first glance what information is contained in the document and navigate quickly to the section of the document they need.

2. *Creating a collection of graphic navigation buttons, with caution.* Make sure they are widely accepted, well understood, and combined with other textual navigation features that make them easy for employees to decode.

3. *Adding search capabilities.* For large collections of sizable documents or smaller collections that are not well categorized, search features can improve retrieval and accessibility of information in your organization.

4. *Using links to improve the utility of your content pages.* Links need to be created or worded in a way that prevents them from distracting from the core content material presented in the corporate portal. Links provide connections to other information

resources, organizational markers (anchors), and reference terms to the current document context.

The most important quality aspects of the corporate portal solution are that the information available is accurate and up-to-date. The operational and strategic decisions made by corporate portal users are only going to be as effective and informed as the information made available to them to make those decisions. If the information is accurate and timely, but employees are not able to find information or need different information to work effectively, then the content presented in the corporate portal solution needs to be reevaluated for usefulness. The issue may be that the information available in the corporate portal is relevant but additional self-service applications or functions are needed to complete or enhance the usability of the corporate portal solution.

Navigation throughout the corporate portal must be well organized, intuitive, and accurate. Be sure that all the links referenced throughout the corporate portal solution work correctly. Having a site map can be very useful in visually representing the information resources available in the corporate portal solution. This visual representation can also be used as another navigation resource to find information throughout the corporate portal solution. As the portal site becomes larger, the site map can serve as a high-level knowledge map for users who are having trouble locating information, or as a training tool to help employees recognize the business process owners and relationships of the information available. An example of a site map for our fictitious case study company, CorporatePortal.com, is shown in Figure 9-5. You may want to consider and evaluate a third-party software package that can create site maps and verify that links are working correctly. An automated solution can minimize maintenance tasks and ensure the quality of your corporate portal solution.

System Intelligence

The current knowledge portal market is beginning to explode, and the future will move in many new directions. Some future opportunities will offer artificial intelligence or a new level of intelligence into the corporate portal arena. The future holds easier ways to

Figure 9-5. CorporatePortal.com site map.

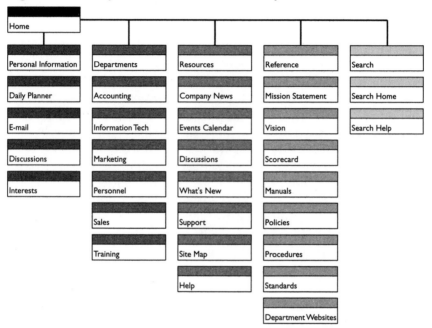

create and manage customized content, community aggregation, information brokering, and other value-added services. Many of these new opportunities tie to e-commerce, information partnering, and new revenue capabilities. The knowledge portal will find a way to integrate the web infrastructure of organizations of all sizes. Although portals were introduced only a few years ago, technology advances will continue to enhance the current functionality and grow into new functions and opportunities for your corporate portal solution.

The extended knowledge portal will continue to serve as the central knowledge desktop for decision processing and content management, connecting employees with information and knowledge experts, and allowing for the management of mission-critical activities of the organization. Additional services will support virtual organizations that can bring channel partners, suppliers, distributors, and customers into the knowledge portal environment.

As you develop your corporate portal strategy, the number of technologies, applications, administration, infrastructure, and security requirements that are integrated into the complete solution are going to be significant. There is not a definitive architecture used to support the corporate portal solution. The iterative implementation of self-service applications into the corporate portal allows you to build the foundation as you build the knowledge management solution. The foundation you are building includes important features that include:

- Data filtering and analysis (solutions that summarize reports and information for clarification specific to a group of employees or identified purpose)
- Information brokering (solutions that serve as a middleman or negotiator to provide the data or material requested by an employee)
- Workflow management (solutions that evaluate and improve process and action activities in your organization)
- Data mining (solutions that attempt to explain or predict patterns in data)
- Content management (solutions that facilitate guidance, control, and structure for unstructured information)
- Mission and task management (solutions that support the creation of a series of activities that are tracked from inception to resolution)
- Communication and collaboration integration (solutions that foster team activities and promote employees sharing ideas and knowledge)
- Personal information management (solutions that provide features for maintaining individual schedules, calendars, tasks, address books, or other personal assistance)
- Risk management (solutions that identify, promote, prioritize, and provide assistance in removing issues or concerns that need to be controlled or resolved)

Personalized Access to Content Checklist

For each business function you've identified and included in the initial phases of the corporate portal solution, please copy the appropriate section (heading and questions), change the heading to match the name of the business function, and answer the following questions with business domain experts in your organization.

PERSONALIZATION REQUIREMENTS

☐ What are the objects that can be personalized in the corporate portal by each user?

☐ How will users initially create their personalized portal?

☐ How will users make ongoing changes to their personalized portal (e.g., adding, renaming, deleting, moving, other)?

☐ Will pre-established templates exist to "jump-start" the users? If so, what are the templates and what will be included on each? Will templates be based on a defined user role?

☐ How does a user specify personal interests, and what information will be affected by this personalization?

☐ Have the personalization requirements for configuration of application functions been defined for the corporate portal solution? These configuration options need to be identified as either (1) managed by each user or (2) managed centrally by the administrator.

☐ Have the personalization requirements for search functions been defined for each user or role?

☐ Have the personalization requirements for collaboration functions been defined for each user or role?

☐ Have the personalization requirements for security features been defined for each user or role and administrators?

CorporatePortal.com Case Study

Portal software applications are being evaluated by CorporatePortal.com to provide the framework for the business functions it wants to share corporatewide. The InfoImage freedom product is being used to complete the analysis activities required to complete the business case. The final selection of a portal software vendor and product will be made during the architecture and design phase of the approved corporate portal project. The portal software application selected must closely match the mission, objectives, and infrastructure of the corporate portal solution. One criterion used to evaluate the portal software application is the personalization options that can be incorporated in the implemented solution.

The IT department will set up and configure new corporate portal users from a template. New users can be created individually or in groups. The employee will be able to open the portal desktop with the standard or template-defined content pages and settings. Help files provide desktop training on how to get started using the portal desktop. Once this training has been completed, users will be allowed to change or update their portal settings and save these new settings. For the first implementation of the corporate portal solution, employees will be able to modify the following elements in the portal desktop:

- *Location of the Main Portal Menu.* It can be at the top of the page (CorporatePortal.com example), on the left side of the portal desktop, or on the right side of the portal desktop.
- *Location of the Content-Relevant Information.* This can be on the left side of the portal desktop (CorporatePortal.com example), the right side of the portal desktop, the top of the page, or other agreed-upon location.
- *Location of Personalization.* This option can be below the main portal menu (CorporatePortal.com example) or removed from the page and included as a tabbed page of content-relevant information.
- *Color and Font Selection.* Users will be able to select different color palettes and font choices that will be reflected in the portal desktop.
- *Content Page Tab(s).* Users can create additional tabs on a content page; they can then add content windows to the new tabbed page.
- *Content-Relevant Information Items.* Users can add user-defined links to the content-relevant information tabbed pages.

FURTHER READING

Kimball, Ralph and Richard Merz. *The Data Webhouse Toolkit: Building the Web-Enabled Data Warehouse.* New York: John Wiley & Sons, Inc., 2000.

Berry, Michael J. A., and Gordon Linoff. *Mastering Data Mining: The Art and Science of Customer Relationship Management.* New York: John Wiley & Sons, Inc., 1999.

KEY POINTS

To prepare the corporate portal strategy, there are several considerations regarding individual identity profiles and personalized access to data. These include:

1. Individual identity is managed through individual profiles and metadata that are used to compile, organize, and document information about the skills, roles, activities, interests, and responsibilities of employees (i.e., people) within your organization.

2. The identity profile is a collection of knowledge about employees in your organization and is composed of the following four objects:

- User profile object
- User preferences object
- Organization chart object
- User identity objects (e.g., skills, activities, roles, interests)

3. To define the corporate portal identity you must determine the attributes regarding each employee who will be represented in the corporate portal solution. The level of detail required is what distinguishes one entity from another so you can guarantee the precise entity (employee) you are referencing is correct.

4. Entity relationship diagrams should be used in the business case to document the preliminary research regarding the unique identity of employees and to verify that the data points or attributes referenced in the corporate portal solution are available in your organization or can be made readily available.

5. The identity schema is the completed ER diagrams; it's used to create the logical outline of the identity profile information required to support the corporate portal solution.

6. The data dictionary or catalog is a definition of the properties used to define the data elements (i.e., attributes) included in the logical data model of the identity schema.

7. Personalized access to content provides decision-making enhancements and effective information management, allowing content filtered specifically for corporate portal users' working styles and preferences. The types of personalization features to evaluate and consider include:

- User personalization
- Navigation personalization
  System intelligence

Use the following checklist to review or analyze the importance of how individual identity is defined and what personalized access requirements should be for your organization's corporate portal solution.

ANALYZING YOUR CORPORATE PORTAL'S INDIVIDUAL IDENTITY AND PERSONALIZED ACCESS TO CONTENT

☐ Are enterprise systems and applications able to cross-reference each other throughout your organization? Would employees benefit from these relationships and cross-references?

☐ Are employees able to organize what content is available on their desktop and how it is arranged or categorized?

☐ Are employees able to understand the navigation of their knowledge desktop and control some aspect of it?

☐ Are employees able to get help through help topics, wizards, and other online solutions? Are employees able to submit questions or give feedback easily?

10

Information Technology Analysis

The purpose of the information technology (IT) analysis is to organize your infrastructure planning and information collection activities for the corporate portal solution. The information collected will allow you to clarify the technologies, hardware, software, and IT personnel that will be necessary to plan, design, develop, deploy, and maintain a corporate portal in your organization. The questions and sections included throughout the information technology analysis should be reviewed and enhanced or removed as necessary for your corporate portal strategy team to create interview sessions that they will want to complete with identified IT experts. Most likely you'll need to create a series of interviews with a variety of experts to collect the complete spectrum of information required. The results of these interviews and meetings will give you the details needed to create the information technology analysis and results section of the business case.

INFORMATION TECHNOLOGY REVIEW

The IT review has been developed to frame discussions surrounding the intranet requirements of your corporate portal solution. The completed IT review provides the answers needed to finish the planning process for infrastructure requirements and establish the corporate portal standards within your organization. This IT review serves two purposes:

- To inform your organization of the important technical, administrative, and cultural aspects of implementing a corporate portal intranet solution
- To lead the corporate portal team to make sound decisions in all areas of intranet planning, based upon the information they discover and on your unique organizational needs and requirements

Participants

The IT review team should include key representatives from your organization's IT department, business domain experts, and members of the corporate portal strategy team. IT representatives should include managers, network and application development personnel, and support staff. Business domain expert representatives should be drawn from groups that have expressed an interest in intranet technology to further their knowledge management and business goals. In most cases the human resources, corporate administration, sales, customer service, and product development groups are among the first departments to be involved in a corporate portal solution. The corporate portal IT issues outlined in this chapter should be reviewed, researched, and documented for inclusion in the business case.

How the Corporate Portal Will Grow

Your corporate portal solution will always be evolving. Content and services will change and grow. Your corporate portal business case needs to encompass not only what it takes to start your corporate portal solution, but also how you expect it to grow and, as important, how that growth will be managed. Many corporate portals begin as the creation of a single self-service application and soon after require several full-time experts to develop, manage, and maintain them. You can expect your corporate portal to mature and grow along a continuum, as shown, to include data sources throughout your organization.

Information Sources and Access Continuum

Local→Regional→National→International

This model predicts upgrades in server, browser, and information technology as well as applications. As the corporate portal solution expands to include additional systems and applications, a greater demand is created for incorporating new and existing services that include additional testing and planning requirements to meet the growing need. Managing this growth is a task of your IT team.

This continuum affects the development, system integration, and maintenance of the corporate portal solution. The integration of the different technologies, applications, services, and system support is critical for providing individual working environments to employees. Determining how to support and enhance personalization requirements while the corporate portal matures is an important planning requirement to be included in the business case.

CORPORATE INTRANET REVIEW

The concept of the corporate portal intranet is a rich, full-function, ubiquitous environment for information dissemination, communication, and application sharing, built on top of open technology standards. An intranet is Internet technology applied within your organization. Web servers deliver web pages in HTML, dynamic HTML (DHTML), extensible markup language (XML), XSL (extensible stylesheet language), and other formats to corporate portal users through browsers. Your corporate portal strategy team needs to review and establish a collection or series of interview questions to evaluate your IT environment. The purpose of these research activities is to assess the current state of, and availability of access to, various systems and their related services, as follows:

- Background (broadly, the current state of your network and intranet resources)
- Messaging infrastructure
- Collaborative and groupware systems
- Intranet strategy (e.g., does current intranet and existing intranet strategy support the proposed corporate portal solution?)
- Internet strategy (e.g., does the current Internet and exist-

ing Internet strategy support the corporate portal solution proposed?)
- Portal software applications
- Enterprise resource planning (ERP) systems
- Search systems (includes services needed to support the corporate portal business functions and self-service application requirements)
- Online help systems (includes requirements and supporting documentation that can provide the right level of assistance and self-discovery from the portal desktop)
- Content management systems
- Line of business (LOB) systems
- Legacy applications
- Data warehouse and data mart systems
- Business intelligence and executive information systems
- Knowledge management systems
- Other (e.g., are there any proprietary systems or custom-built systems that should be evaluated as part of the corporate portal business case?)
- Cultural considerations (an enablement and communication plan that will teach employees about the corporate portal)

To help you gather and research information on each of these systems, you can use the following checklists. The results of your research go into the business case. Note, however, that Internet website planning is not covered as part of this IT review. This IT review is meant to establish a baseline for the skills and experience your organization has with Internet technology.

Background Checklists

As a first step in planning your corporate portal intranet, you must define the current state of your network and intranet resources. The following checklist is designed to help you do that.

User Population and Organizational Environment

☐ What is the total number of locations/offices and where are they geographically located?

☐ How many employees/users are at each of the above-listed locations?

☐ How many of these locations are connected to your wide area network (WAN)?

☐ How many remote locations are there with either dial-up or no access to the corporate network?

☐ How many employees or users are there at each location?

☐ How many remote employees or users are there?

NETWORKING INFRASTRUCTURE

☐ Which network protocols do you support within your organization (e.g., TCP/IP, SPX, NetBIOS)?

☐ Which network operating systems (NOS) do you support within your organization (e.g., NetWare, Windows NT, Windows 2000, UNIX)?

☐ Which directory services (DS) do you support within your organization (e.g., NDS, Active Directory, LDAP)?

☐ What tools or network operating systems do you use to manage your network, including the directory and address structure?

☐ What is the network bandwidth of the local area networks (LANs) at your various sites?

☐ What is the network bandwidth of the WAN connecting your various sites?

☐ What are the known problems with the LAN/WAN at the current time?

☐ What projects are currently in process or planned to improve, add to, or change the current LAN/WAN infrastructure?

REMOTE ACCESS

☐ How do remote users connect to the network?

☐ Approximately how many remote users are there, and what information systems do they commonly access?

INTERNET AND EXTRANET CONNECTIVITY

☐ Do you have a single, centralized Internet connection, or do the various sites have their own direct Internet connections?

☐ What is the bandwidth of your various Internet/extranet connections?

☐ What projects are currently in process or planned to improve, add to, or change your Internet/extranet connectivity?

☐ What is your Internet/extranet security model and structure?

PRIVATE NETWORKS AND EXTRANETS

☐ Do you have any private networks or extranets set up and in place?

☐ What is the bandwidth of these private network connections?

☐ Do you have any plans for setting up, improving, or adding to your existing private network infrastructure, including setting up a virtual private network (VPN) over the Internet?

DESKTOP APPLICATIONS

☐ What is the name and version number of the desktop applications supported within your organization?

APPLICATION DEVELOPMENT

☐ What is the name and version number of the application development tools supported within your organization?

Messaging Infrastructure Checklist

For each messaging system used within your organization, copy the appropriate section (heading and questions) from the following checklist, change the heading to match the name of the system, and answer the questions contained in that section.

MESSAGING SYSTEMS

☐ What is the messaging system's name, manufacturer, and version number?

☐ What operating system platforms does it run on?

☐ What is the current status and plan for this system? If the messaging system is planned or in the process of being implemented, what is the targeted "live" date?

☐ How many users are hosted on this messaging system?

☐ How many remote or disconnected users are hosted on this messaging system?

☐ What standard Internet protocols does this messaging system support (e.g., SMTP, POP3, IMAP, NNTP, LDAP)?

☐ What are the known external interfaces with this system and other messaging systems (e.g., the Internet) and the types of interfaces that are set up (e.g., SMTP, Gateway, Message Transfer Agent, X.500 routing, other e-mail to e-mail connectors)?

☐ Have you recently completed any migrations from an existing messaging system?

☐ Are you planning any consolidations or migrations of existing messaging systems?

Collaborative and Groupware Systems Checklists

For each collaborative and groupware system used within your organization, copy the appropriate section (heading and questions), change the heading to match the name of the system, and answer the questions contained in that section.

COLLABORATIVE AND GROUPWARE SYSTEMS

☐ What is the collaborative or groupware system's name, manufacturer, and version number?

☐ Briefly describe what the system does and how it will be used.

☐ What operating system platforms does it run on?

☐ What is the current status and plan for this system? If the system is planned or in the process of being implemented, then what is the targeted "live" date?

☐ How many users actively use this collaborative or groupware system (do not count those users who only use e-mail)?

☐ How many remote or disconnected users actively use this collaborative or groupware system (do not count those users who only use e-mail)?

☐ What types of collaborative applications are currently being used or in development?

☐ What are the known external interfaces with this system and other groupware systems (e.g., the Internet) and the types of interfaces that are set up (e.g., SMTP, Gateway, Message Transfer Agent, X.500 routing, other e-mail to e-mail connectors)?

☐ How many users will access this system (via the network and remotely)?

Intranet and Internet Strategies Checklist

Your IT department's existing intranet plan and Internet plan must be mentioned in the corporate portal business case. Based on the results of the business process and information needs analysis and the assessment of the current state of your organization's intranet and Internet, you can evaluate whether your intranet and Internet infrastructure can support the proposed corporate portal solution, or whether additional upgrades must be made as part of the submitted proposal. The following checklist is designed to help you collect the information needed.

INTRANET AND INTERNET STRATEGIES

☐ What is your intranet strategy?

☐ What is your Internet presence strategy?

☐ Do you host your own site or is this contracted out?

☐ Which web browsers (e.g., Microsoft IE, Netscape, Mosaic) do you use (include version numbers)?

☐ How many users are currently using each browser?

☐ If you have multiple browsers today, are you in the process of standardizing on one browser, or do you have any plans to standardize?

☐ Which web servers (e.g., Microsoft Site Server/IIS, Lotus Domino, Netscape) do you use (include version numbers)?

☐ What operating system platforms do they run on?

☐ Do you use any application servers, transaction servers, or active application servers (e.g., Microsoft Transaction Server, Net Dynamics, Web Sphere) that may be used to process the business logic or rules in a three- or n-tier architecture system?

☐ What tools do you use for creating your intranet?

☐ How are decisions about your intranet made? Is there an oversight board?
☐ What tools do you use for creating your Internet site?
☐ How are decisions about your Internet presence made? Is there an oversight board?

Portal Software Applications Checklist

You want to consider knowledge portal software applications to implement the corporate portal solution. Consider portal software vendors that support a scalable and distributed collection of portal servers and services. Include in your research the data integration and connectivity support provided by the portal software application and verify these features to your organization's requirements. Your corporate or enterprise portal must support a variety of user communities that are geographically distributed and have unique security requirements. The architecture you deploy must provide a portal platform capable of meeting your current and future user base.

Evaluate the third-party products and enterprise systems that you want to be available within the corporate portal solution. Review the knowledge portal software application's ability to integrate with these products and systems. Determine what functionality the portal software application provides, which of your organization's portal requirements require customization, and what the customization requirements are expected to be. Consider the architecture and flexibility of the corporate portal being proposed to determine how the solution may continue to grow.

The IT development team will benefit from the existing core features and software functions that are provided as part of the portal software application. They'll also benefit from existing software development kits that allow the corporate portal to be programmatically extended to meet your organization's requirements. Your development team should be able to use their current Internet programming standards (e.g., HTML, DHTML, JavaScript, XML/XSL, and Active Server Pages) and the software development kit that comes with the portal software application to create objects for the portal desktop. You want to evaluate the application programming interfaces and software development kits that are available with these portal software applications.

For each portal software application being considered for your organization, copy the appropriate section (heading and questions) from the following checklist, change the heading to match the name of the application, and answer the questions contained in that section.

PORTAL SOFTWARE APPLICATION

☐ What is the portal software application's name, manufacturer, and version number?

☐ Briefly describe the benefits provided.

☐ Briefly describe the weaknesses.

☐ What operating system platforms does it run on?

☐ Which database or data storage platform does it use?

☐ What is the current status and plan for this system? If the system is planned or in the process of being implemented, what is the targeted "live" date?

☐ How many users access this system and how useful is the information provided by the system? Where does it provide good information, bad information, or no information?

☐ What are the known external interfaces with this system and the type(s) of interface available (e.g., batch, text file, pumping technology, CORBA/COM interface, real time)?

☐ What features and services will be available for corporate portal users and self-service applications?

☐ Please submit any current documentation or diagrams that would be helpful in detailing, describing, or clarifying any of the aforementioned topologies, systems, or strategies.

Portal Software Application Administration

The administration element is an important aspect of the corporate portal solution. This impact is primarily on the IT department and corporate portal project team of your organization because they provide the services that maintain the infrastructure, third-party applications, business processes, and IT systems that are part of the corporate portal. It is recommended that the corporate portal business case identify and include a third-party portal application to (1) tie the corporate portal and knowledge management requirements together and (2) the base stability and structure (foundation) to build and grow the corporate portal solution. All types of portal software solutions from many vendors are readily available to research and evaluate. You are interested in a product that meets the corporate portal definition created for your organization, then evaluating the self-service application requirements of your employees and selecting the corporate portal software product that most closely matches these requirements.

The portal products should be evaluated from both an administration and a business requirements perspective as well. The administration issues include:

- Creating the connections and external systems that provide content to the corporate portal.
- Identifying the administration and maintenance requirements of the portal software.
- Setting up and configuring the portal software.
- Adding and removing corporate portal users.
- Determining the knowledge, skills, and training requirements for portal software administrators.
- Obtaining development resources to design, develop, and deploy custom corporate portal requirements.

The business requirements issues include:

- Establishing new business processes or resolving other logistical issues to publish information to the corporate portal.
- Identifying the management, engagement, and team resources to lead the corporate portal initiative for your organization.

For example, a corporate portal administrator is required to create new portal desktop configurations that include content pages and content windows. Figure 10-1 is a picture of Microsoft's Digital Dashboard administration client where an administrator can create a new portal desktop (the Digital Dashboard) and add several content pages. Figure 10-2 represents adding content windows (so-

Figure 10-1. Microsoft Digital Dashboard portal desktop configuration.

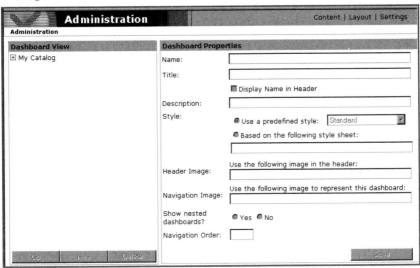

Figure 10-2. Microsoft Digital Dashboard Web Parts (i.e., content windows) configuration.

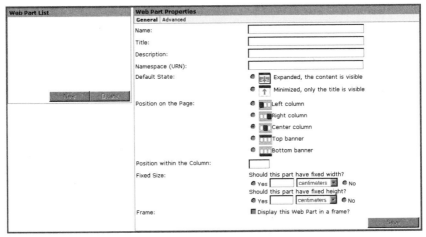

called Web Parts in the Microsoft application) to content pages after they have been created.

For the collection of business functions identified for inclusion in the initial phases of the corporate portal solution, please copy the appropriate section (heading and questions) of the following checklist and answer the questions with business domain experts in your organization.

CORPORATE PORTAL ADMINISTRATION

☐ Which administrator will be responsible for establishing default user interfaces?

☐ Who will be responsible for ongoing maintenance and customization to the user interfaces?

☐ What skills are needed to manage and maintain the corporate portal solution (include all functions of the system, administration requirements, procedures and processes to follow, system maintenance, and common problems)?

☐ What are the training goals and objectives (include all functions of the system, administration requirements, procedures and processes to follow, system maintenance, and common problems)?

☐ What are the methods of delivering training (e.g., classroom, online, computer-based training, desk side)?

☐ What are the required training materials (e.g., handouts, guides, quick reference material)?

☐ What are the logistics for training (e.g., length, topics, location requirements, method of instruction)?

Portal Software Application Security

You must also define the employee security and roles that corporate portal users will need to be assigned to read and perform their required activities from the portal desktop to successfully complete their job requirements. The logged-on user establishes the identity of the corporate portal user. The authenticated user information is used to determine the user's access to the corporate portal and enterprise applications. Each self-service application, software function, and corporate portal feature should be designated permissions (e.g., read, edit, no access) that establish the type of access to be allowed. The corporate portal users should then be assigned to roles (e.g., sales, marketing, manager, administrator) that designate who has rights to access to information, functions, and features throughout the corporate portal. The identified roles should then be assigned to the permissions that have been established to define what each corporate portal user's rights (permissions) are. By establishing roles that represent the activities performed by a group of employees in your organization, you can grant, revoke, or deny permissions for all members of the role at one time. Individual users can be moved from one role to another or added to new roles as their permissions change.

Roles should be established, too, for administrative privileges throughout the corporate portal solution. These roles are necessary for publishing, backing up, and restoring information in the corporate portal. Your organization may require additional administrative privileges for corporate portal developers and security administrators.

The following security requirements should be considered for your corporate portal solution:

• *Ensuring private communications.* If information sent through the intranet needs to be confidential and the integrity of communications made from the corporate portal are critical, then Secure Sockets Layer (SSL) and protocols for private point-to-point e-mail should be considered as part of the security requirements.

• *Verifying identity and authenticating employees.* You should securely identify and authenticate employees through standards-based public key certificate technology.

• *Controlling access to information and resources.* Using administration features and tools available through directories and applications, your organization can control access to information and resources on the Internet and throughout enterprise information sources.

• *Conducting secure transactions.* Your organization must ensure that information received through the corporate portal and the Internet is safe and private. This will include security policies established by your IT department, and types of files (e.g., cookies, ActiveX controls) that are allowed to run on users' desktops.

• *Ensuring software accountability and integrity.* The increasing rate of downloadable content on the Internet presents security risks. Your organization should positively identify the publisher of signed software before users begin downloading it from the Internet and verify that copies of information that reside throughout your organization are accurate and timely.

• *Providing a solid security foundation.* Security needs to be upgradeable to meet the evolving needs of the employees in your organization.

For each business function identified for inclusion in the initial phases of the corporate portal solution, please copy the appropriate section (heading and questions) of the following checklist, change the heading to match the name of the business function, and answer the questions with business domain experts in your organization.

CORPORATE PORTAL SECURITY

☐ What are the overall security requirements for each self-service application and business function?

☐ What (if any) are the criteria that the self-service application and business function must meet in order to be certified and accredited for security purposes?

☐ What safeguards are required for self-service application and business function security?

☐ What are the overall privacy requirements for the self-service application and business function?

☐ Does the organization have a standard policy on privacy, both in the workplace and from a business perspective (e.g., regarding customers, vendors, other suppliers)?

☐ What information is considered to be sensitive or private information?

☐ What safeguards need to be in place to ensure that private or sensitive information remains this way?

☐ Has the business case been reviewed for possible modifications due to security requirements of the corporate portal solution, self-service applications, or business functions?

Enterprise Resource Planning (ERP) Systems Checklist

For each ERP system used within your organization, copy the appropriate section (heading and questions), change the heading to match the name of the system, and answer the questions contained in that section of the checklist.

ERP SYSTEMS

☐ What are the names, versions, and modules of the ERP applications used within your organization?

☐ What operating system and relational database platforms do each of the aforementioned applications run on?

☐ Are you in the process of deploying an ERP system currently, or is deployment complete?

☐ If complete, when was each module that you have installed completed?

☐ What was your experience in the process of implementation?

☐ Did you work with a Big Four consulting organization during the deployment?

☐ Is the consulting firm still involved and, if so, what is it assisting with?

☐ Do you have in-house ERP development resources? If yes, then what do they do?

☐ Do you have in-house experienced database administrators (DBAs) for the relational database platform? If yes, what is their current role and priority?

☐ What would the lead-time be for involvement of your internal DBA and ERP resources in a data integration project for the Internet/intranet?

☐ How are you currently using your ERP data, or how do you expect to use it?

☐ Do you have enterprise data on any other non-ERP systems, such as in homegrown relational database management system (RDBMS) applications or collaborative groupware applications?

☐ Do you use other sources of information to facilitate your business decisions (e.g., the Internet, discussion)?

☐ Are you leveraging your enterprise data on your intranet for any business purpose today?

☐ What is your ERP client deployment strategy?

☐ How do you feel about deploying your ERP system to a large number of users?

☐ Who is or will be using your ERP information?

☐ Do you have disconnected users who can leverage your ERP data, if it were possible?

☐ What is your ERP to intranet/extranet integration strategy?

Enterprise Systems and Applications Checklists

For additional enterprise systems and applications used within your organization, copy the appropriate section (heading and questions), change the heading to match the name of the system, and answer the questions contained in that section of the following checklist.

SEARCH SYSTEMS

☐ What is the search system's name, manufacturer, and version number?

☐ Briefly describe what it does.

ONLINE HELP SYSTEMS

☐ What is the online help system's name, manufacturer, and version number?

☐ Briefly describe what it does.

CONTENT MANAGEMENT SYSTEMS

☐ What is the content management system's name, manufacturer, and version number?

☐ Briefly describe what it does.

Line of Business Systems

☐ What is the line of business system's name, manufacturer, and version number?
☐ Briefly describe what it does.

Legacy Applications

☐ What is the legacy application's name, manufacturer, and version number?
☐ Briefly describe what it does.

Data Warehouse and Data Mart Systems

☐ What is the data warehouse or data mart's name, manufacturer, and version number?
☐ Briefly describe what it does.

Business Intelligence and Executive Management Systems

☐ What is the business intelligence or executive information system's name, manufacturer, and version number?
☐ Briefly describe what it does.

Knowledge Management Systems

☐ What is the knowledge management system's name, manufacturer, and version number?
☐ Briefly describe what it does.

Other System(s) (Additional Systems that Will Be Included in the Self-Service Applications of the Corporate Portal Solution)

☐ What is the other system's name, manufacturer, and version number?
☐ Briefly describe what it does.

Additional Questions

Complete this series of questions for each enterprise system or application—search, online help, content management, LOB, legacy, data warehouse/mart, business intelligence, knowledge management, and other systems—to be included in the corporate portal solution.

☐ What operating system platforms does it run on?

☐ Which database or data storage platform does it use?

☐ What is the current status and plan for this system? If the system is planned or in the process of being implemented, what is the targeted "live" date?

☐ How many users access this system and how useful is the information provided by the system? Where does it provide good information, bad information, or no information?

☐ What are the known external interfaces with this system and the types of interface available (e.g., batch, text file, pumping technology, CORBA/COM interface, real time)?

☐ What features and services will be available for corporate portal users and self-service applications?

☐ Please submit any current documentation or diagrams that would be helpful in detailing, describing, or clarifying any of the aforementioned topologies, systems, or strategies.

Cultural Considerations Checklist

Corporate portals are a new way of working and communicating. Your organization needs to recognize the importance of cultural factors affecting how your employees work together. Discuss with the IT department and business domain experts any concerns they may have with respect to user acceptance of a corporate portal solution.

CULTURAL CONSIDERATIONS

☐ Who is driving the creation on an intranet within your organization?

☐ Is there excitement about the Internet and intranets within your organization?

☐ Is your corporate culture relatively open or relatively closed?

☐ Is there resistance to the notion of sharing information?

CORPORATE PORTAL SOLUTION REVIEW

The corporate portal solution is a central knowledge desktop that allows employees to access information throughout your organization from a browser client. Your corporate portal strategy team must do a complete review of the following areas to define the resources required to implement and maintain the corporate portal solution in your organization:

- *Corporate Portal Management.* Identify the current skills and availability of your network and intranet resources.
- *Administration.* Decide what corporate portal services you will offer now and in the future to achieve your goals.
- *Technical Staff and Support.* Determine the personnel and skills that are necessary to implement the chosen corporate portal services.
- *Resources for Staffing Roles.* Determine the resources required for management, administration, and maintenance of the corporate portal solution.
- *Technical Training.* Define the technical training requirements that need to be considered for the corporate portal solution.

Reviewing these key areas (each of which is detailed further with useful checklists in the following sections) will allow you to make the correct corporate portal decisions for your organization. The results of these information gathering and research activities should then be included in the corporate portal business case.

Corporate Portal Management

A corporate portal solution may begin as a simple proposition. The corporate portal solution is subject to growth that will drive the expansion of the project in every conceivable direction (e.g., infrastructure, complexity, extranet). You need to know how your corporate portal solution can be managed and who will manage and maintain it as it grows. The information collected before project funding is available is open-ended. Your team can nonetheless establish an initial understanding of how large the first phase of the corporate portal is expected to be.

The key project decision maker or corporate champion needs to be identified and working as a member of the corporate portal strategy team. Using the corporate portal vision established by the IT department and business domain experts, a preliminary effort and schedule targets can be determined. This information needs to be documented in the business case establishing a baseline for the corporate portal solution under consideration. Resources in the IT department (identified during the IT interviews and analysis discussed previously) with the appropriate networking, data integration, system security, and other infrastructure skills need to be evaluated. Design, development, deployment, and maintenance of the corporate portal solution demands that these skills are available in your organization.

MODELS FOR CORPORATE PORTAL MANAGEMENT

Management requirements are dependent on the anticipated growth of the corporate portal solution in your organization. Certain functions such as directory services may be centralized, whereas others such as content creation and application development may be decentralized. One of the virtues of open standards is that your corporate portal can easily incorporate different levels of centralization. Use the following checklist to evaluate your management model.

☐ Will overall management of the corporate portal be centralized, balanced, or decentralized?
☐ Will corporate portal administration be centralized, balanced, or decentralized?
☐ Will content creation for the corporate portal be centralized, balanced, or decentralized?
☐ Will corporate portal application development be centralized, balanced, or decentralized?

THE CORPORATE PORTAL IT PLANNING TEAM

Selecting a corporate portal IT team to work on the business case is an important first step. This group must research, review, and analyze the information collected. Using this information, the planning team then documents the corporate portal business case. Another team should be established to take the proposed corporate portal solution in the business case and implement the corporate portal solution. Before assembling your team, ask the following questions:

☐ What skills will be required to manage the corporate portal IT activities and tasks overall?

☐ Will the administration activities be centralized from a single site or across several sites?

☐ Will the responsibilities for administering servers be completed by a single administrator or by a group of administrators?

☐ Who (or what IT group) will be responsible for configuring browsers?

☐ Who (or what IT group) will manage application and content development, testing, and deployment?

☐ Who will represent each of the aforementioned groups as a member of the corporate portal planning team?

☐ How will corporate portal planning team members communicate with each other?

☐ How will the corporate portal planning team communicate with the wider organization and IT department?

CORPORATE PORTAL PILOT MANAGEMENT

Successful corporate portal pilots or reviews of the proposed solution are vital to your overall solution. In some organizations, a special corporate portal pilot team is created to review and provide feedback on the usability and functionality of the corporate portal. The selection of pilot or review teams is an issue that's addressed once the corporate portal project is approved. However, as you plan self-service applications and services, a list of potential pilots is naturally created. Key questions to ask are:

☐ Will a specific corporate portal pilot or review group be created? If so, who will be the initial members of that group?

☐ What roles and responsibilities will the members of the corporate portal pilot or review team have?

☐ How will members of the corporate portal pilot or review team communicate with each other?

☐ How will the corporate portal pilot or review team communicate with the corporate portal project team and the wider organization?

Administration

Administration covers general aspects of infrastructure common to any distributed computing environment, including hardware and software upgrades, backup and disaster recovery, acceptable use policies, management of user access rights and account termination, and product testing. Your organization needs to set policies and determine roles and responsibilities for each area. The following checklists are designed to help you organize the administrative effort.

HARDWARE UPGRADES

☐ Who will determine when hard drive, RAM, CPU, and other server upgrades are necessary?
☐ How will these upgrades be tested?
☐ Who will perform these upgrades?

SOFTWARE UPGRADES

☐ Who will determine when server software upgrades should be adopted?
☐ How will these upgrades be tested?
☐ Who will perform these upgrades?

BACKUP AND DISASTER RECOVERY PLANNING

Your intranet and Internet servers should be covered by the same kind of comprehensive backup and disaster recovery plan your organization uses for other types of servers and data. You may want to establish regular downtime periods to ensure adequate and accepted windows for backing up data.

☐ What backup routine is currently in place?
☐ Are any modifications needed to cover intranet servers or data?
☐ What disaster recovery plan is currently in place?

☐ Are any modifications needed to cover intranet servers or data?

☐ Who will be responsible for backup and recovery of your intranet?

ACCEPTABLE USE

An acceptable use policy for your corporate portal intranet should include information on what kinds of content are expressly permitted and denied, and what kinds of applications corporate portal users are allowed to run. Expect these policies to evolve as your corporate portal does. However, there are administrative, cultural, and even legal ramifications related to the content and use of your corporate portal. Establishing policies in advance can help prevent future problems. Key questions to ask are:

☐ Does your organization have an existing acceptable use policy covering internal network and Internet use, electronic publishing, and what constitutes offensive and/or nonbusiness-use material?

☐ What types of content will not be allowed on the corporate portal?

☐ What types of applications will not be allowed on the corporate portal?

☐ How will acceptable use policies be communicated to all employees?

USER MANAGEMENT

User management relates to the creation, modification, and deletion of user accounts (including mail accounts, if used), the administration of certificates for users, and even access control. Depending on the services your corporate portal is going to provide, user management may be done with the built-in administration features of the portal software. Key questions to review are:

☐ How will user accounts and security be managed (e.g., centrally or by each site)?

☐ Who will be responsible for creating users?

☐ Who will be responsible for creating groups?

Corporate Portal Server Administration

☐ How will server administration responsibilities be assigned, and
to whom?

Each of the corporate portal servers requires administration. Security and performance of the WAN and enterprise systems directly
affect the corporate portal solution, so your server administrators
should be trained in the operating systems and associated applications of the servers they maintain. You may delegate server administration centrally, by site, or by function. Be sure your servers are
secure so that remote access is only available to authorized personnel. Every server requires hardware and software maintenance and
security checks as well. Most require log analysis and user management. An administration program should be created that includes:

- Preventative maintenance
- Regular backups
- Consistent monitoring
- Emergency fallback planning

Technical Staff and Support

Staffing demands on an intranet vary based on a number of factors.
The total number of users and sites served, the number and complexity of applications, the number of servers, and the degree of
centralized application development are the primary variables. In
general, a decentralized, multiple site corporate portal solution requires more staff to support it than a highly centralized, single site.
Your intranet staff will generally be the same staff that supports
the corporate portal solution and must foresee, plan, manage, create, and support the intranet growth inside your organization.
These demands call for distinct intranet skills defined by several
typical roles. The roles needed include:

- *Intranet Manager/Architect*. The intranet manager is the
leader on an intranet team. This person makes the business case
for the intranet to all levels of management, evangelizes the idea
within the organization, and oversees the technical architecture.

Depending on the size of your intranet, you may only need one manager who serves as the architect. This role is responsible for leading the planning of new services and system expansion and managing projects, among other tasks. In larger intranets, you may have one overall architect and a manager for each location or region. Managers and architects are responsible for the overall success of the intranet.

- *Server Administrators.* Server administrators are responsible for the technical operation and security of intranet servers. They need to be highly trained on server operating systems and in the particulars of each type of intranet server they administer. If you do not use a site manager role (see next item), the server administrator may perform those tasks as well.

- *Site Managers.* Site managers are responsible for design and presentation of an intranet site. They need to be highly trained in site design, management, and web application development.

- *Application Developers.* Application developers are responsible for building and maintaining dynamic applications on the intranet. These applications may be built using HTML, DHTML, XML, XSL, C++, Perl, Visual Basic, Visual Basic Script, JavaScript, Java, ActiveX, and other tools. Application developers need to be trained according to the types of applications they are expected to create.

- *Graphic Artists.* Graphic artists are responsible for the graphics and visual details of a site or intranet. They may have a background in multimedia, industrial design, or a similar graphic specialty. They must be skilled in computer graphics and image applications and understand the conventions and constraints of web page design. In smaller intranets, an application developer with art skills often fulfills this role.

- *Help Desk.* Your help desk staff must be trained to support browser users. Corporate portal users may require some training in browser use, searching, and corporate portal navigation. This training should eliminate most calls to the help desk. Additionally, it may be necessary to train a member of the help desk for developers to pose HTML, DHTML, XML, and other design questions to.

Resources for Staffing Roles

New intranet implementers are often surprised at the skill sets and the number of people required to run a mature intranet as a stable, reliable, and responsive enterprise information service. The corporate portal solution presents additional complexities when it comes to connecting and incorporating existing systems into your organization's intranet and the Internet. Expect the corporate portal solution to create new user demands. Therefore, it is important to identify and train (and possibly hire or outsource) the resources necessary for the intranet's and corporate portal's beginning and ongoing support.

INFORMATION TECHNOLOGY STAFFING RESOURCES

☐ Who will be your intranet architect?
☐ Will you have one or more site managers? What will be the criteria for adding site managers (e.g., by department, site, functional group)? Who will be your site managers?
☐ Will you have one or more server administrators? Who will they be? What will be the criteria for adding more administrators as your intranet grows?
☐ Will your organization have one or more application developers? Who will fulfill this role? Will any applications be outsourced or purchased?
☐ Will one or more graphic artists support the corporate portal solution? If so, who will serve in this role?
☐ Is your current help desk or support staff trained in browser setup and use? If not, how will they be trained?
☐ Will publishing and development support be provided to content creators? If so, how?

Technical Training

Training is a key ingredient for the success of your intranet and corporate portal solution. Your technical staff, content creators, and corporate portal users all need varying levels of training. The training requirements for these different groups are outlined as follows:

- *Intranet Manager/Architect Training.* The intranet manager/architect requires some training in the operating systems of your servers and strategic Internet/intranet issues.

This role must be familiar with the tools of site management and application development. The key requirement is the ability to motivate and manage the intranet staff and the communication ability to represent the intranet and corporate portal effort to all levels of management.

- *Server Administrator Training.* Server administrators need to take courses in each type of server they will administer.
- *Site Manager Training.* Site managers need a blend of design, application development, and business skills.
- *Application Developer Training.* Application developers require training according to their knowledge level with different tools (e.g., HTML, DHTML, XML, XSL, C++, Perl, Visual Basic, Visual Basic Script, JavaScript, Java, ActiveX) and the tasks they are assigned.
- *Graphic Artist Training.* Graphic artists are trained in computer art and design generally and in tools such as Adobe Photoshop and Illustrator specifically.
- *Help Desk Training.* Help desk personnel are trained in browser use and available Internet and intranet applications. They should be familiar with the overall architecture of the intranet and the corporate portal solution.
- *End-User Training.* The amount or kind of end-user training for intranets and corporate portal applications is a decision that is determined by the difficulty level of the available applications and the skills of employees in your organization.

KEY POINTS

The ability to implement a corporate portal solution or any other knowledge management initiative requires that the IT department contribute knowledge, time, and resources to the project. A facilitated survey or series of interviews should be created and submitted to the IT department to complete. Once the corporate portal strategy team has worked with members of the IT department to complete the information technology analysis, you need to review and compile the results for your internal corporate portal planning purposes. The summary you create will be added to the corporate portal business case.

11

Business Process and Information Needs Analysis

Research and analysis must first be completed to evaluate the business processes, functions, and types of applications that are going to be initially accessed by the corporate portal. The strategy team works with the business domain experts in the organization to assess the needs and priorities of these processes, functions, and self-service applications. A brainstorming or discovery session allows the business domain experts to begin understanding how a corporate portal can solve several of their business problems and meet their management objectives. Various tools and techniques can be used to assist in the evaluation process. They include:

- Brainstorming
- Opportunity quotient grid
- Analysis matrix

When using these tools and techniques, there are many ways to categorize business processes, functions, or types of applications. For example:

- By roles and responsibilities of employees
- By the processes and activities performed by employees
- By department or workgroups of employees

The final business functions and self-service applications selected for the first phase of the corporate portal solution should include all necessary and many optional elements to make the corporate portal an effective and optimal knowledge management solution.

BUSINESS PROCESS AND INFORMATION NEEDS REVIEW

By evaluating existing business processes that can be improved with better content quality, the corporate portal can provide reliable deployment of web content, the delivery of personalized content, the ability to analyze usage patterns, and the management of site consistency and integrity. The iterative development phases of the corporate portal solution should continuously improve the corporate portal solution based on user behavior and changing business requirements. You need to be able to quickly implement new ideas and technologies, measure their efficiency and business value, and respond accordingly. The goal is to focus on continuous improvement, expand or extend successful activities, and eliminate ineffective processes. The business process and information needs analysis serves two purposes:

- To inform your business domain experts of the values, functions, features, and knowledge desktop advantages of implementing a corporate portal intranet solution
- To lead the corporate portal team to make sound decisions in all areas of application planning based on the information they discover and on your unique organizational needs and requirements

Participants

The business process and information needs team should include key representatives from your organization's information technology (IT) department and business domain experts. Business domain experts include managers, network and application development personnel, and support staff. Business domain expert representatives should be drawn from groups that have expressed an interest in intranet and web technologies to further their knowledge management and business goals. The corporate portal business process and information needs outlined in this chapter should be reviewed, researched, and documented for the business case.

How the Corporate Portal Will Grow

Corporate portals usually begin at one site in your organization that offers core services. As the corporate portal expands, other regions, departments, functional groups, and sites begin creating self-service applications for additional workgroups, departments, or job functions within your organization. Eventually, every employee and business function in your organization may need access to the corporate portal solution. This model of growth, which focuses on scope and interactivity, is a good one for predicting increases in server, network, and personnel resources.

Scope

Self-Service Application→Corporate Portal

Corporate portals grow from a single self-service application to a collection of self-service applications that work together to provide a complete corporate portal solution. During the first phase of the corporate portal project, the primary objective is to deliver different data sources and types of content throughout your organization via the portal desktop. As additional phases of the project are implemented, the corporate portal becomes a universal front-end used to access and manipulate diverse kinds of data sources and applications that remain stored in the back office in their native formats. The corporate portal provides a browser interface to a word processing system, e-mail client, spreadsheets, database user interfaces, multimedia players, enterprise resource planning (ERP) systems, and other enterprise applications and systems.

Interactivity

User Personalization→Navigation Personalization→Behavior Assistance Personalization

Corporate portal solutions typically begin with applications that are complex enough to demonstrate the software functions and universal features of the corporate portal, but generic enough for users in your organization to recognize the advantages and strengths of a knowledge desktop solution. As the scope of corporate portal users and services grow, portal content pages become more dynamic until content is presented to the employee based on configuration information established by their user identity and portal preferences.

This continuum affects the sophistication of the corporate portal solution. The architecture and design of the corporate portal universal features are critical for supporting individual working environments. Determining how to evolve and enhance features that include expanded personalization while the corporate portal matures is an important planning requirement for the business case.

CORPORATE PORTAL SOLUTION IDENTIFICATION

Several trends are driving organizations to deliver and receive valuable information. Whether pulling report pages and documents, pushing report pages and documents, or broadcasting report information, the Web is being used to reach large numbers of employees with hyperlink interaction that facilitates the level of detail each employee requires. The goal is to create a consistent version of information by accessing data sources that have in the past been difficult to leverage. These data sources include:

- *Data Warehouses and Data Marts*. These are systems that serve up online historical information and are specifically designed for predefined report summaries and analysis activities.
- *Operational Systems and Applications*. These include enterprise resource planning (ERP) and line of business (LOB) systems, legacy applications, and customer interaction software (CIS) that define the operational activities of the organization.

The corporate portal solution needs to collate data to support employees with a variety of skills and job requirements. The corporate portal solution should demonstrate access to information from data warehouses, data marts, relational databases, multidimensional databases, web applications, client/server applications, and desktop applications. Once this information is available, employees also need to communicate and collaborate with other knowledge experts in the organization to complete business processes and continually make more informed decisions. The corporate portal desktop is a window to data sources and other employees that can be easily located, navigated, and personalized to meet individual needs. Links to commonly used applications and tools that can be incorporated or launched from the corporate portal solution are therefore important. Online help and documentation minimizes support calls for assistance. Your corporate portal strategy team needs to identify and evaluate your business requirements and information needs by undertaking interviews, meetings, and research activities. The key steps in this review process are listed here; the findings in each case are incorporated into the corporate portal business case.

- *Identifying business functions and applications (discovery).* This process involves the identification of business functions and self-service applications that are best suited for inclusion in the corporate portal solution.

- *Starting with the idea.* The business functions and self-service applications selected have to be refined and decisions made about which ones should be included in the first iteration or initial phases of the corporate portal solution.

- *Describing application functionality.* The highest-level requirements, objectives, and scope of the business functions and corporate portal features are determined for the first iteration or initial phases of the corporate portal solution.

- *Adding data sources.* The strategy team needs to seek out and clearly define the data sources and data points (and any associated issues) that will contribute to the first iteration of the corporate portal solution.

- *Determining search requirements.* This process delineates the corporate portal solution's search requirements for the short term and the search objectives for the long term.

- *Determining online help requirements.* Requirements and objectives for online help and user assistance are determined for the corporate portal solution.

- *Determining collaboration requirements.* Requirements and objectives for communication, discussion forums, and workflow are determined.

- *Providing navigation.* User requirements for locating and traversing information within the corporate portal solution are determined and documented.

- *Providing relevant information.* For each content page, context-sensitive information determined to be relevant or useful to users is identified for the corporate portal solution.

- *Determining personalization requirements.* Personalization features and functions that support and enhance business functions and corporate portal features need to be incorporated into the portal desktop.

- *Determining security requirements.* Decisions about information security requirements are needed to determine what access rights groups of employees will be given when reading or interacting with the data sources presented.

Discovery

For the purpose of planning the corporate portal solution you should review potential business processes and the types of self-service applications that might be best accessed from a central knowledge desktop. You need to work with your business domain experts to assess their business needs and priorities when it comes to self-service applications. A discovery session allows the business domain experts to begin understanding how the corporate portal can help them solve their knowledge management concerns and initiatives. Tools such as brainstorming and the opportunity quotient grid (see Figure 11-1) can be used to objectively identify and prioritize the most important knowledge management business processes and self-service applications to include in the first few iterations of the corporate portal solution.

Figure 11-1. Opportunity quotient grid.

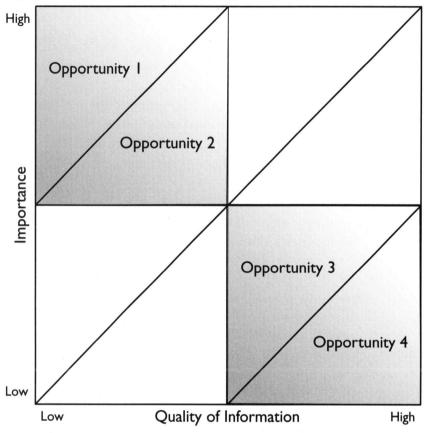

Brainstorming

Brainstorming is a technique that is used during group sessions with business domain experts to inspire conversations about innovative ideas for possible corporate portal business functions or self-service applications and to catalog the ideas and creative thoughts, establishing a collection to be further evaluated and discussed. Brainstorming is most productive during group sessions because team members, working together, can dynamically build upon one another's ideas. This momentum can trigger more ideas and possible solutions to the issues being addressed. The following supplies are needed to complete brainstorming:

- Flipchart or whiteboard
- Markers
- Scribe (to document the activities of the group session)

Depending on the level of detail required, the deliverables from the brainstorming session include:

- A list of ideas generated during the brainstorming session
- Clarification of the ideas generated during the brainstorming session

The ground rules of a general brainstorming session are as follows:

1. Remain focused on the topic.
2. All ideas are considered valid.
3. No judgment or criticism of ideas is allowed.
4. Allow the team to build upon ideas from others within the group.
5. A scribe must document all the ideas in the session on a flipchart or whiteboard.
6. Spelling accuracy is not important during the session.

It is vital to allow innovative discussion while reviewing and expanding upon the topic that defines the purpose of the session. The steps to follow are:

- *Generating the initial list.* Use common brainstorming techniques to identify the first collection of ideas, such as having each person give one idea and go around the room until there are no more ideas. Facilitate or kick off the brainstorming process by suggesting certain core business processes that are shared among several departments or functions in your organization.
- *Discussing the ideas.* Discuss each of the entries in the initial list and come to a general agreement about the meaning and the specific definition of the various business processes. Where necessary, remove duplicate entries or ideas that no longer make sense to the group as a whole. Do not remove

entries that are viewed as critical to one group but not to
another.

- *Documenting the final list.* Write the final lists on the whiteboard or flipchart and label or number each of the entries
  for easy reference. Make sure that the scribe or person taking notes copies down the final list including the label or
  number.
- *Prioritizing the list.* When the list is 80–90 percent complete,
  stop the brainstorming part of the discussion, focus on ar-
  ranging the list into current issues and future issues, and
  assign priorities. This activity will yield the complete list of
  issues that the corporate portal solution must meet to solve
  the current business problems identified and to be considered successful.

The Opportunity Quotient Grid

The goal of the opportunity quotient grid is to compare the
importance of identified business processes and how the quality of
the current information is meeting the business needs. The process
is used to assess the "opportunity quotient" of each business process being considered for inclusion in the corporate portal application. Follow these steps:

1. Hand out the opportunity quotient grid templates (see Figure 11-1) to all of the business domain expert session participants.

2. Ask each business domain expert to independently place
the number or label for each of the business processes identified
during the brainstorming session in the list on the opportunity
quotient grid.

3. Rate the quality of information. "Quality of information"
is a reflection of the current quality or value of information in re-
lation to the business process. A "high" rating would mean that
existing information systems provide excellent, high-quality information to the individuals involved in this business process, and that
the information is in an easily accessible and understandable format. Think of it in terms of efficiency and effectiveness, and combine these factors for an overall rating, between high and low, for
each business process. For example:

- *Efficiency.* How well does the information system work with regards to this process? Is it time-consuming, confusing, or difficult to access? Are many manual transformations required to use the information? Does it require many employees to make the information usable?
- *Effectiveness.* How well does the existing information system support the business process, and does it accomplish what it is intended to? If the process is supposed to provide a specific service or impart a specific type of knowledge, is it successful in doing so?

4. Rate the importance of the information. "Importance" is a reflection of strategic alignment. How well does this business process support core business objectives? Is accurate and timely information critical to the success of this business process and the company's overall objectives? Does it contribute to your ability to meet your objective?

5. Collect all of the opportunity quotient grid documents once everyone has filled out their individual assessments. Then draw the opportunity quotient grid on a whiteboard, starting with the first business process the business domain experts plotted, and combine the results on this single graph. The convergence of the results identifies the first business processes to include in the portal desktop. Continue this process until all of the remaining business processes have been plotted on the combined opportunity quotient grid. If there is a large disparity among the responses, ask the participants to come to a consensus as to where the business process should be placed on the opportunity quotient grid and why.

6. Prioritize the list based on the business processes that fall in the "high importance, low quality" quadrant, as shown in Figure 11-1. Note the diagonal bands that depict opportunities 1–4: Opportunity 1 processes are the first business processes your organization should address, whereas opportunity 4 processes are the last and probably not a good use of resources. The final results of the opportunity quotient grid should be analyzed and the results documented and summarized. This final summary is then presented in the business process and information needs analysis and results section of the corporate portal business case.

Starting with the Idea

Once the collection of business functions and self-service applications have been identified through discovery, you want to prioritize and select the most appropriate business functions for the first iteration of the corporate portal solution. The analysis matrix tool (see Figure 11-2) can be useful to establish the precedence and scope of the business functions, self-service applications, and corporate portal features that provide the most benefit to your organization.

The Analysis Matrix

After all the possible business functions and self-service applications to be evaluated for implementation have been identified, the analysis matrix is used to summarize the decisions made by the business domain experts. The analysis matrix is a tool used to visually identify, by business priorities or goals, the projects or self-service applications your strategy team reviewed and analyzed. The analysis matrix can easily be incorporated in the business case documentation to summarize the self-service applications incorporated in the first phase of the corporate portal. If your organization has already determined the business functions or self-service applications it is planning to implement in the corporate portal solution, then the analysis matrix does not have to be done. The following input is needed to complete an analysis matrix:

- Detailed lists of the projects, self-service applications, or collection of business functions that your organization wishes to analyze, develop, and implement in the corporate portal.
- A detailed list of the business requirements, goals, and other priorities being weighed to determine the most critical project or self-service applications to implement in the corporate portal.

The completed analysis matrix represents the business functions and self-service applications that target the most critical business requirements, goals, or other priorities that need to be addressed by the corporate portal solution. The fundamental steps involved are:

Figure 11-2. Corporate portal analysis matrix.

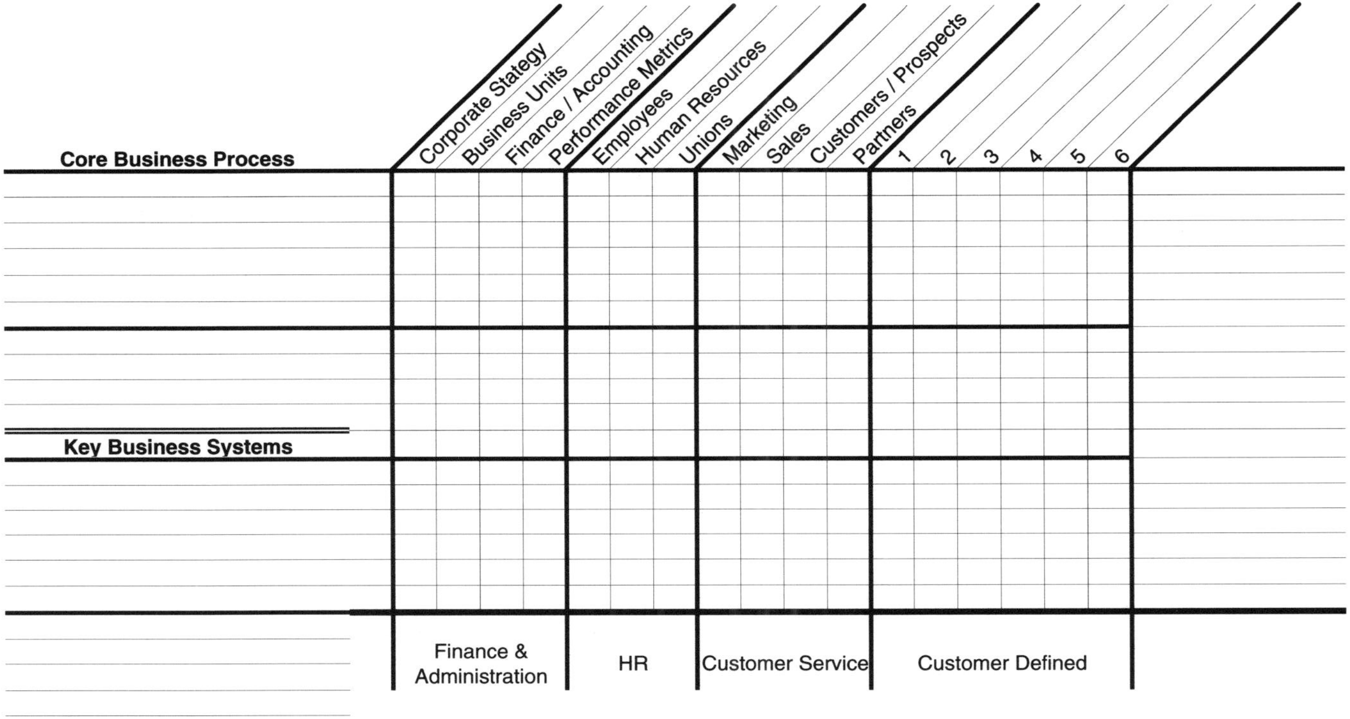

Core Business Process

Corporate Strategy
Business Units
Finance / Accounting
Performance Metrics
Employees
Human Resources
Unions
Marketing
Sales
Customers / Prospects
Partners
1 2 3 4 5 6

Key Business Systems

Finance & Administration | HR | Customer Service | Customer Defined

• Determining which business requirements, goals, or processes must be addressed by the business functions or self-service applications being considered for implementation by the corporate portal solution.

• Recording the basis of any calculations, algorithms, or other assumptions made.

• Completing the analysis matrix using information collected from the interview sessions with the business domain experts.

Goals and Critical Success Factors

After defining the business processes and self-service applications, the next step in reviewing your corporate portal is to discover the goals of executive management (i.e., corporate goals), IT, and business domain experts. Why does your organization want a corporate portal? What is expected from the corporate portal? Discovering the goals of the corporate portal's diverse constituents helps you set up a corporate portal intranet that meets expectations.

Discuss with the business domain experts what the specific goals are for the corporate portal solution. At the same time, you want to identify and discuss what the critical success factors are. One of the best methods is to run a short brainstorming session with the members of the corporate portal strategy team. Guide them in the discussion to collect the corporate portal goals and critical success factors. During this brainstorming process, it is important to involve everyone. One technique is to ask all of the members to think of at least two goals or critical success factors, then go around the room and ask each member, one at a time, for the two goals to be considered. Continue going around the room until there are no more ideas.

Once all of the goals and critical success factors have been generated and no one can think of any other, then go back and discuss each idea. Have the business domain experts prioritize each goal, using a rating system. For example, 1 is a critical goal (i.e., a must-have), 2 is a major goal (i.e., should have), 3 is a nice-to-have feature, and F is a future goal. Some ideas originally thought of may be taken off the list if everyone agrees it is not a valid goal for the project, or it is included or encompassed within another goal. In summary, the steps to follow involve:

- Brainstorming with business domain experts and recording all of the specific goals for the corporate portal solution.
- Evaluating and discussing every idea.
- Prioritizing each goal with a ranking system (e.g., 1 = critical goal, 2 = should have, 3 = nice to have, F = future goals).
- Writing the critical success factor on the whiteboard and verifying this list with the corporate portal team.

Use the following checklists as well as a guide during the brainstorming session with employees—including executives, IT personnel, and business experts—in your company.

IDENTIFYING GOALS AND CRITICAL SUCCESS FACTORS

☐ Are there any goals or critical success factors that are not on this list?

☐ What are the goals and critical success factors of the corporate portal solution?

☐ Which of the goals and critical success factors are high priorities? Low priorities?

CORPORATE GOALS

☐ What are the corporate goals for creating a corporate portal?

☐ What problems is a corporate portal expected to solve?

☐ What improvements does a corporate portal solution bring to your organization?

☐ Are there executives at the corporate level who are sponsoring the creation of a corporate portal?

INFORMATION TECHNOLOGY GOALS

☐ Is the IT department sponsoring the creation of a corporate portal solution?

☐ What are the goals of IT in creating a corporate portal solution?

☐ Are there specific IT-related issues the corporate portal is expected to solve and/or improve (e.g., replace existing knowledge management initiatives)?

Business Domain Experts and User Goals

☐ Are any business units or departments sponsoring the creation of an intranet? Which ones, and why?

☐ Are any of these units willing to participate in a corporate portal pilot program?

☐ What issues do business users believe an intranet can improve/solve?

☐ What are the critical success factors for a corporate portal to be accepted by employees in your organization?

Additional Corporate Portal Requirements

Your corporate portal strategy team needs to complete the following steps in defining the resources required to implement and maintain the corporate portal's content quality and usability in your organization. The results of research activities into the following areas should be included in the corporate portal business case:

- *Goals and Critical Success Factors.* Determine the goals and critical success factors of the business functions and self-service applications included in the corporate portal solution (as discussed in the previous section).
- *Corporate Portal Users.* Identify the business domain experts and user community that will use the first iteration of the corporate portal solution.
- *Documentation.* Determine the documentation requirements for the design, development, deployment, and end user.
- *Corporate Portal Content Management.* Determine the business domain experts responsible for the maintenance and enhancements of corporate portal content and the users responsible for testing the quality and usability of the prototypes created during construction.
- *End-User Training.* Define the end-user training requirements for the corporate portal solution.

Corporate Portal Users

Use the following checklist to identify who the various employees are for the first iteration of the corporate portal solution, as well as other identifiable user groups or communities.

BUSINESS DOMAIN EXPERT AND USER COMMUNITY

☐ Who is responsible for monitoring and providing feedback to improve the business processes or self-service applications after they are implemented in the corporate portal?

☐ Who is responsible for training users on getting started with the corporate portal? Transferring knowledge about the business processes and self-service applications in the corporate portal?

☐ Who is responsible for reviewing the usability and acceptance of the business processes and self-service applications incorporated in the corporate portal?

☐ Who is responsible for reviewing the implementation of software functions and universal features to be included in the corporate portal?

☐ Define the user communities. Where are they located?

☐ What is the intended time frame for deployment of the first phase of the corporate portal solution?

Documentation

Discuss with the business domain experts what the documentation requirements are for the architecture, design, construction, and deployment of the corporate portal solution. Using the following checklist, cover the following areas:

DOCUMENTATION REQUIREMENTS

☐ What are the architecture and design documentation requirements for the corporate portal solution (e.g., flowcharts, object models, network topology, data flow diagrams)?

☐ What coding standards and code documentation standards will be followed for the corporate portal solution (e.g., object-oriented, organization-specific, other)?

☐ How are prototype review sessions to be documented?

☐ What are the end-user documentation requirements (e.g., on-line help, printed quick reference material, other)?

☐ What are the system administrator documentation requirements (e.g., online system help, printed quick reference material, other)?

☐ What other documentation requirements are there?

Corporate Portal Content Management

A corporate portal solution incorporates business functions from across all sections and different functions of your organization. The business domain experts are critical to verify that the material and content used within the corporate portal solution is current and remains pertinent to the employees that need it. You need to know how the content contained in your corporate portal solution will be measured for quality and who will manage and maintain user acceptance as it grows.

MODELS FOR CORPORATE PORTAL CONTENT MANAGEMENT

Content management is dependent on the number of responsibilities or departments that sponsor information in the corporate portal. Within a corporate portal solution certain functions such as personalization content or enhancements may be centralized, whereas others such as content creation and quality of information presented may be decentralized. Identification of business domain experts who are responsible for continual review and enhancements guarantees that the corporate portal will continue to support employees that need the information to make informed decisions. Using the following checklist, cover the following areas:

☐ Have business domain experts been identified to be responsible for the quality and usability of the content presented in the corporate portal?

☐ How will issues identified and enhancements that need to be made to business processes and self-service applications be submitted to the corporate portal IT development team?

☐ How will the business domain experts share ideas and concerns with each other?

☐ What are the checks and balances for the addition of a new business process or self-service application into the corporate portal solution?

CORPORATE PORTAL QUALITY TESTING TEAM

Selecting a group of users to be responsible for reviewing prototype deliveries and providing usability information to the development team during the iterative construction process is suggested. This group can provide feedback to the development team regarding the quality and usability of the corporate portal in general and specifically for business functions and corporate portal features. Using the following checklist, cover the following areas:

☐ Have the employees for the quality testing team been identified?

☐ How will these employees be made aware of their responsibilities and time requirements to complete these activities?

☐ How will structured walkthrough sessions be scheduled, completed, and documented?

☐ How will the results of structured walkthroughs and more informal feedback channels be submitted to the corporate portal project team and the IT development team?

☐ How will the priorities of the issues to be resolved be decided and communicated back to the corporate portal quality testing team?

☐ How will enhancements or new requirements be approved and included in future iterations or phases of the corporate portal solution? How is this information going to be communicated back to the corporate portal development team?

☐ How will the corporate portal project team communicate with the wider organization?

End-User Training

Discuss with the business domain experts their specific training requirements for the corporate portal solution. Using the following checklist, cover the following areas:

END-USER TRAINING

☐ What are the training goals and objectives (include all functions of the corporate portal, administration requirements, procedures and processes to follow, corporate portal maintenance, and common problems)?

☐ What methods will be used for delivering training (e.g., classroom, online, computer-based training, desk side, other)?

☐ What are the required training materials (e.g., handouts, guides, quick reference material, other)?

☐ What are the logistics for training (e.g., length, topics, location requirements, method of instruction)?

☐ What are your end-user training requirements?

☐ What are your executive user training requirements?

☐ Are there other user groups to train (e.g., specific department training requirements)? If so, what are the goals and objectives, methods of delivery, required materials, and logistics of training?

☐ How much training can be implemented through the online help system?

KEY POINTS

The business process and information needs sessions should include key representatives from your organization's information technology department and business domain experts. Business domain experts include managers, network and application development personnel, and support staff. Business domain expert representatives should be drawn from groups that have expressed an interest in intranet technology to further their knowledge management and business goals. The decisions and results of these interviews and meetings should be reviewed, researched, and documented. The summary you create is added to the corporate portal business case.

12

Corporate Portal Storyboard

Think of your corporate portal as a story. Two styles are used to outline or represent your corporate portal story:

- *Storyboard.* A storyboard contains several screen shots or pictures of the proposed corporate portal desktop. These screen shots demonstrate how the self-service applications and corporate portal software features are integrated into the user interface. There might be two or three different layouts created to present how these features can be integrated onto the desktop. On each screen shot created, there will be menu items, hyperlinks, reports, and personalization features as elements of the picture. A series of screen shots are created that demonstrate how the corporate portal desktop changes as these elements are selected.

- *Script.* The script style is similar to walking through the activities an employee will complete when using the corporate portal solution. The self-service applications and features that have been identified from the business process and information needs analysis are broken out into several scripts or "use case" scenarios that describe in detail how the user will interact with the corporate portal. Several scripts should be written to demonstrate how different groups of users will be able to interact with the corporate portal desktop.

The storyboard and script methods should be used together. Creating a storyboard allows you to refine and examine the corporate portal user interface. Once the storyboard is completed, use the scripts to determine the effectiveness of the corporate portal solution as it is defined. The final scripts provide the detailed descriptions required for the validity and credibility review of the corporate portal solution. The storyboard visually demonstrates beyond words that the whole (corporate portal solution) is more than the sum of the parts (self-service applications and business functions).

STORYBOARDING THE CORPORATE PORTAL SOLUTION

Once the scope of the initial phases of the corporate portal solution have been outlined from the business process and information needs analysis, a visual model or storyboard is an excellent way to summarize the benefits of a corporate portal solution and the benefits your organization expects to receive from this knowledge management initiative. The goal is to take the self-service applications and business functions being included in the corporate portal and lay out (or storyboard) what the user interface and different screens would look like and how different types or roles of users will interact with the system. Your corporate portal strategy team should have collected the goals and critical success factors and identified the corporate portal software functions, universal features, and self-service applications to incorporate into the storyboard. The corporate portal solution will be unique based on the information served into the user interface and the personal settings defined by each user. The strategy team may be required to demonstrate a couple of storyboards to represent how a single solution can be focused or tuned to the needs of each corporate portal user.

CorporatePortal.com Case Study

Business domain experts at CorporatePortal.com have identified the initial business functions and self-service applications for the corporate portal solution. The processes and procedures that employees will follow to perform their assigned responsibilities from the portal desktop need to be defined and incorporated into the solution. The preliminary self-service applications include:

- *Corporate Objectives and Metrics.* This information is used to measure CorporatePortal.com objectives, department objectives, and individual employee objectives. It includes a defined set of key financial information, current project (tax and audit) status information, and customer satisfaction metrics for each role in the organization.

- *Document Repository.* An initial corporate document repository is defined and accessed from the portal desktop. This information needs to be distributed throughout several content pages in the corporate portal. The scope of documents and material includes information from departments across the entire organization.

- *Collaboration and Discussion Forums.* The portal desktop allows project teams to collaborate and coordinate their activities (e.g., the ability to join discussions, become a member of a user group, and access instant messaging services).

- *Expert Locator.* Expert locator information that includes employees and their skills and the associated skill level is available from the portal desktop. Employees can locate knowledge workers to ask questions or recruit their assistance in resolving issues. CorporatePortal.com would also like for employee skill information to be cross-referenced with reports and other content in the portal desktop. These employee-to-information relationships can be used to provide collaboration features from content windows and content-relevant information without having to search for a knowledge worker.

- *Personalization.* Employees can choose and personalize how information is organized and presented on content pages in the portal desktop.

The corporate portal software functions and universal features are outlined as follows:

- *Portal Banner.* The portal banner incorporates the Corporate Portal.com logo as well as other company branding information or mantras that help define the organization's image.

- *Portal Menu.* The portal menu is used to implement the highest level of the organization's taxonomy or categorization. Any global features such as help and search that need to be prevalent throughout the corporate portal can easily be incorporated as portal menu features.

- *Personalization.* The personalization features are specific to the personal data assistant (PDA) and personal information management (PIM) functions and universal features provided through the corporate portal solution.

- *Content Page Tabs.* For each content page the content page tabs provide a logical way to organize the collection of related information that is contained on that content page.

- *Content Page.* Each content page contains a logical subset of the complete set of business functions and self-service applications contained in the corporate portal solution.

- *Content Windows.* Each content window contains a logical subset of the collection of information available for the content page. Content windows contain reports, documents, graphs, or links to applications or additional data points. Configuration or setup options can be made available for personalization of the content window information.

- *Content-Relevant Information.* For each tabbed page in the corporate portal solution, the content-relevant information is available to provide additional navigation and detail surrounding the context of the information on the content page. Content-relevant information can contain links to related reports, Internet websites, and knowledge experts. Communication, collaboration, process, and action services can be made available from the content-relevant information section of the corporate portal solution.

Creating the Site Map

Several different types of information need to be made available from the corporate portal user interface. Once the collection of applications, data points, services, reports, business functions, and corporate portal features have been identified, your strategy team and business domain experts must establish a taxonomy or categorization of these objects into the corporate portal solution. As additional business functions and self-service applications are incorporated into the corporate portal solution, the portal menu and navigation decisions continue to evolve. Based on the direction in which the corporate portal grows and feedback received from corporate portal users, the associated taxonomy becomes a feature that is evaluated and updated as new phases of the solution are implemented. The storyboard needs an initial plan for navigation in the corporate portal solution.

Going through the exercise of creating a main portal menu and separating the content that will be available from each menu option results in a site map for the corporate portal. Each main portal menu option translates into content pages, which break down further into content windows and links to additional information. Documenting the complete collection of content pages and links into a central location gives a "big picture" of the corporate portal, or a site map. From the main portal menu and each content page, employees define how to traverse the portal desktop, establishing a navigation plan for the storyboard.

The following checklists are designed to help you establish a site map and navigation scheme for your portal solution. Copy the appropriate section (heading and questions) for the collection of business functions you'll use in the initial phases of the corporate portal solution. With the business domain experts in your organization, answer the questions contained in that section. The information will allow you to create one or two storyboards for the corporate portal business case documentation.

NAVIGATION FEATURES AND TOOLS

☐ Based on the results of business process and information needs analysis, what navigation features and tools are required for each user to complete assigned responsibilities?

☐ How should the navigation features and tools be organized on the corporate portal screens (in terms of logical groupings and tiers within the site)?

☐ What navigation features and tools are required to be standard options (appearing on every corporate portal page)?

☐ What are your initial preferences on the best wording for each navigation option, corporate portal function, and frames or windows of information in the corporate portal?

☐ What is your initial preference for layout of the navigation options and tools?

☐ What menus are available for each user or role?

☐ How should the navigation features and tools be organized on the screen (in terms of logical groupings and tiers within the site)?

☐ What navigation and tools are required to be standard options (appearing on every page)?

☐ What is available from the portal menu?

CORPORATE PORTAL CONTENT

☐ What specific information, reports, and applications will the corporate portal solution need access to? Examples:

  ☐ Policy and procedures manual
  ☐ Knowledge and discussion forums
  ☐ Sales and marketing materials
  ☐ Job postings
  ☐ Online help materials
  ☐ Training materials
  ☐ Department websites
  ☐ Financial reports
  ☐ Enterprise resource planning (ERP) systems
  ☐ Line of business (LOB) systems
  ☐ Data warehouses and data marts
  ☐ Relational database management systems
  ☐ Desktop applications
  ☐ Content management applications
  ☐ Other applications
  ☐ Other tools and utilities

☐ How are these applications going to be made available and accessed from the corporate portal?

CorporatePortal.com Case Study

To create a CorporatePortal.com site map, the company has to review the business functions and corporate portal features being incorporated into its portal desktop. The main portal menu options include:

- *Personal Information*. PDA and PIM features, applications, and services fall in this category.
- *Departments*. The department category is structured along the same logic as the organization chart.
- *Resources*. The resources category incorporates general information about CorporatePortal.com. This includes information that needs to be disseminated widely, or "pushed" to users, regarding the organization (e.g., company news and events and frequently used services such as online help and support).
- *Reference*. The reference category is similar to resources but includes information that is used less frequently and is more static in nature. Examples are policies, procedures, and department websites. Updates to material available from the reference portal menu that need to be pushed to corporate portal users should be included as "company news" with a link to new reference material so employees are aware of these updates.
- *Search*. The search category is unique. Based on the taxonomy that CorporatePortal.com has implemented, search could have been included as an option in the resources portal menu item. The decision was made to separate the search feature and search online help as its own portal menu item to make this option more prevalent than other resource options.

Each of the main portal menu options (primary items) has a collection of options (secondary items) that can be selected (see Figure 12-1). This menu hierarchy can be implemented as drop-down menus from the main portal menu or as content page tabs on each content page. The secondary items that are available from the main portal menu include:

Personal Information

- Daily planner
- E-mail
- Discussions
- Interests

Departments

- Accounting
- Information technology
- Marketing
- Personnel
- Sales
- Training

Resources

- Company news
- Events calendar
- Discussions
- What's new
- Support
- Site map
- Help

Reference

- Mission statement
- Vision
- Scorecard
- Manuals
- Policies
- Procedures
- Standards
- Department websites

Search

- Search home
- Search help

The primary menu options are represented as the first-level options in the hierarchy. The secondary items are available once a portal menu option has been selected and are represented as file folders in Figure 12-1. In several cases there are additional levels of break-out for items presented in the portal desktop. For example, under the main portal menu Reference option there is a secondary menu

Figure 12-1. CorporatePortal.com site map (content pages).

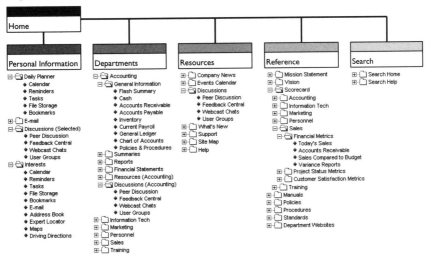

option for Scorecard information. Depending on the employee role of the portal user, the accounting, information technology, marketing, personnel, sales, or training content page will be presented. Each employee role is defined as a "portal profile" attribute value. Departments and employees have corporate objectives that are measured by financial metrics, project status metrics, and customer satisfaction metrics. The portal desktop presents the separate Scorecard reports and material for each employee in a content page tab for each set of metrics.

The portal desktop is laid out in sections that are positioned in the same consistent locations. The portal banner, main portal menu, and personalization features are all stacked at the top of the portal desktop. These features are pervasive for the first phase of the portal desktop. The content-relevant information and content page section of the portal desktop are dynamic based on the portal menu option selected. The standard presentation used for the business case has the content-relevant information on the left appearing as file folders with the content page and content windows on the right. Additional presentation options can be considered by CorporatePortal.com based on the portal software solutions evaluated and the usability decisions made during prototype reviews of the corporate portal solution.

Defining the Roles

The information-gathering activities completed by the corporate portal strategy team results in the identification of several types of information and requirements—security and administration requirements, identification of the business functions and self-service applications, and the complete collection of portal software features and functions. Using these initial results the corporate portal user community can be organized into roles or groups of users with like responsibilities or interests. Each role has similar business expectations and requirements for the information available in the corporate portal, therefore all the employees in a specific role want the exact same reports, background material, notifications, and shared information to be presented in the corporate portal. The individual portal desktops can be organized with different information on different content pages. This lends enough individuality (to make the portal desktop appealing to how each user wants to work) and enough commonality (to make collaboration and knowledge-sharing possible).

To help you define the roles for your portal solution, use the following checklist. For each business function identified for the initial phases of the corporate portal solution, copy the appropriate section (heading and questions), change the heading to match the name of the business function, and answer the questions contained in that section.

USER ROLES IDENTIFIED

☐ Based on the identified user communities in your organization, what groups of employees should be listed as users of the corporate portal solution?

☐ Are there any other organizations or groups of users who should have access to the corporate portal solution?

☐ What members of the IT department should have roles in the corporate portal solution?

☐ Are there any users or groups of users who should not have access to the corporate portal solution?

☐ Are there any existing systems or applications that need to access the corporate portal solution?

ROLES DEFINED

For each role identified, answer the questions in this section.

☐ What role does this group of users have in the corporate portal solution?

☐ Is this role similar to that of other roles? For example, can users in the sales manager role do everything that employees in the sales representative role do, plus some other functions?

BUSINESS FUNCTIONS OUTLINED FOR ROLES

For each role identified, answer the questions in this section.

☐ Which actions or events should each role be allowed to perform?

☐ Which events or actions are not allowed for a particular role to perform? Are there any exceptions?

☐ Which report or views should the role be allowed to see or generate? Which ones should the role not be allowed to see?

☐ What process and actions does the role need to perform with each data point or collection of information?

☐ Can you combine any of the tasks or activities into a single task or activity? Would it be beneficial to do so?

☐ Are there any trivial tasks or activities that should be automated for the corporate portal solution?

☐ Are tasks and activities being performed where they make the most sense?

☐ Are there additional steps or tasks that need to be performed to complete a defined process?

☐ What are the links or connections between the various processes?

CorporatePortal.com Case Study

Each self-service application must be reviewed from the perspective of several employee roles. These include:

- Accounting
- Information technology (IT)
- Marketing
- Personnel
- Sales
- Training

There are different levels of security and access to information for each of these employee roles. For example, the sales role includes sales managers and sales representatives. Payroll, financial, and other reports can contain employee-specific information. Sales representatives are only able to access report information that is specific to their accounts, customers, and sales. Sales managers are able to access information specific to themselves and the information of all sales representatives that report to them.

Defining the Content Page

The site map you created defines a hierarchy for the corporate portal solution. The first level (primary) can be used to define the main portal menu items. The second level (secondary) can be used to define the content pages for the initial phases of the corporate portal solution. As the corporate portal solution continues to expand, additional levels will be added to the site map. These additional levels require both (1) new navigation solutions and (2) additional content pages. There are several initial approaches to consider when outlining the content pages.

Option 1: Portal Menu Primary and Portal Menu Secondary. Let's use the Departments portal menu option as an example. When the Departments item is selected, a drop-down list appears with the department names (e.g., Accounting, IT, Marketing, Personnel, Sales, Training) for the user to select from. Each option selected presents a different content page.

Option 2: Portal Menu Primary and Content Page Tabs Secondary. When the Departments item is selected, a default content page appears with the department names (e.g., Accounting, IT, Marketing, Personnel, Sales, Training) as content page tab names. Each content page tab selected presents a different content page.

The CorporatePortal.com storyboard is based on this approach where the department names appear on the content page tabs and the default content page of accounting. General information appears in the content page (see Figure 12-2).

Option 3: Portal Menu Primary and Content-Relevant Information Secondary. When the Departments item is selected, a default content page appears with the department names (e.g., Accounting, IT, Marketing, Personnel, Sales, Training) on one of the content-relevant information tabbed pages. Each department name selected from the content-relevant information section presents a different content page.

For the combined business functions identified for the initial phases of the corporate portal solution, copy the appropriate sec-

Figure 12-2. Portal menu for Accounting department.

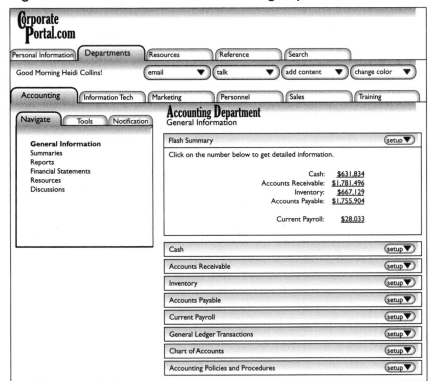

tion (heading and questions) from the following checklist and answer the questions contained in that section.

Content Pages Defined

☐ Based on the results of the business process and information
needs analysis, what activities or tasks have been identified for
inclusion in the corporate portal solution?

☐ What is the information necessary to present in the corporate
portal?

☐ What should be the layout of each corporate portal web page?

☐ What other corporate portal software functions should be included to support each user in the performance of his or her
role or activities?

☐ How should the information and reports be organized and presented on each corporate portal page (in terms of logical groupings and tabs within the content page)?

☐ What information and reports can be enlarged to full screen in
the corporate portal?

☐ What will be the size of each frame or section in the corporate
portal? Can the user change the size?

CorporatePortal.com Case Study

Based on information collected through interviews and research,
the content pages that have been identified can be sketched and
reviewed with business domain experts. These sketches provide a
framework for adding clarification and usability to the portal desktop. The collection of portal pages is outlined. In several cases
there are secondary menu options that are repetitive throughout
the CorporatePortal.com site map. For example, there are several
iterations of the Discussions content page. The Resources/Discus-
sions content pages include topics and material for the entire
CorporatePortal.com organization. The Accounting/Discussions
content pages are filtered to include topics and material specific to
the accounting department. The Discussions content pages that
are accessed from the Personal Information menu option are filtered based on topics and material the employee has selected.

There is a link to the Resources/Discussions for the employee to access a complete listing of topics and material from the Accounting/Discussions and Personal Information/Discussions content pages.

Defining the Content Windows

After defining the first level (main portal menu) and second level (content pages) of the portal desktop, your storyboard is demonstrating the navigation scheme. The next step or the third level is to build the substance or content of the storyboard. In the portal desktop, the third level defines the content windows for each of the content pages. In many cases a content window can logically belong on more than one content page. This is acceptable. It is much easier for employees to navigate the corporate portal and locate information if material, reports, and links can be found in several locations. Consider the following approaches when outlining the content windows:

Option 1: Portal Menu Secondary. The navigation paradigm for option 1 includes selecting the Departments item from the portal menu. A cascading menu option with the secondary menu options (e.g., Accounting, IT, Marketing, Personnel, Sales, Training) is made available from a drop-down list for the user to select from. Assuming that the Accounting item is selected, the content page options (e.g., General Information, Summaries, Reports, Financial Statements, Resources, Discussions) can be made available from three separate user interface locations. These include:

- A second cascading menu option on the portal menu
- The content page tabs
- The content-relevant information section

Option 2: Content Page Tabs Secondary. Assuming the Departments portal menu option has been selected from the portal menu, the department names (e.g., Accounting, IT, Marketing, Personnel, Sales, Training) will appear as content page tab names. Each content page tab selected presents a different content page. Once the Accounting item is selected, the content page options (e.g., General Information, Summaries, Reports, Financial Statements, Resources, Discussions) can be made available from two separate user interface locations. These include:

- A cascading menu option on the content page tabs
- The content-relevant information section

The CorporatePortal.com storyboard is based on this approach where the Accounting content page options (see Figure 12-2) are available from the content-relevant information section of the corporate portal.

Option 3: Content-Relevant Information Secondary. Assuming the Departments portal menu option has been selected from the portal menu, the department names (Accounting, Information Tech, Marketing, Personnel, Sales, Training) appear on one of the content-relevant information tabbed pages. Once the Accounting item is selected, the content page options (General Information, Summaries, Reports, Financial Statements, Resources, Discussions) can be made available from two separate user interface locations. These include:

- A cascading menu option from the content-relevant information section
- The content page tabs

The following checklist is designed to help you define content windows for your corporate portal. For each business function identified to be included in the initial phases of the corporate portal solution, copy the appropriate section (heading and questions) and answer the questions contained in that section.

Content Windows Defined

☐ Based on the collection of information you've identified for each content page, what applications, data, services, reports, business functions, and corporate portal features will be included inside content windows?

☐ What personalization features will be available for each content window (e.g., maximize to full page, minimize to title bar only, remove, move to another content page tab)?

☐ What should be the default layout of content windows for the content page?

☐ What other corporate portal software functions will be included to support each user in the performance of his or her role or activities?

☐ How should the information and reports be organized and presented on each corporate portal page (in terms of drill-down and queries within the content window)?

☐ What information and content windows can be enlarged to full screen in the corporate portal?

☐ What will be the size of each content window in the corporate portal? How can the user change the size?

CorporatePortal.com Case Study

The content windows to be included on several of the content pages have been defined in the CorporatePortal.com site map. The content windows are the lowest-level items in the outline presented in Figure 12-1. There will be several formats and uses for how information is presented in content windows. In most cases hyperlinks are contained within content windows to perform an action or locate additional information. Examples of these different types of content windows in the CorporatePortal.com implementation include:

• *Drilling into reports.* Content windows contain report summary information with hyperlinks to more detailed information (see Figure 12-3). There can be several levels of hyperlinks built into these reports. When designing reports, determine the levels of detail beforehand, so employees using a reporting tool or software application can continue performing their responsibilities.

• *Submitting a request.* Content windows allow employees to request additional information. A request form is completed and the results are returned to the user (see Figure 12-4). Activities that require user input, such as completing corporate forms and submitting search requests, benefit from wizards that help complete the

Figure 12-3. Content window for drilling into reports.

Flash Summary	setup ▼

Click on the number below to get detailed information.

Cash:	**$631,834**
Accounts Receivable:	$1,781,496
Inventory:	$667,129
Accounts Payable:	$1,755,904
Current Payroll:	$28,033

Cash	setup ▼

The following information is as of [current date and time]

General Ledger Account	Account Description	Amount
000-1100-00	Cash - Operating Account	$407,381.89
000-1101-00	Cash - Bank of America	$9,007.84
000-1102-00	Cash - Bank One	$18,302.17
000-1103-00	Cash Chase Bank	$6,007.94
000-1104-00	Cash - First National Bank	$7,909.80
000-1105-00	Cash - Wells Fargo Bank (Atlanta)	$12,697.77
000-1106-00	Cash - Wells Fargo Bank (Chicago)	$7,501.90
000-1107-00	Cash - Wells Fargo Bank (Denver)	$6,963.24
000-1110-00	Cash - Payroll	$139,080.67
000-1120-00	Cash - Flexible Benefits Program	$345.32
000-1130-00	Petty Cash	$319.54
000-1140-00	Savings	$16,316.12
Total		**$631,834.20**

form or help topics that define the fields that need to be completed before the form can be submitted.

• *Selecting a link.* Content windows contain hyperlinks to other sections in the same document or open new content windows with new information. The example presented in Figure 12-5 opens a second content window with the requested tax form displayed on the screen.

Personalization features are associated with content windows. The Setup option allows the content window to be collapsed to the title or expanded to display the title and contents (see Figure 12-6).

Figure 12-4. Content window for submitting a request.

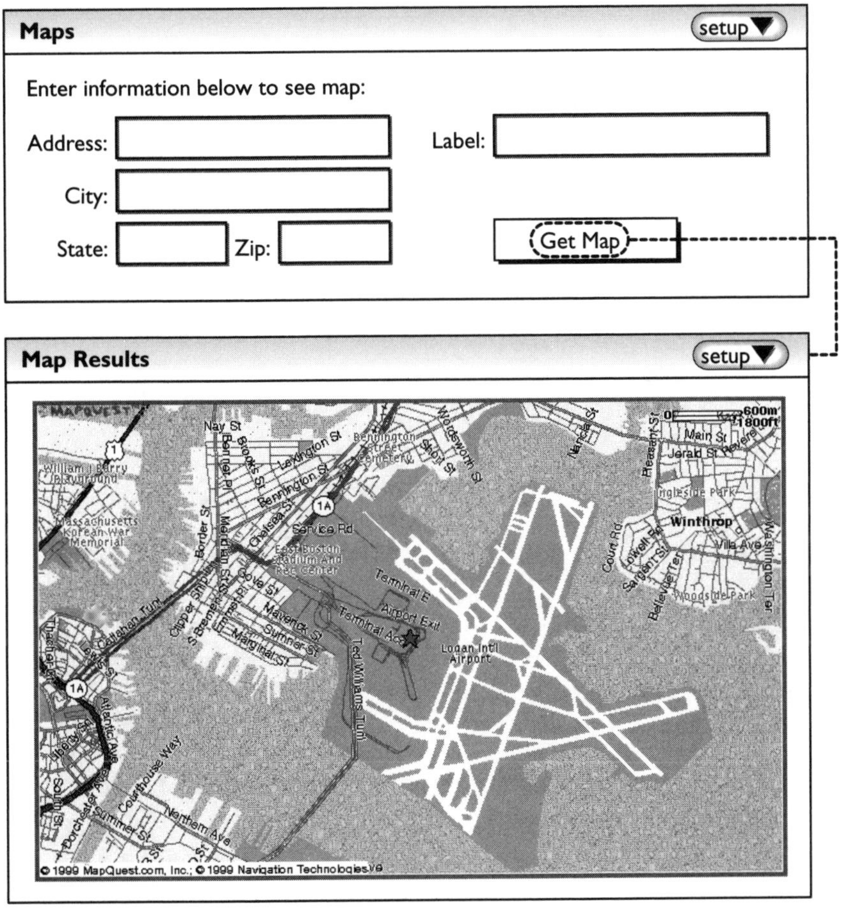

There can be additional features to forward the information presented in the content window in an e-mail message or to create a discussion topic that references or includes the content window information. There could also be options to contact the content owner or additional knowledge experts when employees need them.

Defining the Content-Relevant Information

To complete the storyboard you want to visit the content pages one more time to review what should be included in the content-

Figure 12-5. Content window for selecting a link.

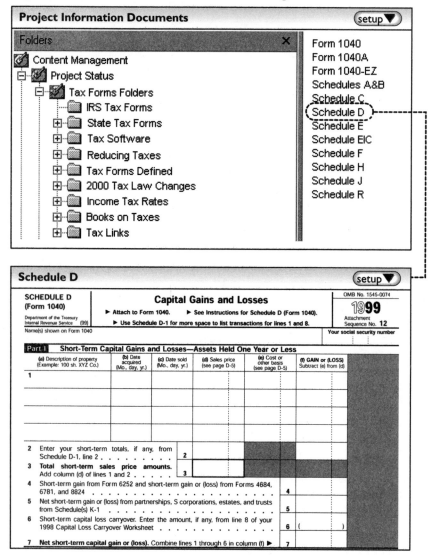

Figure 12-6. Content window for setup options.

Flash Summary		Setup ▼
Click on the number below to get detailed information.		Collapse Expand Forward Discussion Experts Refresh
Cash:	$631,834	
Accounts Receivable:	$1,781,496	
Inventory:	$667,129	
Accounts Payable:	$1,755,904	
Current Payroll:	$28,033	

relevant information section. Several different types of information need to be considered. From the perspective of the employee role that will be using the content page, various tools, services, hyperlinks to related topics, applications, reports, knowledge experts, discussion forums, and other corporate portal features (e.g., online help or search) must be available. Before the advent of the corporate portal, employees had to open several applications from their workstation to complete different activities. The portal desktop brings the ability to complete a variety of activities from a single location. The content-relevant information provides an additional benefit by bringing new procedures, tips and tricks, lessons learned, and related material to employees while they are doing the job. A selection of material and links can be included in the content-relevant information section of the portal desktop; however, you want the information to be context-sensitive to the content page and content windows presented on the screen. Since the content-relevant information is based on the context of the current content page, the categories available in the content-relevant information section can be static or dynamic, depending on the requirements of the roles using the content page.

For each business function you've identified for the initial phases of the corporate portal solution, copy the appropriate section (heading and questions) of the following checklist and answer the questions contained in that section.

CONTENT-RELEVANT INFORMATION DEFINED

☐ Based on the collection of information you've identified for each content page, what applications, data, services, reports, business functions, and corporate portal features will be included in the content-relevant information section?

☐ What categories and tabs need to be created to organize the content-relevant information?

☐ Are some of the options in the content-relevant information section only available by role? For example, do users in the sales manager role have the same options available as users in the sales representative role?

☐ How should the information and options be organized and presented in each content-relevant information tab (e.g., outline controls, toolbar)?

☐ When an item is selected from the content-relevant information section, how is the option made available to the user (e.g., it's launched in a new window, replaces the content of the content page)?

☐ Are additional navigation features needed to support the options available from the content-relevant information section?

CorporatePortal.com Case Study

CorporatePortal.com has identified a paradigm to categorize content-relevant information in the portal desktop. The initial plan is to sketch the content-relevant information using the same four tab definitions for each content page. This requires that the tab definitions be specific enough for employees to understand and generic enough to house several types of information hyperlinks. In the content-relevant information paradigm for the CorporatePortal.com storyboard, the categories identified include:

• *Navigate.* The navigate category or tab in the content-relevant information section contains links to data points and other content pages that are pertinent to the current content page open in the corporate portal. These include:

1. Additional content pages available for the accounting department
2. Knowledge experts who can provide additional information if needed

3. Discussion forums to introduce new topics
4. Chat rooms to talk to other users online
5. White papers to research topics of interest
6. Department websites to learn more about specific objectives, processes, and procedures
7. Other data points that need to be made available

- *Tools.* From the tools tab, users can:

1. Access applications that need to be launched to perform activities outside the scope of the corporate portal.
2. Perform content management activities for the accounting department.
3. Forward information from the content page to selected users.
4. Create a notification that pushes information on important issues associated with the current content page to other users.
5. Start any workflow or process and action tasks associated with the context of the content page.
6. Access other utilities that have been identified as useful to the user's job.

- *Notification.* The notification category included in the content-relevant section permits:

1. User-created notifications that are directly related to the content page or the organization
2. New discussion items that provide useful information to users as their assigned tasks and responsibilities are completed
3. White papers that are relevant to the context of the content page or content page windows available

Defining Personalization Features

The storyboard only demonstrates how personalization features are incorporated into the portal desktop and where the user will access these features. The corporate portal strategy team must determine what personalization options should be available in the first phases of the corporate portal solution. Begin by evaluating what features need to be consistent for your organization in the portal desktop; this provides a framework that employees can easily recognize. After these fixed points have been established, you want to provide as many user-customization opportunities as possible.

For the combined business functions identified for the initial phases of your corporate portal solution, copy the appropriate section (heading and questions) of the following checklist and answer the questions contained in that section.

PERSONALIZATION DEFINED

☐ What personalization features have been identified to be included in the corporate portal solution?

☐ Are some personalization features available all the time and others only available on content windows or other corporate portal features?

☐ What categories, tabs, or buttons need to be created to organize the personalization features?

☐ Should a section of the corporate portal solution be designated to store global personalization options?

☐ When a portal desktop personalization feature is added or updated, how is the option made available to the user? Is an approval process required? Are administrative tasks or activities required? Do any other processes or procedures need to be completed?

☐ Are additional navigation features needed to support the options available from the personalization options?

GRAPHICS

☐ What will be the default graphics, font, and color schemes of the corporate portal?

☐ How should your organization's logo and color scheme be integrated into the user interface?

☐ Does your organization have existing graphics standards that will govern the user interface?

☐ Will there be multiple color schemes?

☐ How will the user select (and subsequently change) the color scheme according to their preferences?

CorporatePortal.com Case Study

The personalization section of the portal desktop gives employees access to their e-mail and online chats with their peers. It also gives them the ability to add and update the material presented on the content page, and to select colors and fonts in the portal desktop. In the CorporatePortal.com implementation, the personalization section offers these specific options:

- All PIM options accessible from the e-mail option
- Interactive discussions and online interactions accessible from the talk option
- The ability to add, remove, and move content windows and content page tabs on each content page from the add content option in the personalization section
- The ability to change graphics and color themes from the change color option

Business domain experts at CorporatePortal.com have determined that employees want content pages to be consistent across the organization for all the main portal menu options except the Personal Information menu option. For the content pages available from the Departments, Resources, Reference, and Search main portal menu options, the employee can create additional portal page tabs and add content windows to the content pages created. The Personal Information content pages contain content page tabs that the employee defines with a unique collection of content pages, content windows, and content-relevant information specific to the responsibilities and material each employee selects.

SCRIPTING THE CORPORATE PORTAL SOLUTION

The script that is created to accompany the storyboards can also be referred to as "use case" scenarios or event models. The goal is to check that the self-service applications and business functions outlined for the corporate portal solution are well defined and complete. The script is a step-by-step walkthrough of the storyboards from the perspective of a user or role with respect to (1) all the information that needs to be available and (2) the activities or tasks that need to be done to successfully complete a business process. These scripts are often used later in the development cycle when preparing test plans and other testing activities. Scripts focus on the actions and activities to be completed for each business function, who is responsible for each step of the tasks or activities along the way, and how the different users or roles interact with each other during these tasks and activities.

For each business function included in the portal desktop, you must identify all the steps to be completed from start to finish. There may be multiple start and finish states. Once the collection of steps has been defined, determine each role that is directly and indirectly responsible for each step. The goal is to identify and define all of the different steps of each business function that a particular user or user role would be expected to perform. This should all be done from the perspective of the employee roles and their interaction with the corporate portal solution. This activity should yield enough information to create an event analysis matrix that identifies each role in a column and the steps or events of the business functions in the rows. A symbol or mark where the roles and steps cross completes the analysis matrix.

Using the information about how tasks or activities are completed from start to finish and the roles involved in the process, you can create a script or scenario for each role involved in a business function. By role, determine what information is directly and indirectly related to the current step of the business function and how it can be represented in the portal's content pages, content windows, and content-relevant information section. This exercise also lets you identify the actual and expected usage of the corporate portal, which will be an important piece of information for the business case. The strategy team must determine how many storyboards and scripts need to be included in the corporate portal business case documentation.

For each business function to be included in the initial phases of the corporate portal solution, copy the appropriate section (heading and questions) of the following checklist and answer the questions contained in that section.

SCRIPT OR USE CASE SCENARIO DESIGN

☐ Based on the collection of business functions included in the corporate portal solution, have the step-by-step processes of each business function been identified?

☐ What roles are involved or included in each step or event?

☐ Are some of the steps or events only available by role? For example, do users in the sales manager role have access to the same information, processes, and actions as users in the sales representative role?

☐ How should the information and options for each business process be organized and presented using the corporate portal solution, software functions, and universal features?

☐ What components of the corporate portal solution should be consistent for the user community to work effectively together?

☐ What components of the corporate portal solution can be personalized or changed by each member of the user community to allow them to work efficiently as individuals?

CorporatePortal.com Case Study

Several scripts need to be written for each employee role and the employee's expected interaction with the corporate portal solution. These scripts are used to verify that the storyboard sketches accurately reflect the benefits and usage of the portal desktop. Using the document repository self-service application and the sales manager role, a sample script has been documented. The activity is to update the sales campaign strategy templates and procedures for tax projects. The sales manager is expected to complete the following activities and tasks:

1. The sales manager must research the types of tax projects CorporatePortal.com sells the most of and the types of customers who buy them. To complete this research the sales manager uses several areas in the portal desktop. From the Reference/Scorecard

content page, the Financial Metrics and Project Status Metrics information helps identify the types of tax projects and customers being researched (see Figure 12-7). Additional accounting information will be researched from the Departments/Accounting content pages.

2. The sales manager must discuss the research results with other sales managers and interested employees throughout CorporatePortal.com to establish and verify conclusions. The results of the research are posted as a discussion topic from Resources/Discussions in the Peer Discussions content page (see Figure 12-8).

3. The sales manager must create and update the sales campaign strategy templates and procedures. Any reports, documents, and other material used to research and write the new sales campaign strategy templates and procedures are created and stored using the Personal Information/Interests/File Storage content page of the portal desktop (see Figure 12-9).

4. The sales manager must review the new material with other sales managers and sales representatives at CorporatePortal.com.

Figure 12-7. Storyboard page 1: researching tax projects.

Corporate Portal.com

Personal Information	Departments	Resources	Reference	Search

Good Morning Heidi Collins! email ▼ talk ▼ add content ▼ change color ▼

Financial Metrics	Project Status Metrics	Customer Satisfaction Metrics

Navigate	Tools	Notification

Reference
Scorecard

Mission Statement
Vision
Scorecard
Manuals
Policies
Procedures
Standards
Department Websites

Project Status Pivot Table				setup ▼
Q2 2000 Revenue				
	▶Project A	▶Project B	▶Project C	▶Project D
▼ **ACME Office Supply**	$78,683	$59,945	$42,158	$48,776
▶ Planning	$56,000	$26,344	$22,366	$20,000
▼ Project Definition	$22,683	$33,601	$19,792	$28,776
▼ Analysis	$18,637	$30,258	$2,604	$26,976
Data Gathering	$9,761	$28,282	$1,717	$25,000
Recomendations	$8,876	$1,976	$887	$1,976
▼ Documentation	$1,000	$1,580	$656	$1,000
Audit Report	$1,000	$1,580	$656	$1,000
▼ Delivery	$3,046	$1,763	$16,532	$800
Report Review	$2,309	$776	$6,654	$700
Final Presentation	$737	$987	$9,878	$100

Figure 12-8. Storyboard page 2: discussing research results.

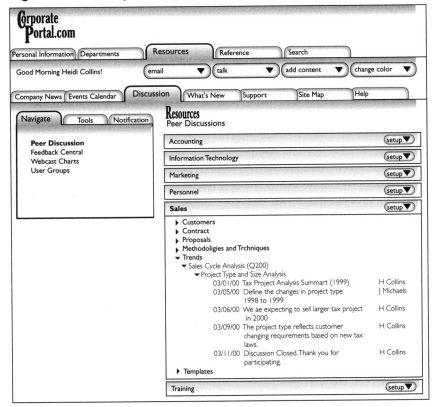

The first version of the sales campaign strategy templates and procedures are posted for peer review from Resources/Discussions in the Peer Discussions content page (see Figure 12-10).

5. The sales manager incorporates the feedback and publishes the new sales campaign strategy templates and procedures. The sales manager continues to lead the peer discussion of the sales campaign strategy material and writes the final versions of the sales campaign strategy templates and procedures. The final versions of these documents are posted in the Documentum application from content pages available in the Departments/Sales options (see Figure 12-11).

6. The sales manager schedules a webcast seminar to present the new sales campaign strategy templates and procedures to

Figure 12-9. Storyboard page 3: using file storage to review and update new tax project sales strategy templates.

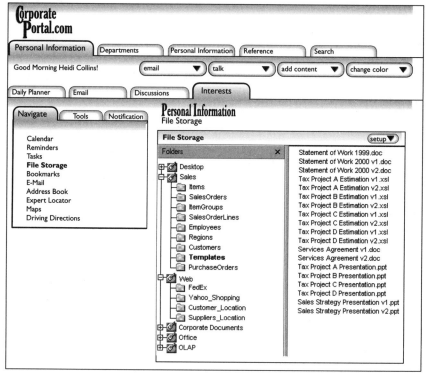

any interested CorporatePortal.com employees. Using the Re-
sources/Discussions menu option and the Webcast Chats content
page (see Figure 12-12), the sales manager can schedule the seminar.

7. The sales manager posts the webcast seminar in the
CorporatePortal.com Events Calendar so that interested employees are aware of the upcoming event. Using the Resources/Events
Calendar menu option and associated content pages (see Figure
12-13), the webcast seminar is posted to the calendar.

KEY POINTS

Corporate portal storyboards and associated scripts should be included as a section of the business case. The visual representation

Figure 12-10. Storyboard page 4: discussing new tax project strategy templates.

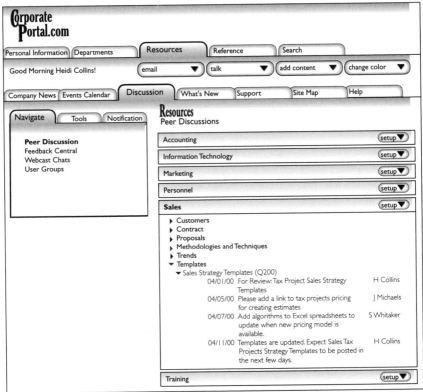

of the corporate portal user interface can clarify the value propositions of the corporate portal solution for your organization. A series of storyboards accompanied by a script can establish how activities, tasks, responsibilities, and corporate information will be combined in a single user interface that allows a user to work effectively with personalization features that provide organization and structure unique to each employee. You need to make the storyboards available in a variety of formats (e.g., black and white for making copies of the business case and color for presentations). The storyboard and script summary you create becomes a section in the corporate portal business case.

Figure 12-11. Storyboard page 5: publishing new tax project strategy templates.

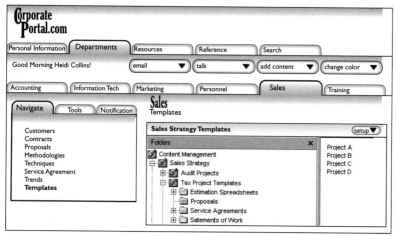

Figure 12-12. Storyboard page 6: scheduling a tax project strategy webcast.

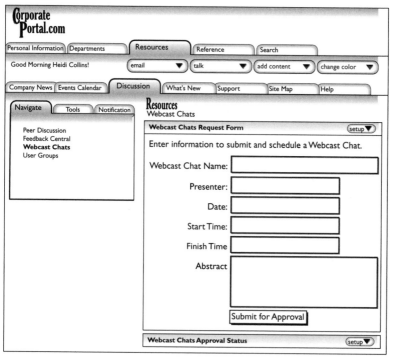

Figure 12-13. Storyboard page 7: reviewing the CorporatePortal.com events calendar.

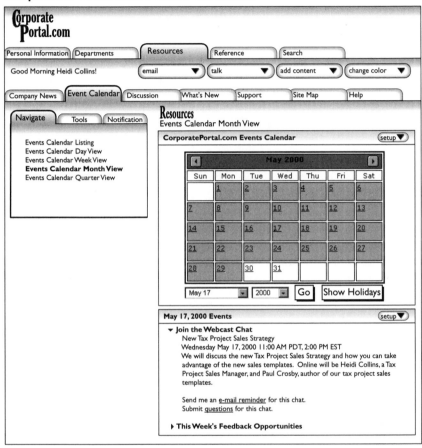

13

Financial Metrics Analysis

The financial results presented in the executive summary of the business case reflect the credibility and effectiveness regarding the corporate portal recommendations and conclusions. Decision makers and executives want to know whether the corporate portal solution can accomplish the proposed benefits before reading a full presentation of financial results. The financial metrics section of the business case presents the complete answer. The executive summary documents the specific measurements that the business case conclusions and proposal are based on. Make certain that the executive summary also includes details on how the financial measurements are going to be used. The types of measurements that you may want to consider include:

- Net cash flow
- Discounted cash flow (DCF)
- Internal rate of return (IRR)
- Payback period
- Total cost of ownership (TCO)
- Return on investment (ROI)
- Cost/benefit analysis

EVALUATING FINANCIAL CONSEQUENCES

The financial consequences of implementing a corporate portal solution are measured several different ways in a business case. Each approach has a unique purpose and definition that can be used to evaluate financial consequences. It is important that you document the line items that are included in several financial calculations to support the expected benefits your organization will realize from a corporate portal solution. Three of these are:

- Cost of ownership
- Return on investment
- Cost/benefit analysis

An effective conclusion must be documented and should concentrate on supporting the objectives of the corporate portal solution. The conclusions and formal recommendation should be included in the executive summary of the business case and be used to remind the decision makers to give special consideration to the important contingencies and dependencies regarding your corporate portal proposal. You should create a baseline of your corporate objectives and how well they are being achieved before the portal desktop is implemented. Continue to measure your corporate objectives after the portal desktop is implemented to determine if there has been any improvement and what impact the corporate portal solution has contributed.

Cost of Ownership (COO)

Cost of ownership calculations are often included in the business case when expensive capital items need to be considered. The cost of ownership includes the total cost of acquiring, installing, using, maintaining, changing, and disposing of the asset across an extended period of time (e.g., most or all of the useful life). There are some pros and cons when using this metric:

- *Cost of ownership is always more than the purchase price.* The additional costs to consider are installation, support, maintenance, administration, and other services. Decisions will have to be made regarding the costs that are included in the analysis and why.
- *A cost of ownership analysis does not include any financial benefit information.* Consequently, there are some limita-

tions in a cost of ownership analysis. There will not be enough information available to create a return on investment analysis. In addition, the COO analysis will have to be supported by other financial metrics to provide decision criteria in the business case.

- *Cost of ownership results are presented as cost totals.* As such, results can be easily compared to corporate budget information.

To evaluate if a cost of ownership calculation should be included in the financial metrics of the corporate portal solution, consider the following questions.

Cost of Ownership (COO) Calculation

☐ Does a lot of expensive capital equipment have to be purchased for the corporate portal solution?

☐ Do you need to present total cost information that can be compared to corporate budget information?

☐ If you have answered yes to the previous questions, would a cost of ownership (COO) calculation be a useful financial metric to include in the corporate portal business case?

☐ Is a COO calculation required for corporate budget information?

Return on Investment (ROI)

Return on investment is used to measure the performance of an organization and is usually a reference to return on invested capital (i.e., total income/total capital). For the corporate portal solution, ROI is defined as the return (incremental) gain of a business activity or project (i.e., total return/total investment). When using this calculation in your corporate portal business case, be certain to clearly define for a specified period of time how "return" and "investment" are to be interpreted. An ROI calculation is appropriate if the expected return and investment cost are clearly related to each other, occur over a short period of time, and can be presented with a simple explanation. If ROI is difficult to present as a quantitative value, you should focus on other financial metrics such as net cash flow, discounted cash flow, internal rate of return, or payback period in your business case.

To evaluate if an ROI calculation is to be included in the financial metrics of the corporate portal solution, consider the following questions.

RETURN ON INVESTMENT (ROI) CALCULATION

☐ Is there a relationship between expected return and investment cost that occurs over a short period of time?

☐ Do you need to present financial information that measures the performance of your organization?

☐ If you have answered yes to the previous questions, would a return on investment (ROI) calculation be a useful financial metric to include in the corporate portal business case?

☐ Is an ROI calculation required for the corporate portal business case?

Cost/Benefit Analysis

A cost/benefit analysis presents a collection of positive and negative impacts that are weighed against each other and summarized. This type of analysis is commonly used to evaluate proposals or projects and would be useful to consider for the corporate portal business case. The cost/benefit analysis must clearly identify the timing of expected inflows and outflows as well as their costs and benefits. The cost/benefit analysis is a mechanism for including discussions regarding nonquantified benefits or costs. The research done to define the benefits of a corporate portal solution and a knowledge management initiative should be included as part of the cost/benefit analysis. For example, the ability to make better, more informed decisions is a benefit of the corporate portal solution, but it is difficult to apply a monetary value. These types of cost and benefit items therefore require that the corporate portal strategy team determine exactly how a monetary value will be assigned. A time-based cash flow summary (see Figure 13-1) can be created from the cost/benefit analysis. This information is useful for creating other financial metrics such as net cash flow, discounted cash flow, internal rate of return, or payback period.

Figure 13-1. Time-based cash flow summary.

Cash Inflows (outflows) ($ in $1,000's)	For year ending last day of					
	June 1996	June 1997	June 1998	June 1999	June 2000	Total
Benefits/Gains	$6,400.0	$7,337.0	$7,379.6	$8,108.1	$15,708.9	$44,933.6
Operating Expenses	($6,119.0)	($6,888.0)	($6,625.0)	($6,765.0)	($6,621.0)	($33,018.0)
Net Operating Inflow (Outflow)	$281.0	$449.0	$754.6	$1,343.1	$9,087.9	$11,915.6
Tax Savings (Tax) on Inflow/Outflow	($88.4)	($147.2)	($254.1)	($463.6)	($3,170.8)	($4,124.1)
Asset Purchase	($3,011.2)	($512.4)	($300.5)	($10.0)	($110.0)	($3,944.1)
Tax Savings from all Depreciation Expense	$230.0	$378.4	$306.1	$169.9	$138.6	$1,223.0
Net Cash Flow	($2,588.6)	$167.8	$506.1	$1,039.4	$5,945.7	$5,070.4

Benefits/Gains Cash Inflows (outflows) ($ in $1,000's)	For year ending last day of					
	June 1996	June 1997	June 1998	June 1999	June 2000	Total
Maintenance Cost Savings	$420.0	$462.0	$508.2	$559.0	$614.9	$2,564.1
Faster Response Time	$780.0	$780.0	$780.0	$780.0	$780.0	$3,900.0
Avoided Mainframe Upgrade	$0.0	$350.0	$0.0	$0.0	$6,741.7	$7,091.7
Avoided Hiring	$1,200.0	$1,200.0	$900.0	$800.0	$700.0	$4,800.0
Improved Profits	$2,500.0	$3,000.0	$3,600.0	$4,320.0	$5,184.0	$18,604.0
Freed-Up Professional Time	$1,500.0	$1,545.0	$1,591.4	$1,649.1	$1,688.3	$7,973.8
Total Benefits/Gains	$6,400.0	$7,337.0	$7,379.6	$8,108.1	$15,708.9	$44,933.6

Operating Expenses Cash Inflows (outflows) ($ in $1,000's)	For year ending last day of					
	June 1996	June 1997	June 1998	June 1999	June 2000	Total
Administration Expenses	($1,058.0)	($1,246.0)	($1,246.0)	($1,246.0)	($992.0)	($5,788.0)
Management Expenses	($364.0)	($368.0)	($393.0)	($393.0)	($393.0)	($1,911.0)
Personnel Expenses	($3,554.0)	($4,251.0)	($4,323.0)	($4,468.0)	($4,578.0)	($21,174.0)
Facilities Expenses	($198.0)	($198.0)	($198.0)	($198.0)	($198.0)	($990.0)
Services Expenses	($700.0)	($465.0)	($130.0)	($125.0)	($125.0)	($1,545.0)
Other Expenses	($245.0)	($360.0)	($335.0)	($335.0)	($335.0)	($1,610.0)
Total Operating Expenses	($6,119.0)	($6,888.0)	($6,625.0)	($6,765.0)	($6,621.0)	($33,018.0)

To evaluate whether a cost/benefit analysis should be included in the financial metrics of your corporate portal solution, consider the following questions.

COST/BENEFIT ANALYSIS

☐ Is there a need to evaluate nonquantified benefits or costs?

☐ Is there a need to present a collection of positive and negative impacts that can be weighed against each other and summarized?

☐ If you have answered yes to the previous questions, is a cost/

benefit analysis a useful financial metric to include in the corporate portal business case?

☐ Is a cost/benefit analysis required for the corporate portal business case?

CORPORATE PORTAL FINANCIAL MODEL

A key element of the business case will be the corporate portal financial models. You may determine that the only financial metric that needs to be done for the business case is a cash flow statement. For more complex business cases, a complete financial model may include several cash flow statements with supporting material, a cost and benefit model, and other tables and graphs needed to clarify key elements. The financial metrics to consider or evaluate for the corporate portal business case include:

- Net cash flow
- Discounted cash flow
- Internal rate of return (IRR)
- Payback period
- Cost and benefit models

Net Cash Flow

The focus for net cash flow is cash coming into the organization and cash flowing out of the organization over a defined period of time. The net cash flow measure is used in several other financial metrics. The formula for net cash flow is:

$$\text{Net Cash Flow} = \text{Cash Inflows} - \text{Cash Outflows}$$

The cash flow statement (see Figure 13-2) reflects the amount of cash that will be gained or lost for a specified amount of time. A corporate portal business case may want to include a cash flow stream to demonstrate actual cash inflow and outflow information. The cash flow stream is important for budgeting and business planning purposes and can be used for other financial metrics. The cor-

Figure 13-2. Cash flow statement.

A Simple Cash Flow Statement

	Year 1	Year 2	Year 3	Total
Benefits (Cash Inflows)	$1,000	$2,500	$4,000	$7,500
Costs (Cash Outflows)	($1,600)	($1,200)	($1,100)	($3,900)
Net Cash Flow	($600)	$1,300	$2,900	$3,600

porate portal project team can use this information as a starting point to manage the project and optimize overall results.

To evaluate if a net cash flow calculation needs to be included in the financial metrics of your corporate portal solution, consider the following questions.

NET CASH FLOW CALCULATION

☐ Is there a requirement to state the amount of cash that will be gained or lost over a specified period of time?

☐ Is a cash flow stream important to demonstrate actual cash inflow and outflow information?

☐ If you have answered yes to the previous questions, would a net cash flow calculation be a useful financial metric to include in the corporate portal business case?

☐ Is a net cash flow calculation required for the corporate portal business case?

Discounted Cash Flow

The discounted cash flow is a cash flow summary that has been adjusted to reflect the time value of money. Financial members of the decision-making team will want to review cash flows on a discounted and nondiscounted basis. This information is used to compare investments or purchases using the present value of money. This applies the idea that the money available now should be valued higher than an identical amount of money that would be received in the future. The money available now could be invested and would be worth the initial value plus the gain or interest. Exactly how much the present value should be discounted from the future value is determined by (1) the amount of time between now and future payment and (2) an interest rate that is based on the current rate of return. The formula for a future payment expected would be:

Present Value = (Future Value) / $(1.0 + \text{Interest Rate})^n$

The exponent n refers to the number of periods being referenced. Periods can reference years, months, or any other time period identified. Be certain that the interest rate represents the appropriate period (e.g., year, month). You should consider including a discounted cash flow as part of the corporate portal business case under certain circumstances, such as when:

- A comparison about different uses for money or an investment scenario is presented.
- The business case covers a time period of two or more years.
- Cash inflows and cash outflows are expected to change significantly over time.
- Two or more alternative cases are being evaluated with different cash flow timing considerations within the same analysis period.

Consider two different investment scenarios for computer equipment (see Figure 13-3). Each case calls for an initial cash outlay of $10,000, and each case returns a total of $20,000 over the next two years, creating a net gain of $10,000. The returns are realized on different schedules with a different present value of each year's return. These calculations were completed using a 10 percent interest rate in both cases. The net present value (NPV) is the sum of the two years' calculated present value less the initial investment. The scenario with the higher net present value (all other factors being equal) is the better investment or scenario. Early large returns in the first year (option 1) led to a better net present value than smaller returns in the first year (option 2).

To evaluate if a discounted cash flow calculation needs to be included in the financial metrics of your corporate portal solution, consider the following questions.

Discounted Cash Flow Calculation

☐ Do different uses for money or investment scenarios need to be presented in the business case?

Figure 13-3. Discounted cash flow.

10% Interest Rate

Timing	Option 1 Net Cash Flow	Option 1 Present Value	Option 2 Net Cash Flow	Option 2 Present Value
Now	-$10,000	-$10,000	-$10,000	-$10,000
Year 1	$ 6,000	$ 5,455	$ 2,000	$ 1,818
Year 2	$ 6,000	$ 4,959	$ 2,000	$ 1,653
Year 3	$ 4,000	$ 3,005	$ 4,000	$ 3,005
Year 4	$ 2,000	$ 1,366	$ 6,000	$ 4,098
Year 5	$ 2,000	$ 1,242	$ 6,000	$ 3,726
Total	$10,000	NPV = $ 6,026	$10,000	NPV = $ 4,300

☐ Does the business case cover a time period of two or more years?

☐ Are cash inflows and cash outflows expected to change significantly over time?

☐ Do different cash flow timing considerations for the same analysis period need to be presented in the business case?

☐ If you have answered yes to the previous questions, would a discounted cash flow calculation be a useful financial metric to include in the corporate portal business case?

Internal Rate of Return (IRR)

The internal rate of return is another version of the cash flow summary that has been adjusted for the time value of money. The definition of internal rate of return is the discount rate at which the total present value of future cash flows equals the cost of the investment. You are determining the interest rate where net present value is equal to zero. Using the same discounted cash flow data from Figure 13-3 and applying different interest rates (see Figure 13-4), then graphing the results (see Figure 13-5), you will notice that as the interest rate used in the calculation increases, the resulting net present value decreases. The internal rate of return is near 38 percent in the first case (option 1) and 22 percent in the second case (option 2). The internal rate of return provides information regarding how high interest rates would have to reach to eradicate the value of the investment. The scenario with the higher internal rate of return is the better investment as long as these scenarios can be equally compared.

To evaluate whether an IRR calculation needs to be included in the financial metrics of the corporate portal solution, consider the following questions.

INTERNAL RATE OF RETURN (IRR) CALCULATION

☐ Is there a requirement for a cash flow summary that has been adjusted to reflect the time value of money?

☐ Do you need to determine the interest rate where net present value is equal to zero?

☐ If you have answered yes to the previous questions, would an

(text continues on page 324)

Figure 13-4. Discounted cash flow (calculated internal rate of return).

10% Interest Rate

Timing	Option 1 Net Cash Flow	Option 1 Present Value	Option 2 Net Cash Flow	Option 2 Present Value
Now	-$10,000	-$10,000	-$10,000	-$10,000
Year 1	$ 6,000	$ 5,455	$ 2,000	$ 1,818
Year 2	$ 6,000	$ 4,959	$ 2,000	$ 1,653
Year 3	$ 4,000	$ 3,005	$ 4,000	$ 3,005
Year 4	$ 2,000	$ 1,366	$ 6,000	$ 4,098
Year 5	$ 2,000	$ 1,242	$ 6,000	$ 3,726
Total	$10,000	NPV = $ 6,026	$10,000	NPV = $ 4,300

20% Interest Rate

Timing	Option 1 Net Cash Flow	Option 1 Present Value	Option 2 Net Cash Flow	Option 2 Present Value
Now	-$10,000	-$10,000	-$10,000	-$10,000
Year 1	$ 6,000	$ 5,000	$ 2,000	$ 1,667
Year 2	$ 6,000	$ 4,167	$ 2,000	$ 1,389
Year 3	$ 4,000	$ 2,315	$ 4,000	$ 2,315
Year 4	$ 2,000	$ 965	$ 6,000	$ 2,894
Year 5	$ 2,000	$ 804	$ 6,000	$ 2,411
Total	$10,000	NPV = $ 3,250	$10,000	NPV = $ 675

30% Interest Rate

Timing	Option 1 Net Cash Flow	Option 1 Present Value	Option 2 Net Cash Flow	Option 2 Present Value
Now	-$10,000	-$10,000	-$10,000	-$10,000
Year 1	$ 6,000	$ 4,615	$ 2,000	$ 1,538
Year 2	$ 6,000	$ 3,550	$ 2,000	$ 1,183
Year 3	$ 4,000	$ 1,821	$ 4,000	$ 1,821
Year 4	$ 2,000	$ 700	$ 6,000	$ 2,101
Year 5	$ 2,000	$ 539	$ 6,000	$ 1,616
Total	$10,000	NPV = $ 1,225	$10,000	NPV = -$ 1,741

40% Interest Rate

Timing	Option 1 Net Cash Flow	Option 1 Present Value	Option 2 Net Cash Flow	Option 2 Present Value
Now	-$10,000	-$10,000	-$10,000	-$10,000
Year 1	$ 6,000	$ 4,286	$ 2,000	$ 1,429
Year 2	$ 6,000	$ 3,061	$ 2,000	$ 1,020
Year 3	$ 4,000	$ 1,458	$ 4,000	$ 1,458
Year 4	$ 2,000	$ 521	$ 6,000	$ 1,562
Year 5	$ 2,000	$ 372	$ 6,000	$ 1,116
Total	$10,000	NPV = -$ 303	$10,000	NPV = -$ 3,416

50% Interest Rate

Timing	Option 1 Net Cash Flow	Option 1 Present Value	Option 2 Net Cash Flow	Option 2 Present Value
Now	-$10,000	-$10,000	-$10,000	-$10,000
Year 1	$ 6,000	$ 4,000	$ 2,000	$ 1,333
Year 2	$ 6,000	$ 2,667	$ 2,000	$ 889
Year 3	$ 4,000	$ 1,185	$ 4,000	$ 1,185
Year 4	$ 2,000	$ 395	$ 6,000	$ 1,185
Year 5	$ 2,000	$ 263	$ 6,000	$ 790
Total	$10,000	NPV = -$ 1,490	$10,000	NPV = -$ 4,617

Figure 13-5. Total discounted cash flow (internal rate of return).

	Option 1 NPV	Option 2 NPV
10% Interest Rate	$6,026	$4,300
20% Interest Rate	$3,250	$675
30% Interest Rate	$1,225	-$1,741
40% Interest Rate	-$303	-$3,416
50% Interest Rate	-$1,490	-$4,617

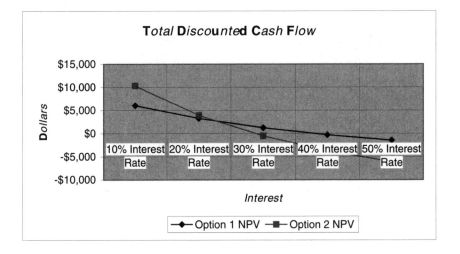

internal rate of return (IRR) calculation be a useful financial
metric to include in the corporate portal business case?
☐ Is an IRR calculation required for the corporate portal business
case?

Payback Period

The payback period is a metric that is used to take an investment
and risk perspective of the plan or scenario and its estimated cash
flow stream. The payback period is the length of time required to
recover the cost of an investment and is usually measured in years.
The investment with the shorter payback period is the better investment with less risk. To calculate a payback period, the positive
cash inflows at some point must outweigh the cash outflows. The
calculation does not reflect the time value of money or money coming in after the investment is recovered. The plan or investment
with the shortest payback period is defined as being less risky as-

suming that the longer the payback period is, the more uncertain returns are expected to be.

As an example, consider the scenario of a $10,000 software purchase that is expected to improve productivity that is valued at $6,000 per year for the next three years (see Figure 13-6). The total paid back by the end of year two is $12,000, and the total paid back by the end of year three is $18,000. The original purchase was $10,000, so the payback period is greater than one year and less than two years. The payback period formula is:

$$\text{Year Value} = \text{Year Payback Is Realized}$$
$$\text{Low Value} = \text{Investment} - \text{Total Paid Back in Year 1}$$
$$\text{High Value} = \text{Total Paid Back in Year 2} - \text{Total Paid Back in Year 1}$$
$$\text{Payback Period} = \text{Year Value} + ((\text{Low Value} / \text{High Value}))$$
$$\text{Payback Period} = 1 + ((10{,}000 - 6{,}000) / (12{,}000 - 6{,}000))$$
$$\text{Payback Period} = 1 + (4{,}000 / 6{,}000) = 1.67 \text{ Years}$$

To evaluate if a payback period calculation needs to be included in the financial metrics of the corporate portal solution, consider the following questions.

PAYBACK PERIOD CALCULATION

☐ Is there a requirement for an estimated cash flow stream with an estimated length of time required to recover the cost of an investment?

☐ Is there a requirement for a cash flow summary that is not adjusted to reflect the time value of money?

☐ If you have answered yes to the previous questions, would a payback period calculation be a useful financial metric to include in the corporate portal business case?

Figure 13-6. Payback period.

	Paid Out	Paid Back	Total Paid Back
Year 1	$10,000	$6,000	$6,000
Year 2	$0	$6,000	$12,000
Year 3	$0	$6,000	$18,000

☐ Is a payback period calculation required for the corporate portal business case?

Cost and Benefit Models

Cost (or expense) and benefit models provide a framework for identifying and organizing all line items implied by the corporate portal features and the boundaries of analysis. The cost and benefit data to be included in the corporate portal business case should be documented as specific line items. A well-analyzed presentation of the cost and benefit models provides an effective means of assuring decision makers that the business case includes all relevant line items. To build or design the cost and benefit model, consider grouping together cost or benefit items that have common sources or other logical relationships to each other. The groups should be organized along one or more dimensions, creating a matrix that outlines the impact of the cost or benefit. The model identifies and organizes the cost and benefit line items with boundaries that describe how or where they are measured.

The corporate portal business case financial models and metrics involve uncertainty since they project results into the future. The business impact or results represent the corporate portal strategy team's view of the most likely outcome. Decision makers reviewing these results will have additional questions. Use the following checklist to prepare to address these concerns.

EVALUATING UNCERTAINTY

☐ What happens if some of the assumptions change?
☐ How likely is this set of results? How likely are other possibilities?
☐ What must happen in order to obtain the results published in the corporate portal business case?
☐ What can be done to maximize results?

A sensitivity analysis can be included to compare several possibilities in the financial metrics section of the corporate portal business case. To evaluate if a cost and benefit model or a sensitivity analysis needs to be included in the financial metrics of the corporate portal solution, consider the following questions.

COST AND BENEFIT MODEL

☐ Is there a requirement for a framework that identifies and organizes all line items implied by the corporate portal features and the boundaries of analysis?
☐ If you have answered yes to the previous question, would a cost and benefit model be a useful financial metric to include in the corporate portal business case?
☐ Is a cost and benefit model required for the corporate portal business case?

SENSITIVITY ANALYSIS

☐ Is there a requirement for a framework for comparing several alternatives and different assumptions of the financial models?
☐ If you have answered yes to the previous question, is a sensitivity analysis a useful financial metric to include in the corporate portal business case?
☐ Is a sensitivity analysis required for the corporate portal business case?

ASSUMPTIONS AND METHODS

The financial metrics tell the financial story surrounding the corporate portal solution. The credibility of the information included in the business case depends heavily on the data sources, results, and assumptions incorporated in the financial metrics. To convince decision makers that the financial metrics are valid, consider and document the assumptions and methods included in the final documentation. The type of information to document includes:

- Assumptions
- Boundaries
- Data sources and methods

Assumptions

All assumptions need to be explicitly recorded in the business case. The documentation of how assumptions were made regarding the research and analysis of financial metrics guarantees that readers and decision makers will be able to understand the material contained in the business case. This documentation should have the following features:

• *Prediction.* The corporate portal business case presents some information that is based on future financial results that change over time. Examples are prices, salaries, and the cost structure used in the organization, among others. The corporate portal business case may include computer hardware purchases that expand over several years. What price information do you include in the business case for purchases made in the future? You have the option of using current prices or a projected future price based on market trends. The choice you make needs to be clearly documented as an assumption. Make sure that you are consistent and apply this assumption the same way throughout the business case.

• *Clarification.* Choices have to be made when presenting future events in the corporate portal business case. These types of choices include estimates of purchases made from one year to the next or the number of IT employees supporting the corporate portal solution from one period to time to the next. What percentage of hardware purchases are expected to made this year versus next year? You have several options that are all equally acceptable. The choice you make is an assumption and will need to be documented.

• *Simplification.* When collecting or documenting information on a fact that has unavailable or difficult-to-acquire details, an assumption is required. You may be required to list salary information for system administrators. It may be impossible or impractical to disclose the salary information for these employees. A more logical solution is to assume the average salary of a system administrator in your organization.

For each assumption identified and included in the financial metrics of the corporate portal solution, consider the following questions.

Assumptions Defined

☐ Do all the data sources, supporting materials, and paradigms regarding predictions included in the financial models validate the corporate portal proposal?

☐ Have all the clarifications regarding the selection of options used to create the financial models for the corporate portal proposal been identified?

☐ Have any assumptions made to simplify an algorithm or estimate a cost or benefit in the financial models been identified and documented as part of the business case?

Boundaries

Boundaries define the range of analysis along several dimensions, providing rules for what financial data belongs in the business case. The boundaries selected give your corporate portal strategy team an outline of the costs and benefits, identifying where the financial impacts come from. Boundary statements are necessary for the corporate portal business case. The dimensions that need to be evaluated include:

- Time
- Geography or location
- Organization or function
- Technology

For each boundary identified to be included in the financial metrics of the corporate portal solution, please copy the appropriate section (heading and questions) of the following checklists and answer the questions contained in that section.

Time

☐ When does the analysis period begin? When does it end?

☐ Is the analysis synchronized with calendar years, fiscal years, program plans, or project plans?

GEOGRAPHY OR LOCATION

☐ Does the analysis refer to a specific site or location? Does the analysis refer to multiple sites or locations?

☐ Does the analysis cover a specific location only (e.g., executive offices, accounting department workstations)?

ORGANIZATION OR FUNCTION

☐ Does the analysis cover a specific workgroup or department? Does the analysis cover the entire organization?

☐ Does the analysis apply to only certain business functions (e.g., accounting, marketing, sales)?

☐ Does the analysis apply to certain user communities or roles?

TECHNOLOGY

☐ Does the analysis include computer software and computer hardware?

☐ Does it include purchasing equipment and equipment maintenance?

Data Sources and Methods

Your corporate portal business case must describe data sources along with the methods used to assign cost and benefit values. Models identify and organize the cost and benefit line items, and the boundaries determine how they are measured. Identify the data source used to establish cost or benefit information and the methods used to assign the cost and benefit values. Briefly describe the cost allocation method used to define the cost estimates. When defining the benefits, be certain to identify the source and the rationale applied to all gains that have been assigned as arbitrary values.

For each of the data sources and methods included in the financial metrics of the corporate portal solution, consider the following questions.

Data Sources Defined

☐ Have all the data sources used to create the financial models included in the corporate portal business case been identified and documented?

Methods Defined

☐ Have all the methods and approaches used to create the financial models included in the corporate portal business case been identified and documented?

CorporatePortal.com Case Study

The business processes and self-service applications proposed for the first implementation of the corporate portal solution need to be analyzed for direct increases in revenue, direct reduction in expenses, and increased satisfaction of corporate portal users. The initial implementation provides knowledge sharing among project team members. The increased information to additional knowledge workers should allow questions, problems, and answers to be resolved 25–50 percent faster and more accurately. This results in the ability to increase revenue by completing additional tax and audit engagements each month or quarter using the current number of employees. The focus on current corporate and individual objectives and their measurements allows employees to concentrate on completing activities that will provide the most benefit for the entire organization. The reduction in expenses is possible by providing reports online, which gives users the ability to submit additional queries and searches from the portal desktop. There should also be a reduction in help requests to use enterprise systems and applications. These features reduce the number of requests and information intermediary activities required by IT department employees. Provided that the corporate portal weaknesses are managed and minimized as risks, there should be acceptance of the portal desktop by key users of the application.

The first phase of the corporate portal solution will be completed in twenty-four months from start date, will affect 360 users at

CorporatePortal.com, and is estimated to cost between $1,050,000 and $1,200,000. There are several data integration and data mart creation activities that will be included and completed as part of the corporate portal solution. The initial corporate portal pilot team will begin using the first prototype of the solution five or six months after the project has been approved. There will be ongoing support and training for the corporate portal solution, primarily during the first year of the portal project, but it is considered a critical component of user acceptance and a successful implementation. The support and training cost is expected to be 10–15 percent of the total cost of the corporate portal solution. The payback period is eighteen months, and the return on investment is 133 percent.

CorporatePortal.com has defined the cost and benefit model for the initial phase of the corporate portal solution. The details of the cost and benefit model can be seen in Figure 13-7. The current monthly cost for each line item has been identified. The future monthly cost based on the implementation of a corporate portal solution has been calculated for each line item. The difference between these two values defines the expected monthly savings. The monthly savings can only be recognized after the business functions, self-service applications, and portal desktop features have been implemented. A start date of when monthly savings should be realized is included. The net present value and level of risk identified have also been included. The line items identified by CorporatePortal.com include:

Benefits

- Reducing cost to produce financial metric reports (e.g., sales, accounts receivable and flash reports, and reports that drill into details).
- Reducing cost to produce accounting reports (e.g., summary reports, exception reports, profit and loss, budget versus actual).
- Reducing cost to produce ad hoc report requests.
- Reducing cost to analyze reports (e.g., financial metric reports, accounting reports).
- Reducing cost to publish corporate and department content.
- Increasing total corporate revenue from increased operating

income as a result of actions being taken sooner due to information being constantly available.

- Reducing total corporate expenses as a result of better and faster decisions being made.

Cost

- Corporate portal development cost (e.g., planning, requirements analysis, architecture and design, development, deployment, training)
- Hardware and software
- IT support and administration staff (two analysts)
- Business domain experts (e.g., publishing corporate content, publishing department content, publishing policies and procedures, creating online help)

The financial analysis assumes a two-year time frame for analyzing the cost and savings aspects of the corporate portal solution and is summarized in Figure 13-8. The savings and cost information has been grouped into three categories of risk:

- *Low Risk.* CorporatePortal.com can control and directly affect the cost savings of these line items.

- *Medium Risk.* These line items are controlled by employees who are able to use the corporate portal solution, interpret the information presented in the portal desktop, and have an indirect impact on the savings of the corporate portal solution.

- *High Risk.* These line items are controlled by the acceptance of the corporate portal solution by CorporatePortal.com employees. The impact on savings is subjective, and the outcome requires establishing a community of corporate portal users.

KEY POINTS

There are different approaches, each with a variety of definitions, that can be used to evaluate the financial consequences of implementing a corporate portal solution. It is important that the strategy team includes and documents the line items that are included

(text continues on page 336)

Figure 13-7. CorporatePortal.com cost and benefit model.

	Current Monthly Cost		Future Monthly Cost		Monthly Savings	Start Date	Net Present Value[2]	Risk
Description	Amount	Assumptions[1]	Amount	Assumptions[1]				
Benefits								
1 Reduce cost to produce Financial Metric Reports (Sales, Accounts Receivable, Flash Reports, drilling into details)	$3,690	90 hrs/mo @ $41/hr	$0	100% reduction	$3,690	Q3/00(7/1/00)	$57,794	Low
2 Reduce cost to produce Accounting Reports (Summary Reports, Exception Reports, Profit and Loss, Budget Versus Actual)	$4,920	120 hrs/mo @ $41/hr	$0	100% reduction	$4,920	Q3/00(7/1/00)	$77,059	Low
3 Reduce cost to produce ad hoc report requests	$6,560	160 hrs/mo @ $41/hr	$0	100% reduction	$6,560	Q4/00(10/1/00)	$84,567	Low
4 Reduce cost to publish corporate and department content	$7,380	180 hrs/mo @ $41/hr	$0	100% reduction	$7,380	Q4/00(10/1/00)	$95,138	Low
5 Reduce cost to analyze reports (Financial Metric Reports, Accounting Reports)	$198,000	10 hrs/mo/Mgr @ $60/hr	$118,800	40% reduction	$79,200	Q4/00(10/1/00)	$1,020,993	Med
6 Increase in total corporate revenue from increased operating income as a result of actions being taken sooner due to information being constantly available								
a) Total Corporate Revenue	$10,600,000	Revenue	$106,000	1.0% increase				
b) Total Corporate Operating Income	$1,484,000	Operating Income	$1,498,840	1.0% increase	$14,840	Q4/00(10/1/00)	$191,307	High
7 Reduction in total corporate expenses as a result of better and faster decisions being made								
a) Total Corporate Expenses	$8,700,000	Expenses	$8,691,300	0.1% reduction	$8,700	Q4/00(10/1/00)	$112,155	High
Subtotal:					$125,290		$1,639,014	

Total Revenue Increase and Cost Reduction (Low Risk): $314,559
Total Revenue Increase and Cost Reduction (Low & Medium Risk): $1,335,552
Total Revenue Increase and Cost Reduction (Low, Medium & High Risk): $1,639,014

Description	Current Monthly Cost		Future Monthly Cost		Monthly Savings	Start Date	Net Present Value[2]	Risk
	Amount	Assumptions[1]	Amount	Assumptions[1]				
Cost								
1 Corporate Portal development cost (Planning, Requirements Analysis, Architecture and Design, Development, Deployment, Training)								
a) Planning			$25,000	One time cost	($25,000)	Q1/00(1/1/00)	($25,000)	Low
b) Requirements Analysis			$67,000	One time cost	($67,000)	Q3/00(7/1/00)	($63,507)	Low
c) Architecture and Design			$104,000	One time cost	($104,000)	Q3/00(7/1/00)	($98,578)	Low
d) Development			$480,000	One time cost	($480,000)	Q4/00(10/1/00)	($443,418)	Low
e) Deployment			$201,000	One time cost	($201,000)	Q4/00(10/1/00)	($185,681)	Low
f) Training			$4,800	12 days @ $400/day	($4,800)	Q4/00(10/1/00)	($61,878)	Low
2 Hardware and Software			$150,000	One time cost	($150,000)	Q2/00(4/1/00)	($145,985)	Low
3 IT Support and Administration Staff								
a) Two Analysts			$4,920	120 hrs/mo @ $41/hr	($4,920)	Q4/00(10/1/00)	($63,425)	Low
4 Business Domain Experts (Publishing Corporate Content, Publishing Department Content, Publishing Polices and Procedures, Creating Online Help)								
a) Six Departments			$7,380	180 hrs/mo @ $41/hr	($7,380)	Q4/00(10/1/00)	($95,138)	Low
Subtotal:							($1,182,612)	
Total Cost (Low Risk):							($1,182,612)	
Total Cost (Low & Medium Risk):							($1,182,612)	
Total Cost (Low, Medium & High Risk):							($1,182,612)	
Summary								
Net Total Savings (Low Risk):							-$868,053	
Net Total Savings (Low & Medium Risk):							$152,940	
Net Total Savings (Low, Medium & High Risk):							$456,402	
ROI (Low Risk)(%)							27%	
ROI (Low & Medium Risk)(%)							-113%	
ROI (Low, Medium & High Risk)(%)							139%	
Payback Period (Low Risk)(months)							90	
Payback Period (Low & Medium Risk)(months)							21	
Payback Period (Low, Medium & High Risk)(months)							17	

Legend
[1] Fully burdened salary based on the following:
  - Analyst - $85,000/yr ($41/hr)
  - Business Domain Expert - $85,000/yr ($41/hr)
  - Director or Manager - $125,000/yr ($60/hr)
[2] Project life of 24 months, internal cost of money of 11%

Figure 13-8. CorporatePortal.com cost and benefit analysis results.

	Low Risk	Medium Risk	High Risk
Costs	$1,182,612	$1,182,612	$1,182,612
Savings	($868,053)	$89,515	$392,977
Return on Investment	27%	108%	133%
Payback Period	90	22	18

in the corporate portal business case, the time period evaluated, and the assumptions used to calculate the financial metrics. An effective conclusion must be documented and should concentrate on supporting the objectives of the corporate portal solution. The conclusions and formal recommendation should be included in the executive summary of the business case and used to remind the decision makers to give special consideration to the important contingencies and dependencies regarding your corporate portal proposal. The financial metrics information you create is then added as a section in the corporate portal business case.

14

Preliminary Project Plan and Timeline

The corporate portal project needs to be a well-established sequence of activities with a recognized beginning and ending. The focus of the corporate portal project plan is to achieve an identified objective in a specified time frame. Several established parameters such as time, cost, available resources, and quality standards need to be adhered to as the identified tasks of the corporate portal project are completed.

Various management, coordination, and communication skills are used to monitor all aspects of the corporate portal project. Your corporate portal project team must use effective tools, applications, and planning activities to coordinate the project from accepted proposal (start) to first phase implementation (finish). Your corporate portal project team must store, track, and display project information to verify that team members are aware of the schedule, their specific responsibilities, and the current status of the project at all times.

CORPORATE PORTAL PROJECT DEFINITION

The corporate portal solution requires that your project team use engagement management practices to provide early indications of potential issues. Work has to be coordinated and communicated with the development team. Best practices allow the project team to deliver a complete solution with the appropriate documentation, on schedule, and within budget. The engagement management practices your team adopts have aspects of project integrity, construction integrity, and product integrity and stability. Several of the areas to concentrate on when establishing the preliminary corporate portal project plan and associated timeline include:

- *Risk Management.* Areas of risk to try to minimize on a corporate portal project include issues that affect the schedule, executive support of the project, changing requirements, software limitations, hardware limitations, and development skills, among others.
- *A Detailed User Interface Prototype.* Several interface prototype iterations that the business domain experts and corporate portal user community can evaluate for effectiveness and usefulness need to be scheduled and completed. This review or pilot team must be available during all phases of the project. The feedback and input of these employees can ensure that the user community accepts the corporate portal solution delivered.
- *A Realistic Schedule.* The schedule that is introduced to successfully implement the first phases of the corporate portal solution must account for the initial risks identified. Although it is impossible to know the impact of each of the risks, it is important that you must attempt to create a schedule that allocates time to researching and resolving risks. This research allows the preliminary project plan to be as realistic as possible. The results should be documented as part of the corporate portal business case.
- *A Quality Assurance Plan.* The identification of the quality characteristics that are expected to be included in the corporate portal solution provides information regarding the types of quality tasks that need to be included in the project plan.
- *Detailed Task Lists.* The identification of the tasks to be completed to successfully implement a corporate portal solution provides most of the information required to allocate the appropriate resources and follow the progress of the project. Each task that you define likely consists of several steps that must be executed successfully before the identified task itself is to be considered complete. In many cases tasks have relationships or dependencies with each other.

Project Definition Identified

One of the first steps to complete when beginning the process of establishing a preliminary project plan is documenting the goals and objectives of the corporate portal solution. The level of detail collected during the information technology analysis (covered in Chapter 10) and the business process and information needs analysis (covered in Chapter 11) determines how specific the corporate portal project plan and, in turn, the business case ends up being. The corporate portal strategy team should concentrate its research and analysis around project complexity, constraint identification, and corporate portal objectives while establishing a preliminary project plan for the corporate portal solution.

For each phase of the corporate portal's preliminary project plan and the timeline section of the business case, please copy the appropriate section (heading and questions) of the following checklists and answer the questions contained in that section.

PROJECT COMPLEXITY

- ☐ How much planning will be required for each phase of the corporate portal solution?
- ☐ How large will the corporate portal project team need to be to successfully implement each phase of the project?
- ☐ What skill sets are needed for the corporate portal project team?
- ☐ Are new procedures or technologies required?
- ☐ Is there a defined or limited budget?
- ☐ Do some tasks depend on the completion of other tasks, or are there several collection of steps or tasks that need to be coordinated?

CONSTRAINTS IDENTIFIED

- ☐ What will be the cost to implement each phase of the corporate portal solution?
- ☐ What are the deadlines or other time constraints?
- ☐ What approval processes are required?

CORPORATE PORTAL PROJECT DEFINITION

☐ What is the scope of each phase of the corporate portal solution?

☐ Who is affected (e.g., corporate portal project team, development team, user community)?

☐ What is the expected time frame to complete the corporate portal solution?

☐ What will indicate or signal the end of each phase of the corporate portal solution?

Project Manager Role Identified

To successfully implement the corporate portal solution, a project manager needs to be identified. This person is responsible for the coordination, collation, and dissemination of the corporate portal project information. During the initial stages of the project, the project manager works with other members of the project team, business domain experts, and executive managers to define the objectives and priorities of the corporate portal project. The next step for the project manager is to outline a path to accomplish the selected objectives. Once the corporate portal project has started, the project manager is responsible for supervising the progress, assessing the impact of schedule variations, and maintaining an updated or current project plan. After each of the project milestones has been reached or an objective is achieved, the project manager completes a status report or a project evaluation report to document the strengths and weaknesses of the project. This information is used to evaluate the future direction of the corporate portal project and to continue to effectively plan the next phases of the project.

Software Development Activities

The corporate portal business case needs to address the software life cycle approach being followed to implement the solution. The software life cycle is defined in the project plan and timeline as the activities that constitute the corporate portal project. The strategy team must make certain that it understands not only the activities it must complete but also what it means in terms of time and complexity when estimating the risks, return on investment, and scope of the proposed corporate portal solution that will be included in the business case. The following activities must be completed by the corporate portal development team and recommended in the business case:

- *Requirements Analysis* (i.e., the activities and research that establish the user description of the corporate portal functionality defined in detail)
- *System Design* (i.e., the software solution and infrastructure that will facilitate or be used to create the corporate portal solution identified in the user requirements)
- *Program Design* (i.e., the mechanics or pseudo instructions and algorithms that will best implement the corporate portal solution design)
- *Program Implementation* (i.e., the construction of the corporate portal solution)
- *Testing* (i.e., verification that the corporate portal solution performs as defined)
- *Delivery* (i.e., acceptance of the corporate portal solution by the employees who will use the portal desktop)
- *Maintenance* (i.e., support for the deployed corporate portal solution and identification of additional features and enhancements requested for future development phases)

There are several inherent problems and risks associated with software development that apply to the corporate portal. For example:

- Requirements are constantly changing, and the employees are not aware of what these changes will be in advance.
- Frequent changes are difficult to manage, and trying to establish checkpoints for planning and cost estimation is difficult.
- Phased development requires that a distinction exist between the corporate portal solution under development and the corporate portal solution in production. Any new release of the corporate portal must be backward-compatible with the production solution.

Several methodologies have been proposed to deal with these inherent problems. One popular approach is the waterfall model (see Figure 14-1). It provides a linear look at the system life cycle with easily identifiable milestones that are referenced during the development of the corporate portal solution. However, a solution as complex as a corporate portal requires an iterative approach that can address changes in requirements.

One possible iterative solution to consider is the spiral model (see Figure 14-2). This approach can identify and assign priorities to risks. A series of prototypes are created that have the waterfall model activities associated with each round or cycle in the spiral. Once a risk has been successfully resolved, the next round of the

Figure 14-1. The waterfall model of the software life cycle.

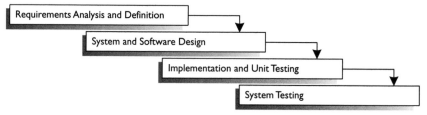

Figure 14-2. The spiral model of the software life cycle (Boehm).

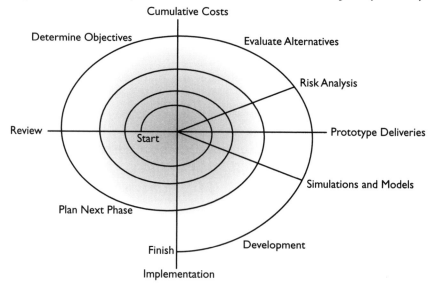

process begins. There are several types of prototypes that may be created to resolve the current set of corporate portal risks identified. These include:

- *Illustrative Prototype*. Develop the user interface with a set of storyboards.
- *Functional Prototype*. Implement and deliver an operational corporate portal solution with minimum functionality, then add additional functionality based on the risks identified.
- *Exploratory Prototype*. Implement part of the corporate portal solution to learn more about the system and user requirements.
- *Revolutionary Prototype or Specification Prototype*. Implement a draft version of the corporate portal solution to be evaluated before the final version of the corporate portal solution is constructed. The draft version of the corporate portal solution is discarded before development begins on the final version.
- *Evolutionary Prototype*. Each version of the prototype is reviewed and enhanced to become the final corporate portal solution deliverable.

During an actual corporate portal project you'll be called on to deal with iterations that include out-of-order activities and additional revisions or refinements based on new information received during project construction. The goal of the corporate portal strategy team is to understand the software development activities, understand the risks involved to determine how they are going to minimized, and identify the tools and techniques used to create a quality corporate portal solution that can be delivered in time and within budget.

PROJECT PLAN DEFINITION

After identifying the objectives of the project, you'll need to decompose the corporate portal project into several components or building blocks. These include:

- Tasks
- Milestones
- Resources

Your strategy team must create a high-level set of tasks to meet the preliminary objectives identified for the first phases of the corporate portal solution. Third-party project management software applications are excellent tools for establishing an initial project plan. These applications can quickly recalculate schedules and allow the project manager to see how changes in one part of the project will affect the overall plan. Reviewing the credibility of tasks, adjusting schedule dates, and juggling available resources can be quickly done with project management applications. There are several communication and dissemination activities that will need to be completed as well. These include:

- The ability to manage requests, document results, and make presentations
- The ability to keep team members informed of only the tasks and activities unique to each employee
- The ability to produce reports that reflect the current state or progress of the corporate portal project

The project phases and their associated schedules should be created before the first task in the project begins. Once the project has started, the project manager can oversee the tasks as they occur and make adjustments to the schedule as required. When adjustments to the schedule are necessary, the results and changes must be communicated to everyone in the organization associated with the corporate portal project. Project phases include:

- *Creating the initial project schedule.* This activity needs to be completed before the corporate portal project begins. The result of this activity should be the initial pass of the tasks, schedules, and resources for the first phases of the corporate portal solution.

- *Managing the project and adjusting to changes.* The project manager must track the status of tasks and determine whether each task is proceeding as planned. When tasks fall behind schedule, the project manager must evaluate whether the corporate portal objectives can still be achieved. The project plan should be adjusted as necessary. The project manager should always be trying to anticipate the unexpected. These unexpected occurrences may be a resource that's unavailable, a budget that's been reduced, or the addition of new requirements. Since project tasks are often interdependent, these types of changes often affect the entire project.

• *Communicating results and progress.* The corporate portal project team typically involves employees from several different workgroups or departments. It is important to communicate project schedules and expectations to the team members and their supervisors. When corporate decision makers need information about the progress of the project, a variety of reports, discussion postings, and presentations can be used to reflect the status and progression of the corporate portal project effectively.

• *Evaluating the performance of the completed corporate portal project.* As the project progresses, all the information relating to tasks, resources, and costs needs to collected and evaluated. At the close of the project this collection of information is used to assess the effectiveness of the original corporate portal project plan. This analysis is then used to improve the planning and implementation of future projects.

For each phase of the corporate portal solution that you've included in the preliminary project plan and timeline section of the business case, please use the following checklist and answer these questions contained in that section.

ANALYZING YOUR CORPORATE PORTAL'S PRELIMINARY PROJECT PLAN AND TIMELINE

☐ What tasks and steps are needed to accomplish the objectives of the corporate portal solution?

☐ What resources, tools, or other utilities are needed to accomplish the objectives of the corporate portal solution?

☐ What is the expected cost to implement this phase of the corporate portal solution?

☐ How will progress made on the corporate portal solution be presented to inform other interested employees in your organization about the status of the corporate portal project?

Tasks

Tasks, also called steps, are all the items that have to be completed in the project plan to define the scope of each corporate portal objective. The result is the project task list or scope of work. One approach to create the task list is to outline the high-level tasks and proceed to drill into each high-level task, establishing a list of associated elements or steps. As each group of tasks expands into multiple elements and steps, a hierarchy called a work breakdown structure (WBS) begins to emerge. The WBS outlines the steps to be completed in a sequence that is determined by the nature of the type of project. As each step in the task list is reviewed and placed (or replaced) in the hierarchy, the tasks are identified as sequential or concurrent.

The amount of time required to complete a step is referred to as the duration of the step. It is a good idea to establish the duration of each task when the task list is created. Task duration estimates are usually identified by:

- Historical information
- Knowledge experts
- Intuition

The most reliable duration estimate comes from historical data that has been collected from previous project plans. The next most reliable source is to interview individuals who have some knowledge about a task or have completed the task in the past. Intuitive data comes from an employee who has completed a similar task in the past and has some idea how to estimate the duration of the task at hand.

Milestones

A milestone is the completion of a group of related tasks or an identified phase of the corporate portal project. Milestones are used as checkpoints for the project. Creating milestones helps you organize tasks into logical groups or sequences. They are an excellent way to note and summarize the progress of the project. Once a group of related tasks are recognized as completed, then the checkpoint or milestone has successfully been reached. Once all the milestones have been completed, the corporate portal project is complete. The steps for identifying and documenting milestones in the corporate portal preliminary project plan and timeline include:

- Listing several important tasks of the corporate portal project.
- Determining which of the tasks listed are dependent on each other.
- Determining which of the tasks can be completed simultaneously.
- Determining which of the tasks are repeated throughout the corporate portal project.
- Determining any task constraints (such as specific dates).
- Determining which tasks are related.
- Determining which tasks represent parts of the same process.
- Determining which tasks complete a phase in the project.
- Identifying points in the project that represent milestones.

Resources

Resources must be assigned to the corporate portal project team to complete the tasks identified in the project plan. Resources include people, tools, utilities, equipment, and other items recognized as necessary to complete or perform a task. One consideration for the preliminary corporate portal project plan is identifying what the availability of resources will be when trying to implement the project plan. This entails:

- *Identifying the employees, workgroups, or departments needed to complete a specific task.* This effort provides the most flexibility in the corporate portal business case using titles or other general descriptions of the resources required.

- *Identifying the equipment you need to complete each task.* The business case only requires identification of equipment for which special arrangements need to be made. You may also want to identify equipment that is only available in limited supplies.

- *Identifying the facilities that are needed to complete each task.* Office space, conference rooms, or server rooms may have to be reserved. You should only plan for facilities that require special arrangements to reserve.

CorporatePortal.com Case Study

The first phase of the corporate portal solution for CorporatePortal.com is scheduled to be completed in less than 450 days, or twenty-four months from the date the project begins. The first prototype of the solution will be in use by a selected group of corporate portal users five or six months into the project. The tasks have been grouped together based on their type. Types of tasks include requirements analysis, design, development, and deployment. Some tasks must be completed before others can start, while several of the tasks can be completed simultaneously. These task relationships have been excluded in this case study, but can easily be included at a later date using a project plan application. The project plan and timeline information will be summarized and included in CorporatePortal.com's business case. The details are outlined in the "CorporatePortal.com Project Plan and Timeline."

CorporatePortal.com Project Plan and Timeline

Requirements Analysis

Activity	Duration
Preparation	7.50 days
• Assign corporate portal planning resources.	
• Conduct corporate portal documentation review.	
• Prepare initial project plan.	
IT Development Team Meeting	1.00 day
• Prepare for IT development team meeting.	

Activity	Duration
• Hold IT development team meeting. • Document IT development team meeting. • Milestone: IT development team meeting complete.	
Business Domain Expert Meeting • Prepare for business domain expert meeting. • Hold business domain expert meeting. • Document business domain expert meeting. • Milestone: Business domain expert meeting complete.	1.25 days
Information Gathering • Do preparation and research. • Hold information technology analysis meeting. • Hold business process and information needs analysis meeting. • Conduct follow-up interviews. • Do analysis.	9.50 days
Infrastructure Requirements Documented • Create the infrastructure requirements draft document. • Review with the IT department. • Create the infrastructure requirements final document.	4.00 days
Business Requirements Documented • Create the business requirements draft document. • Review with the business domain experts.	8.00 days

Activity	Duration
• Create the business requirements final document.	
Executive Sponsor Approval • Milestone: Executive signature. • Post final documentation and deliverables.	1.25 days
Requirements Analysis Total	32.50 days (7.65%)

Architecture and Design

Activity	*Duration*
Preparation • Assign corporate portal design resources. • Conduct corporate portal documentation review. • Update project plan.	4.00 days
Project Plan Review • Review project plan with IT development team. • Review project plan with business domain experts.	3.00 days
Information Gathering • Do preparation and research. • Create storyboards and scripts. • Identify corporate portal software functions. • Determine training requirements. • Study user acceptance testing requirements. • Milestone: Information gathering complete.	25.00 days
Architecture and Design Documentation	18.00 days

Activity	Duration
• Identify proof-of-concept activities.	
• Create the architecture and design draft document.	
• Review with the IT department.	
• Review with business domain experts.	
• Create the architecture and design final document.	
Executive Sponsor Approval	2.00 days
• Milestone: Executive Signature.	
• Post final documentation and deliverables.	

Design Total	52.00 days (12.24%)

Development

Activity	Duration
Preparation	4.00 days
• Assign corporate portal design resources.	
• Conduct corporate portal documentation review.	
• Update project plan.	
Project Plan Review	2.00 days
• Review project plan with IT development team.	
• Review project plan with business domain experts.	
Development Plan	5.00 days
• Create draft of detailed development plan.	
• Review with the IT department.	
• Milestone: Create final detailed development plan.	

Activity	*Duration*
Infrastructure	13.00 days
• Confirm infrastructure requirements.	
• Secure hardware and software.	
• Install hardware and software.	
• Perform installation validation.	
• Create backup schedule.	
• Milestone: Development environment setup complete.	
Data Mart (Data Source) Development	28.00 days
• Create data mart specification.	
• Build data mart.	
• Build data integration extraction.	
• Build data integration transformation.	
• Build data integration load.	
• Set up security configuration.	
• Set up administration configuration.	
• Validate data mart.	
Self-Service Application Development	36.00 days
• Create detail design specification.	
• Code construction.	
• Set up security configuration.	
• Set up administration configuration.	
• Validate self-service application.	
Corporate Portal Development	32.00 days
• Create detail design specification.	
• Code construction.	
• Set up security configuration.	
• Set up administration configuration.	
• Validate corporate portal solution.	

Activity	Duration
Search	20.00 days
• Create detail design specification.	
• Code construction.	
• Build search catalogs.	
• Set up security configuration.	
• Set up administration configuration.	
• Validate search.	
Content Management	20.00 days
• Create detail design specification.	
• Code construction.	
• Build process and action functionality.	
• Set up security configuration.	
• Set up administration configuration.	
• Validate content management.	
Collaboration	5.00 days
• Create detail design specification.	
• Code construction.	
• Validate collaboration.	
Messaging	5.00 days
• Create detail design specification.	
• Code construction.	
• Validate collaboration.	
Prototype Reviews	20.00 days
• Define prototype review scope.	
• Schedule review.	
• Hold review.	
• Document required changes.	
• Update the project plan and budget.	

Activity	*Duration*
Infrastructure Quality Assurance	7.00 days
• Create infrastructure test plan.	
• Milestone: Validate corporate portal infrastructure.	
Development Quality Assurance	26.00 days
• Create development test plan.	
• Execute unit test plans.	
• Execute data integration test plans.	
• Execute system test plans.	
• Milestone: Validate corporate portal solution.	
Documentation	17.00 days
• Create end-user documentation.	
• Create technical documentation.	
• Review documentation.	
• Milestone: Documentation complete.	
Development Total	240.00 days (56.47%)

Deployment

Activity	*Duration*
Deployment Plan	3.00 days
• Draft detailed deployment plan.	
• Review with business domain experts.	
• Milestone: Create final detailed deployment plan.	
Infrastructure	8.50 days
• Confirm infrastructure requirements.	
• Secure hardware and software.	
• Install hardware and software.	
• Perform installation validation.	
• Create backup schedule.	

Activity	Duration
• Milestone: Production environment setup complete.	
Deployment Preparation	40.00 days
• Secure IT department resources.	
• Arrange administrator technical training.	
• Arrange developer technical training.	
User Acceptance	26.00 days
• Execute user acceptance testing.	
• Collect feedback.	
• Implement required modifications.	
• Milestone: User acceptance complete (sign-off).	
Production Deployment	20.00 days
• Make corporate announcement.	
• Perform client configuration and setup.	
• Roll out end-user training.	
• Support hand-off from development to administration.	
Wrap-up Meeting	3.00 days
• Prepare for wrap-up meeting.	
• Hold wrap-up meeting.	
• Document lessons learned.	
• Post all project documents.	
• Create corporate portal project abstract/summary.	
• Milestone: Corporate portal project complete.	
Deployment Total	100.50 days (23.64%)

Corporate Portal Project Total	425.00 days (100.00%)

KEY POINTS

The corporate portal preliminary project plan and timeline can easily be created from a third-party project management software application. The results of the initial tasks, milestones, and resources compiled to achieve the corporate portal project's objectives are to be included in the preliminary project plan and timeline section of the corporate portal business case. Be sure to include:

- *An Assessment of Your Corporate Portal Project and Its Objectives.* Define the complexity of the first phases of your corporate portal solution and identify any constraints that must be included. Formulate objectives that are specific to the scope of the corporate portal project, the user community that is affected, and the timeline that needs to be met.

- *A List of Project Tasks, Milestones, and Resources.* The objective is to generate a list of the initial key tasks and durations. You want to concentrate on the relationship between tasks that identify which tasks depend on each other, which tasks occur repeatedly, and what milestones and resources are required to complete identified tasks.

- *A Refinement of the Project Plan.* The initial outline of the corporate portal solution needs to be created. The strategy team must identify the skills and procedures needed to implement the first phases of the corporate portal solution. Any constraints identified (e.g., fixed costs, deadlines, or communication about the project status) must be documented.

15

CorporatePortal.com Business Case

CorporatePortal.com is a fictitious business. The following business case is an adaptation of the case studies available throughout earlier chapters in this book. Although no appendices are included in this extended example, in most cases you will want to include additional reference or supporting material as part of your final business case. Review Chapter 4 for additional details regarding the sections and appendices to include in a corporate portal business case.

Mission Statements

The CorporatePortal.com mission defines the organization and is continually referenced to successfully identify and measure its goals and objectives. The internal infrastructure and systems implemented at CorporatePortal.com are designed to assist in the execution of this mission. A corporate portal solution has been analyzed and is being proposed to improve the ability of employees to understand and complete corporate objectives, fulfilling the organization's mission. The company's mission and the supporting corporate portal mission have been used to define the benefits of a corporate portal solution at CorporatePortal.com.

Organization Mission

CorporatePortal.com will provide customers with the highest-quality tax and audit services with an emphasis on solving all of our related customers' needs and satisfaction by applying a well-organized set of operating procedures and methodologies.

Corporate Portal Mission

The mission statement for the corporate portal solution has been established "to bring critical business and financial information to the desktop of employees, and to allow the users of that information to analyze and act upon the data to make consistent and timely business decisions."

Executive Summary

A corporate portal solution offers several business advantages for CorporatePortal.com. There are many different enterprise applications and systems that employees are responsible for understanding and using to complete assigned tasks throughout the organization. Employees are only responsible for understanding and using the systems that directly affect their responsibilities. This means that employees have to navigate through or ignore unwanted material; consequently, the material that employees want is not easily found or easily accessible. Streamlining communication and processes requires that employees be familiar with applications, documents, manuals, and the expertise areas of other knowledge workers. CorporatePortal.com is evaluating a corporate portal solution for the primary purpose of making a wide collection of relevant information and data sources available to all employees and for the secondary purpose of improving communication and interaction among these employees.

The objectives and unique opportunities offered by the corporate portal solution for CorporatePortal.com include:

- The ability to retrieve information from corporate information technology (IT) systems and present the results according to the roles, specific tasks, and preferences of individual employees.
- The ability to present employees with information relevant to their daily tasks without making them search for it.

- The ability to gather information about each employee, facilitating communication between the people who need information and the people who can supply the information. For instance, an account manager may need to learn the details of a customer's tax audit from the consulting team leader responsible for composing and documenting the results. By knowing the name of the customer, the account manager would be able to use a few mouse clicks to locate the name of the team leader and contact him or her via e-mail, telephone, or other tools available.

- The ability to let employees act on the information presented in the desktop without requiring them to switch to a different system or interface for the purpose of sharing the information and collaborating with other employees.

- The ability to present a desktop interface through a web browser that requires minimal technical training.

- The ability to support multiple business processes for a single department, a single process across multiple departments, or multiple processes across multiple departments.

Business Need and Opportunity

There is no other solution available at CorporatePortal.com that provides a desktop interface to consolidate a complete collection of corporate information, content management, team collaboration and coordination, and personal information management. The corporate portal will facilitate centralizing enterprise information and coordinating business functions for all employees. The services and self-service applications facilitated through the corporate desktop will allow employees to share knowledge and find answers they need to make informed decisions.

Corporate Portal Definition

A portal is an intranet "window" that presents information to users and an intranet "door" that allows users to pass through to reach the selected destinations. The corporate portal creates the central location where navigation services are available for employees to find information, launch applications, interact with corporate data, identify collaborators, share knowledge, and make decisions. The definition of a corporate portal is:

> A browser-based application that allows knowledge workers to gain access to, collaborate with, make decisions, and take action on a wide variety of business-related information regardless of the employee's virtual location or departmental affiliations, the location of the information, or the format in which the information is stored.

Financial Metrics Statement

The first phase of the corporate portal solution will be completed in twenty-four months from start date, will affect 360 users at CorporatePortal.com, and is estimated to cost between $1,050,000 and $1,200,000. There will be ongoing support and training for the corporate portal solution, primarily during the first year of the portal project, which is considered a critical component of user acceptance and a successful implementation. The support and training cost is expected to be 10–15 percent of the total cost of the corporate portal solution. The payback period is eighteen months, and the return on investment is 133 percent.

The financial analysis assumes a two-year time frame for analyzing the cost and savings aspects of the corporate portal solution and is summarized in Figure 15-1. The savings and cost information has been grouped into three categories of risk:

- *Low Risk.* CorporatePortal.com can control and directly affect the cost savings of these line items.

- *Medium Risk.* These line items are controlled by employees understanding how to use the corporate portal solution, interpret

Figure 15-1. CorporatePortal.com cost and benefit analysis results.

	Low Risk	Medium Risk	High Risk
Costs	$1,182,612	$1,182,612	$1,182,612
Savings	($868,053)	$89,515	$392,977
Return on Investment	27%	108%	133%
Payback Period	90	22	18

the information presented in the portal desktop, and have an indirect impact on the savings of the corporate portal solution.

- *High Risk.* These line items are controlled by the acceptance of the corporate portal solution by CorporatePortal.com employees. The impact on savings is subjective, and the outcome will require establishing a community of corporate portal users.

Key Characteristics of a Corporate Portal

There are several characteristics that can be incorporated into the corporate portal solution for the organization to take advantage of. They include (among others):

- *Support for Making Better Decisions.* The structure and content available from the corporate portal desktop should provide the appropriate detail and direct access to information throughout CorporatePortal.com for employees to improve and enhance decisions they make while doing their jobs and completing their assigned responsibilities.

- *Semantics.* The corporate portal solution provides the framework to create a consistent view of the organization through the use of consistent terminology and navigation hierarchies.

- *Information Organization and Search Capabilities.* This characteristic allows the portal solution to be focused on the layout of individual desktop screens organized around the way employees work rather than around the applications they use. An additional feature is to provide search features to locate documents and information available inside CorporatePortal.com or on the World Wide Web.

- *Direct Access to Knowledge and Resources.* The central portal desktop provides a single point-of-access for employees to focus on the most important aspects of their jobs, personalized objectives, summarized reports, discussion forums, and the experience of other knowledge workers to complete their assigned responsibilities.

- *Direct Links to Reports, Analysis, and Queries.* Summarized or status information that needs to be tracked, published, and presented is incorporated into the portal desktop. These reports provide several services that include information to (1) educate employees and (2) evaluate and measure the success of the organization's performance objectives and defined metrics.

• *Direct Links to Related or Relative Data Points.* This benefit encapsulates the ability to traverse content inside the portal desktop that is relevant to the primary responsibilities and interests of the employee.

• *Personalized Access to Content.* Personalization provides the ability and functionality required for each employee to organize, define, and rearrange the portal desktop to work effectively and efficiently.

Structure and Important Features of the Corporate Portal Solution

There are combinations of software functions working together in the portal desktop to implement these identified characteristics in the corporate portal solution. Portal software vendors provide development environments to integrate enterprise information and third-party products into the portal desktop. The most common software functions that portal software solutions will need to support include:

• *Data Points and Integration.* The data points and integration element includes the ability to access information from a wide range of internal and external information sources and display the resulting information in the single-point-of-access desktop.

• *Taxonomy.* The taxonomy or categorization element provides information context and semantics specific to the organization. The taxonomy established needs to be logical and easily recognized or understood by employees using the corporate portal.

• *Search.* The search element will need to support searches across the enterprise, the World Wide Web, and third-party search engine catalogs and indexes. The user will need for the portal solution to support search queries that can be run on a scheduled basis or as an immediate request.

• *Help.* The help element provides assistance when using the corporate portal solution. Help should be available for both corporate portal features and specific features of business functions. Help features to be included are simple pop-up help when a mouse is held down over a menu option, context-sensitive help for information that is supposed to be entered in a specific field, and detailed help on a specific topic or issue.

• *Content Management.* The publishing and distribution, or content management, element supports content creation, authorization, and inclusion in or exclusion from corporate portal content collections. New policies, procedures, forms, templates, announcements, schedules, and much more will be published and included in the CorporatePortal.com portal desktop.

• *Process and Action.* The process and action element enables the corporate portal user to initiate and participate in business processes included in the portal desktop.

• *Collaboration and Communication.* The collaboration and communication element gives employees the ability to work together in a qualitatively better way by facilitating a shared, virtual desktop (collaboration), supporting electronic messaging (communication), and adding collaboration and communication features to business processes (coordination).

• *Personalization.* The personalization element is a critical component that allows employees to define a unique working environment that is organized and configured specifically to their responsibilities and activities. Decision-making capabilities are optimized to each portal user's working style and content preferences.

• *Presentation.* The presentation element is the user's visual experience and interaction with the portal desktop that encapsulates all of the corporate portal's functionality. All of the software functions or elements mentioned previously must be supported in the presentation element in a format that is flexible enough to allow intuitive use and easy navigation throughout.

• *Administration.* The administration element provides two services. The first is deployment and maintenance activities, or tasks associated with the corporate portal system. The second is what can be uniquely configured (1) by an administrator for the corporate portal system and (2) by each user through corporate portal personalization.

- *Security.* The security element provides a description of the levels of access each user or groups of users are allowed for each portal application and software function included in the corporate portal. The types of access allowed include no access, reader, or editor, among others.

Corporate Portal Solution Overview

CorporatePortal.com determines that employees are having several problems with the current intranet and existing applications. Employees are not aware of material and manuals in the organization. Awareness and use of this material would allow employees with similar job descriptions to make consistent decisions and reduce the need to ask questions regarding current processes. The mission and objectives for CorporatePortal.com need to be incorporated into the objectives and daily activities of every employee. There will be measurements (i.e., scorecard information) defined for corporate and department objectives that are centrally located and easily referenced to help employees establish priorities. CorporatePortal.com would like to provide all employees with a corporate taxonomy to serve the purpose of (1) creating a menu hierarchy to navigate available documentation and systems and (2) providing semantics to create a common vocabulary. The final benefit CorporatePortal.com would like to take advantage of is better team communication and collaboration on customer projects and internal projects.

Critical Success Factors

After completing the internal evaluation of existing systems and solutions, the company has recognized that several corporate objectives are only partially being met. The corporate portal solution will bring corporate and personal objectives to every employee, providing awareness and opportunity to improve corporate performance and achieve the corporate mission. CorporatePortal.com is interested in taking advantage of existing technologies, systems, and applications. The corporate portal solution is being evaluated to enhance existing enterprise systems to improve how decisions are made and provide knowledge-sharing aspects to existing processes. The goals and critical success factors identified for the corporate portal solution include:

- Improvements and enhancements of the decision cycle
- A consistent view of the organization
- Information organization and search capabilities
- Direct access to corporate knowledge and resources
- Direct links to reports, analysis, and queries
- Direct links to related or relative data
- Personalized access to content

Additional research and interviews need to be completed to determine how a corporate portal solution will address this list of critical success factors. The corporate portal software functions and universal features that describe how each of the critical success factors can be measured will be included in the requirements analysis documentation. The corporate portal solution will incorporate business functions and self-service applications that are evaluated to meet these objectives and provide the most value to employees.

Information Technology Analysis

A review of the corporate infrastructure has been completed. This research provided valuable information about the current state of the corporate wide area network. A preliminary estimate of how many corporate portal users will be supported in the first phase of the portal solution has been determined. These users will need to have workstations with web browser software and access to the applications, systems, and data sources that are going to be used through the portal desktop. The first implementation of the corporate portal will target approximately 360 users and will need to be supported by two IT employees. The IT employees will be responsible for portal development, deployment, maintenance, and administration of the corporate portal solution.

CorporatePortal.com is interested in recruiting employees in several departments of the organization to establish sets of corporate objectives and measure their performance. The systems that have been targeted to provide data for these metrics are the current financial system (i.e., Oracle Financials), the tax and audit project management system (i.e., Oracle RDBMS), and customer satisfaction reports (i.e., Oracle RDBMS). These Oracle-based systems are well established and supported by the IT department. The portal desktop will use reports and query results from available Oracle databases and views to present performance results and metrics to employees.

There are several sources available throughout CorporatePortal.com to find documents. The documents consist of Microsoft Word documents, Excel spreadsheets, PowerPoint presentations, e-mail messages, project files, Adobe PDF files, and others. These documents are shared through the CorporatePortal.com website and Microsoft Exchange public folders and on network file servers. Documentum is the content management application that will be evaluated and considered for implementation at CorporatePortal.com to consolidate and easily locate structured and unstructured information throughout the organization. Employees will share and interact with information available in enterprise systems and the corporate document repository from the portal desktop.

Microsoft Outlook is the messaging and e-mail system implemented at CorporatePortal.com. There is a need for structured discussion forums and project team knowledge sharing. Employees under-access the current feedback and bulletin board applications at CorporatePortal.com. The corporate portal will provide centralized access to instant messaging (i.e., online chat) and discussion forums at the desktop for employees. A project team collaboration application will be evaluated and included as part of the corporate portal solution to coordinate specific tax and audit project knowledge and associated activities.

Business Process and Information Needs Analysis

The benefits of a corporate portal solution have been discussed with business domain experts at CorporatePortal.com. These discussions have allowed business domain experts to review their current work processes and consider how a corporate portal could improve the working environment of their employees. The preliminary self-service applications have been identified to benefit employees in the CorporatePortal.com organization. These applications include:

- Key financial information, current project (i.e., tax and audit) status information, and customer satisfaction metrics, all of which should be summarized and easily available in the corporate portal desktop
- A corporate document repository that can be accessed from both a standard menu hierarchy and a search engine
- A shared portal workspace where project teams can collaborate and coordinate their activities
- An expert locator that allows employees to locate other knowledge workers for their assistance in resolving identified problems.
- Discussion forums and instant messaging
- A desktop interface that consolidates these identified self-service applications and lets employees choose and personalize how this pertinent information is organized and presented

The corporate portal solution initially being considered needs to support integration with data sources in CorporatePortal.com that are responsible for financial systems, project (tax and audit) systems, customer satisfaction systems, document management systems, messaging and collaboration systems, search engines, and project management systems. A CorporatePortal.com menu hierarchy will need to be implemented in the portal solution to allow navigation to information and knowledge experts available. Help features will need to be identified, developed, and supported from the portal desktop. The corporate portal solution will include and support the personal information management (PIM) requirements of employees.

Corporate Portal Team Members and Business Domain Experts

The corporate portal strategy team includes three individuals whose combined backgrounds represent employee management skills, project management skills, business process analysis, and several years' experience with CorporatePortal.com. The executive sponsor of the corporate portal solution is the vice president of sales. He will be directly involved in all aspects of the corporate portal solution. Some of these activities include approving the requirements for the first phase of the corporate portal project, managing the corporate portal budget, and working directly with the corporate portal development team through the implementation of the corporate portal solution. A senior project manager from the IT department will work closely with the corporate portal sponsor and concentrate primarily on the technical infrastructure, administration, risk management and the establishment of priorities for the corporate portal project.

Business domain experts and employees from the accounting, information technologies, marketing, personnel, sales, and training departments will be recruited as pilot team members. The pilot team will complete the business functions and self-service application requirements for the first phase of the corporate portal solution. This group will be involved in several prototype reviews and usability acceptance of the final corporate portal implemented at CorporatePortal.com.

Corporate Portal Storyboard and Script

Several scripts have been written for each employee role and their expected interaction with the corporate portal solution. These scripts were used to verify that the corporate portal solution identified by business domain experts at CorporatePortal.com accurately reflects the benefits and usage of the portal desktop. Using the document repository self-service application to be included in the corporate portal solution and the example of the sales manager role, a sample script of how employees will use and interact with the portal desktop has been documented. The sales manager activity is to update the sales campaign strategy templates and procedures for tax projects. The activities and tasks the sales manager is expected to complete are outlined as follows:

   1. The sales manager will need to research the types of tax projects CorporatePortal.com sells the most of and the key customers for these projects. There are several areas in the portal desktop the sales manager will use to complete this research. From the Reference/Scorecard content page, the financial metrics and project status metrics information will help identify the types of tax projects and customers being researched (see Figure 15-2). Additional accounting information will be researched from the Departments/Accounting content pages.

   2. The sales manager will need to discuss the research results with other sales managers and interested employees throughout CorporatePortal.com to establish and verify conclusions. The results of the research will be posted as a discussion topic from Resources/Discussions in the Peer Discussions content page (see Figure 15-3).

   3. The sales manager will need to create and update the sales campaign strategy templates and procedures. Any reports, docu-

Figure 15-2. Storyboard page 1: researching tax projects.

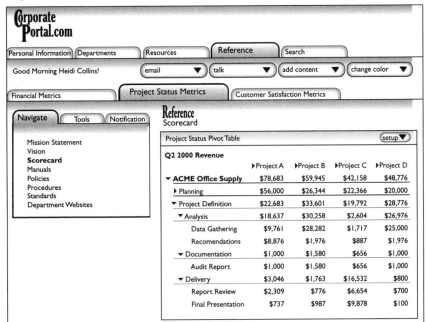

Figure 15-3. Storyboard page 2: discussing research results.

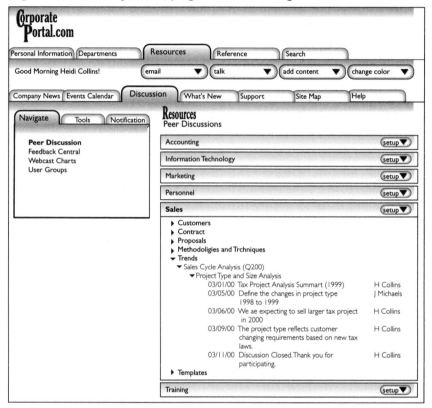

ments, and other material used during the researching and writing of the new sales campaign strategy templates and procedures will be created and stored using the Personal Information/Interests/File Storage content page of the portal desktop (see Figure 15-4).

4. The sales manager will need to review the new material with other sales managers and sales representatives at Corporate-Portal.com. The first version of the sales campaign strategy templates and procedures will be posted for peer review from Resources/Discussions in the Peer Discussions content page (see Figure 15-5).

5. The sales manager will incorporate the feedback and publish the new sales campaign strategy templates and procedures. The sales manager will continue to lead the peer discussion of the

Figure 15-4. Storyboard page 3: using file storage to review and update new tax project sales strategy templates.

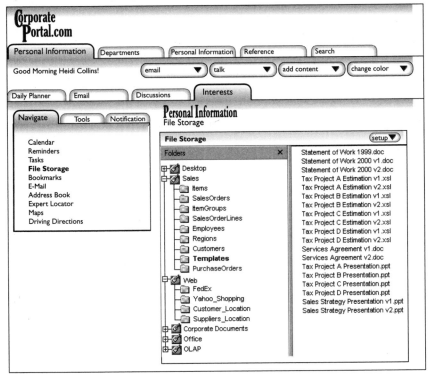

sales campaign strategy material and write the final versions of the sales campaign strategy templates and procedures. The final versions of these documents will be posted in the Documentum application from content pages available in the Departments/Sales options (see Figure 15-6).

6. The sales manager will schedule a webcast seminar to present the new sales campaign strategy templates and procedures to any interested CorporatePortal.com employees. Using the Resources/Discussions menu option and the Webcast Chats content page, the sales manager can schedule the seminar (see Figure 15-7).

7. The sales manager will post the webcast seminar in the corporate events calendar so that interested CorporatePortal.com employees will be aware of the upcoming event. Using the Re-

Figure 15-5. Storyboard page 4: discussing new tax project strategy templates.

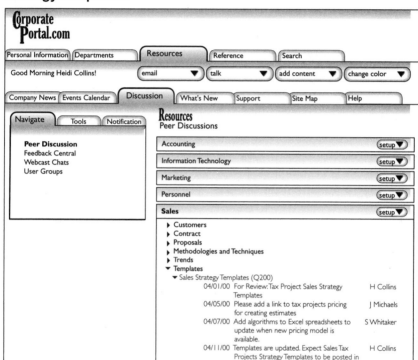

sources/Events Calendar menu option and associated content pages, the sales manager posts the webcast seminar to the calendar (see Figure 15-8).

Financial Metrics Analysis

CorporatePortal.com has defined the cost and benefit model for the initial phase of the corporate portal solution. The details of the cost and benefit model can be seen in Figure 15-9. The current monthly cost for each line item has been identified. The future monthly cost based on the implementation of a corporate portal solution has been calculated for each line item. The difference between these

Figure 15-6. Storyboard page 5: publishing new tax project strategy templates.

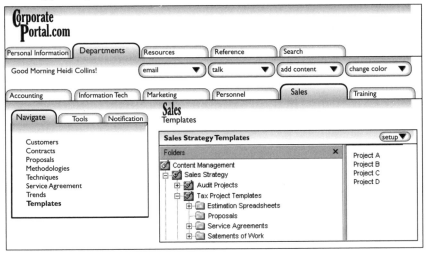

two values defines the expected monthly savings. The monthly savings can only be recognized after the business functions, self-service applications, and portal desktop features have been implemented. A start date of when monthly savings should be realized is included. The net present value and level of risk identified have also been included. The line items identified by CorporatePortal.com include:

Benefits

- Reducing cost to produce financial metric reports (e.g., sales, accounts receivable, flash reports, and reports that drill into details).
- Reducing cost to produce accounting reports (e.g., summary reports, exception reports, profit and loss, budget versus actual).
- Reducing cost to produce ad hoc report requests.
- Reducing cost to analyze reports (e.g., financial metric reports, accounting reports).
- Reducing cost to publish corporate and department content.
- Increasing total corporate revenue from increased operating

Figure 15-7. Storyboard page 6: scheduling a tax project strategy webcast.

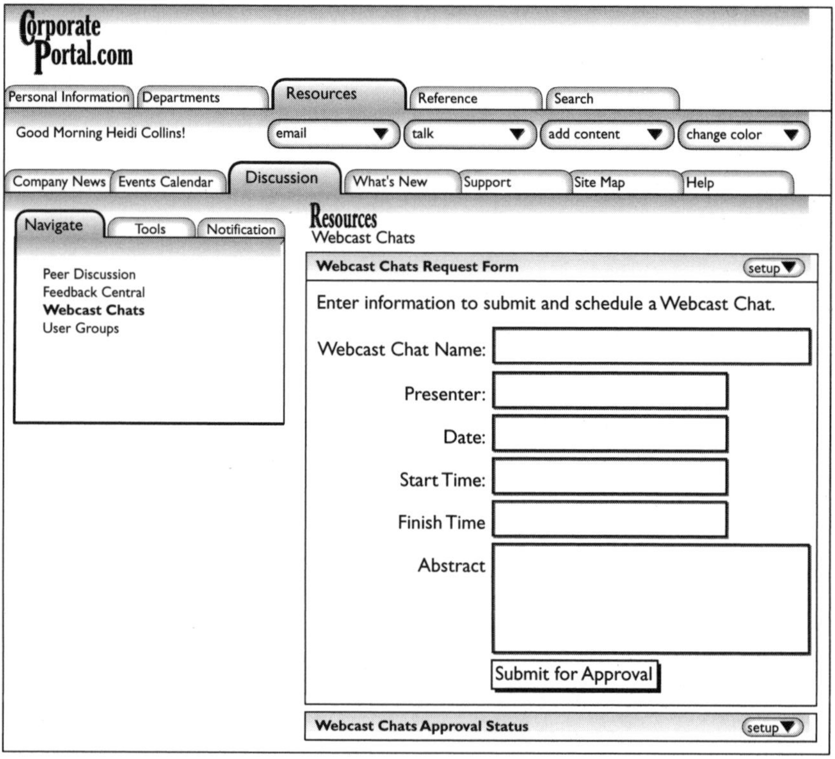

income as a result of actions being taken sooner due to information being constantly available.
- Reducing total corporate expenses as a result of better and faster decisions being made.

Cost

- Corporate portal development cost (e.g., planning, requirements analysis, architecture and design, development, deployment, and training)
- Hardware and software
- IT support and administration staff (two analysts)
- Business domain experts (e.g., publishing corporate content, publishing department content, publishing policies and procedures, creating online help)

Figure 15-8. Storyboard page 7: reviewing the CorporatePortal.com events calendar.

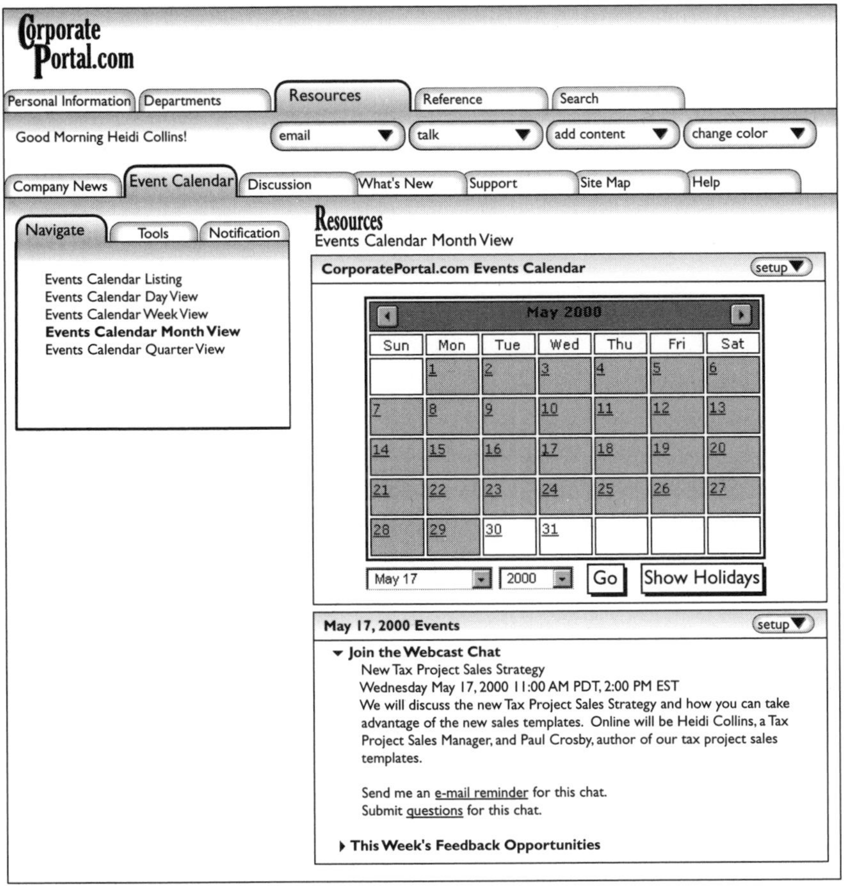

Staged Delivery Analysis

The corporate portal solution will be implemented using a phased delivery process following the accepted IT department software life cycle approach. The software life cycle is defined in the project plan and timeline as the activities that will constitute the first phase of the corporate portal project. The skills of the corporate portal development team members have been identified. The appropriate team will be recruited to complete the corporate portal solution and will be led by the project's executive sponsor. Additional steps will be

(text continues on page 378)

Figure 15-9. CorporatePortal.com's cost and benefit model.

Description	Current Monthly Cost Amount	Current Monthly Cost Assumptions[1]	Future Monthly Cost Amount	Future Monthly Cost Assumptions[1]	Monthly Savings	Start Date	Net Present Value[2]	Risk
Benefits								
1 Reduce cost to produce Financial Metric Reports (Sales, Accounts Receivable, Flash Reports, drilling into details)	$3,690	90 hrs/mo @ $41/hr	$0	100% reduction	$3,690	Q3/00(7/1/00)	$57,794	Low
2 Reduce cost to produce Accounting Reports (Summary Reports, Exception Reports, Profit and Loss, Budget Versus Actual)	$4,920	120 hrs/mo @ $41/hr	$0	100% reduction	$4,920	Q3/00(7/1/00)	$77,059	Low
3 Reduce cost to produce ad hoc report requests	$6,560	160 hrs/mo @ $41/hr	$0	100% reduction	$6,560	Q4/00(10/1/00)	$84,567	Low
4 Reduce cost to publish corporate and department content	$7,380	180 hrs/mo @ $41/hr	$0	100% reduction	$7,380	Q4/00(10/1/00)	$95,138	Low
5 Reduce cost to analyze reports (Financial Metric Reports, Accounting Reports)	$198,000	10 hrs/mo/Mgr @ $60/hr	$118,800	40% reduction	$79,200	Q4/00(10/1/00)	$1,020,993	Med
6 Increase in total corporate revenue from increased operating income as a result of actions being taken sooner due to information being constantly available								
a) Total Corporate Revenue	$10,600,000	Revenue	$106,000	1.0% increase				
b) Total Corporate Operating Income	$1,484,000	Operating Income	$1,498,840	1.0% increase	$14,840	Q4/00(10/1/00)	$191,307	High
7 Reduction in total corporate expenses as a result of better and faster decisions being made								
a) Total Corporate Expenses	$8,700,000	Expenses	$8,691,300	0.1% reduction	$8,700	Q4/00(10/1/00)	$112,155	High
Subtotal:					$125,290		$1,639,014	

Total Revenue Increase and Cost Reduction (Low Risk): $314,559
Total Revenue Increase and Cost Reduction (Low & Medium Risk): $1,335,552
Total Revenue Increase and Cost Reduction (Low, Medium & High Risk): $1,639,014

Description	Current Monthly Cost		Future Monthly Cost		Monthly Savings	Start Date	Net Present Value[2]	Risk
	Amount	Assumptions[1]	Amount	Assumptions[1]				
Cost								
1 Corporate Portal development cost (Planning, Requirements Analysis, Architecture and Design, Development, Deployment, Training)								
a) Planning			$25,000	One time cost	($25,000)	Q1/00(1/1/00)	($25,000)	Low
b) Requirements Analysis			$67,000	One time cost	($67,000)	Q3/00(7/1/00)	($63,507)	Low
c) Architecture and Design			$104,000	One time cost	($104,000)	Q3/00(7/1/00)	($98,578)	Low
d) Development			$480,000	One time cost	($480,000)	Q4/00(10/1/00)	($443,418)	Low
e) Deployment			$201,000	One time cost	($201,000)	Q4/00(10/1/00)	($185,681)	Low
f) Training			$4,800	12 days @ $400/day	($4,800)	Q4/00(10/1/00)	($61,878)	Low
2 Hardware and Software			$150,000	One time cost	($150,000)	Q2/00(4/1/00)	($145,985)	Low
3 IT Support and Administration Staff								
a) Two Analysts			$4,920	120 hrs/mo @ $41/hr	($4,920)	Q4/00(10/1/00)	($63,425)	Low
4 Business Domain Experts (Publishing Corporate Content, Publishing Department Content, Publishing Polices and Procedures, Creating Online Help)								
a) Six Departments			$7,380	180 hrs/mo @ $41/hr	($7,380)	Q4/00(10/1/00)	($95,138)	Low
Subtotal:							($1,182,612)	
Total Cost (Low Risk):							($1,182,612)	
Total Cost (Low & Medium Risk):							($1,182,612)	
Total Cost (Low, Medium & High Risk):							($1,182,612)	
Summary								
Net Total Savings (Low Risk):							-$868,053	
Net Total Savings (Low & Medium Risk):							$152,940	
Net Total Savings (Low, Medium & High Risk):							$456,402	
ROI (Low Risk)(%)							27%	
ROI (Low & Medium Risk)(%)							113%	
ROI (Low, Medium & High Risk)(%)							139%	
Payback Period (Low Risk)(months)							90	
Payback Period (Low & Medium Risk)(months)							21	
Payback Period (Low, Medium & High Risk)(months)							17	

Legend

[1] Fully burdened salary based on the following:
- Analyst - $85,000/yr ($41/hr)
- Business Domain Expert - $85,000/yr ($41/hr)
- Director or Manager - $125,000/yr ($60/hr)

[2] Project life of 24 months, internal cost of money of 11%

taken once all project team members understand the activities they need to complete and what the work means in terms of time and complexity when estimating the risks, understanding budget constraints, and verifying the scope of the proposed corporate portal solution. Several activities that will be completed by the corporate portal development team will be recommended in the business case. These include:

- *Requirements Analysis* (i.e., activities and research that will establish the user description of the corporate portal functionality defined in detail)
- *System Design* (i.e., the software solution and infrastructure that will facilitate or be used to create the corporate portal solution identified in the user requirements)
- *Program Design* (i.e., the mechanics or "pseudo instructions" and algorithms that will best implement the corporate portal solution design)
- *Program Implementation* (i.e., the construction of the corporate portal solution)
- *Testing* (i.e., verification that the corporate portal solution performs as defined)
- *Delivery* (i.e., acceptance of the corporate portal solution by the employees using the portal desktop)
- *Maintenance* (i.e., support of the deployed corporate portal solution and identification of additional features and enhancements requested for future development phases)

There are several inherent problems and risks associated with software development that apply to the corporate portal. These include:

- Requirements are constantly changing, and the employees are not aware of what these changes will be in advance.
- Frequent changes are difficult to manage, and trying to establish checkpoints for planning and cost estimation is difficult.
- Phased development requires that a distinction exist between the corporate portal solution under development and the corporate portal solution in production. Any new release of the

corporate portal will need to be backward-compatible with the production solution.

Preliminary Project Plan and Timeline

The first phase of the corporate portal solution for CorporatePortal.com will be completed in less than 450 development days or twenty-four months from the date the project begins. There are several data integration and data mart creation activities that will be included and completed as part of the corporate portal solution. The initial corporate portal pilot team will begin using the first prototype of the solution five or six months after the project has been approved. The tasks have been grouped together based on their type. Types of tasks include requirements analysis, architecture and design, development, and deployment. Some tasks must be completed before others can start, while several of the tasks can be completed simultaneously. These task relationships have been excluded in this case study, but they can easily be included at a later date using a project plan application. The project plan and timeline information will be summarized and included in the corporate portal business case. The details include:

Requirements Analysis

Preparation	7.50 Days
IT Development Team Meeting	1.00 Days
Business Domain Expert Meeting	1.25 Days
Information Gathering	9.50 Days
Infrastructure Requirements Documented	4.00 Days
Business Requirements Documented	8.00 Days
Executive Sponsor Approval	1.25 Days
Requirements Analysis Total	32.50 Days (7.65%)

Architecture and Design

Preparation	4.00 Days
Project Plan Review	3.00 Days
Information Gathering	25.00 Days

Architecture and Design Documentation	18.00 Days
Executive Sponsor Approval	2.00 Days

Architecture and Design Total	52.00 Days (12.24%)

Development

Preparation	4.00 Days
Project Plan Review	2.00 Days
Development Plan	5.00 Days
Infrastructure	13.00 Days
Data Mart (Data Source) Development	28.00 Days
Self-Service Application Development	36.00 Days
Corporate Portal Development	32.00 Days
Search	20.00 Days
Content Management	20.00 Days
Collaboration	5.00 Days
Messaging	5.00 Days
Prototype Reviews	20.00 Days
Infrastructure Quality Assurance	7.00 Days
Development Quality Assurance	26.00 Days
Documentation	17.00 Days

Development Total	240.00 Days (56.47%)

Deployment

Deployment Plan	3.00 Days
Infrastructure	8.50 Days
Deployment Preparation	40.00 Days
User Acceptance	26.00 Days
Production Deployment	20.00 Days
Wrap-up Meeting	3.00 Days

Deployment Total	100.50 Days (23.64%)

Corporate Portal Project Total	425.00 Days (100.00%)

Bibliography

Abrams, Rhonda M. *The Successful Business Plan: Secrets and Strategies.* Palo Alto, Calif.: Running 'R' Media, 1999.

Adams, Bob. *Complete Business Plan: Writing a Business Plan Has Never Been Easier.* Holbrook, Mass.: Adams Media Corporation, 1998.

Altbach, Philip G. *Knowledge Context: Comparative Perspectives on the Distribution of Knowledge.* Albany, N.Y.: State University of New York Press, 1987.

Berry, Michael J. A., and Gordon Linoff. *Mastering Data Mining: The Art and Science of Customer Relationship Management.* New York: John Wiley & Sons, Inc., 1999.

Brackett, Michael H. "Business Intelligence Value Chain." *DM Review* (March 1999).

———. "Transforming Disparate Data." *DM Review* (October 1998).

Brick, Bob, and Jean Henry. "Enterprise Portals: Not Just Information Delivery." Manhasset, N.Y.: CMP Media Inc. (November 1999).

Calkins, Matt, and Michael Beckley. "The Ten Rules of Personalization." Oklahoma City: Appian Corporation, 1999.

Catapult, Inc. *Microsoft Project 98: Step By Step.* Redmond, Wash.: Microsoft Press, 1997.

Cohen, Brent L., James D. Seabolt, R. Wayne Thompson, and John S. Williams. "Finding the Solution to Data Mining: A Map of the Features and Components of SAS Enterprise Miner Software Version 3." Cary, N.C.: SAS Institute, Inc., 1999.

Coleman, David. *Groupware: Collaborative Strategies for Corporate LANs and Intranets.* Paramus, N.J.: Prentice Hall, 1996.

"The Convergence of Business Intelligence and Knowledge Management." Cary, N.C.: SAS Institute, Inc., 1999.

"Corporate Portal Architecture: Special Report on InfoImage Freedom." Boston: The Delphi Group, November 1999.

Cunningham, Ann M., and Wendy Wicks. *Changing Roles in Information*

Distribution, Report Series, 1994. Philadelphia: National Federation of Abstracting, 1993.

Davydov, Mark M. "EIP: The Second Wave." *Intelligent Enterprise Magazine* (March 2000).

Eckerson, Wayne. "Analyst Insight: E-Intelligence Framework." *DM Review* (February 2000).

"The Eight Key Factors in Evaluating Balanced Scorecard Systems." Cambridge, Mass.: Pilot Software, Inc. (1999).

"E-Intelligence: Creating Knowledge from E-Business and E-Commerce Data." Cary, N.C.: SAS Institute, Inc. (1999).

English, Larry P. "Information Quality in the Knowledge Age." *DM Review* (October 1999).

"Enterprise Reporting: A Critical Environment for Securing Data Knowledge." Boston: Aberdeen Group, Inc. (July 1998).

Finkelstein, Clive. "A Visible Solution: Enterprise Information Architecture." Waltham, Mass.: Visible Systems Corporation (2000).

Fleming, Jennifer. *Web Navigation: Designing the User Experience.* Cambridge, Mass.: O'Reilly and Associates, 1998.

"The Freedom to Succeed: An Analysis of the Corporate Portal Market and a High-Level View of Freedom's Key Concepts and Features." Phoenix: InfoImage, Inc. (August 1999).

Gonzalez, Steven Jon. "Developing a Good Data Model." *DM Direct* (November 1997).

Harrington, Jan L. *Relational Database Design: Clearly Explained.* Chestnut Hill, Mass.: AP Professional, 1998.

Hickson, Tony. "Mine Your Own Business." Information Systems Engineering Department of Computing and Department of Electrical and Electronic Engineering (May 1996).

Hummingbird Communications, Ltd. "Web-Based Business Intelligence and the Lowest Cost of Ownership Imperative." *DM Review* (March 2000).

"InfoImage Architecture for Federated Portals: An Introduction to the Federated Portal and a Discussion of Its Distributed Architecture." Phoenix: InfoImage, Inc. (August 1999).

Inmon, Bill. "Information Management: Charting the Course: Fact Tables in the Warehouse." *DM Review* (November 1999).

Kelly, Chip, and Don Hendersen. "The Impact of Web Technology on Enterprise Decision Support Systems." Cary, N.C.: SAS Institute, Inc. (1996).

Kimball, Ralph, and Richard Merz. *The Data Webhouse Toolkit: Building the Web-Enabled Data Warehouse.* New York: John Wiley & Sons, Inc., 2000.

Kimball, Ralph, Laura Reeves, Margy Ross, and Warren Thornthwaite. *The Data Warehouse Lifecycle Toolkit: Expert Methods for Designing, Developing, and Deploying Data Warehouses*. New York: John Wiley & Sons, Inc., 1998.

Korab, Holly. "Striking Gold in Mountains of Data." Champaign, Ill.: NCSA Automated Learning Group (August 1997).

Levin, Adina. "Relationship Management Critical to Web Success." *DM Review* (March 1999).

Leymann, Frank, and Dieter Roller. *Production Workflow Concepts and Techniques*. Paramus, N.J.: Prentice Hall, 1999.

Lynch, Patrick J., and Sarah Horton. *Web Style Guide: Basic Design Principles for Creating Web Sites*. New Haven, Conn.: Yale University Press, 1999.

McConnell, Steve. *Code Complete: A Practical Handbook of Software Construction*. Redmond, Wash.: Microsoft Press, 1993.

McIntyre, John, Mark Moorman, Richard King, and Edward Walker. "A Formula for OLAP Success: Using Online Analytical Processing to Transform Data into Knowledge." Cary, N.C.: SAS Institute, Inc. (1996).

Microsoft Corporation. "The Basics of Interface Design." *MSDN Library*, 2000.

———. "Creating Submenus." *MSDN Library* (2000).

———. "Creating a User Interface." *MSDN Library* (2000).

———. "Designing for Usability." *MSDN Library* (2000).

———. "Designing a User Assistance Model." *MSDN Library* (2000).

———. "Designing with the User in Mind." *MSDN Library* (2000).

———. "Developing Applications Using the Application Framework." *MSDN Library* (1999).

———. "Interface Styles." *MSDN Library* (2000).

———. "The Microsoft Internet Security Framework: Technology for Secure Communication, Access Control, and Commerce." *MSDN Library* (1996).

———. "Menu Title and Naming Guidelines." *MSDN Library* (2000).

———. "The Need for Collaboration in the Corporate World." Redmond, Wash.: Industry Solutions White Paper (1999).

———. "Negotiating Menu and Toolbar Appearance." *MSDN Library* (2000).

———. "Taking Business Web Sites to the Next Level." *MSDN Library* (2000).

———. "Toolbars." *MSDN Library* (2000).

———. "When Things Go Wrong: Interacting with Users." *MSDN Library* (2000).

Missroon, Alan M. "Demystifying the Balanced Scorecard." *DM Direct* (May 1999).

Murray, Gerry. "Automating Content Integration with Autonomy." New York: International Data Corporation (2000).

———. "Making Connections with Enterprise Knowledge Portals." New York: International Data Corporation (1999).

Oellermann, William. "Site Server Personalization and Membership for Intranets." *Microsoft Internet Developer* (January 2000).

Olson, Craig. "Know Your Data: Data Profiling Solutions for Today's Hot Projects." *DM Review* (March 2000).

Orfali, Robert, Dan Harkey, and Jeri Edwards. *The Essential Client/Server Survival Guide,* 2nd ed.. New York: John Wiley & Sons, Inc., 1996.

"Portals with a Purpose: Accelerating Decision Quality and Velocity." Waltham, Mass.: Kinetic Information (January 2000).

"The Quality Data Warehouse: Serving the Analytical Needs of the Manufacturing Enterprise." Cary, N.C.: SAS Institute, Inc. (1999).

Reynolds, Hadley, and Tom Koulopoulos. "Enterprise Knowledge Has a Face." Manhasset, N.Y.: CMP Media, Inc. (March 1999).

Russom, Philip. "New Directions for Knowledge Management Software." *DM Review* (October 1999).

"SAS Rapid Warehousing Methodology." Cary, N.C.: SAS Institute, Inc. (1998).

Schmidt, Marty J. "Business Case Essentials: A Guide to Structure and Content." Boston: Solution Matrix Ltd. (1999).

Schmidt, Marty J. "The IT Business Case: Keys to Accuracy and Credibility," *Solution Matrix Ltd.* (1999).

———. "What's a Business Case and Other Frequently Asked Questions." Boston: Solution Matrix Ltd. (1999).

Shepherd, John B. "Data Migration Strategies." *DM Review* (June 1999).

Simon, Alan. *90 Days to the Data Mart: Step-by-Step Guide to Planning, Designing, and Building Data Marts.* New York: John Wiley & Sons, Inc., 1998.

Szuprowicz, Bohdan O. *Search Engine Technologies for the World Wide Web and Intranets.* Charleston, S.C.: Computer Technology Research Corporation, 1997.

Thomsen, Erik. "Decision Support: It's an Uncertain World." *Intelligent Enterprise Magazine* (December 1998).

"TopTier Business Intelligence: Achieve a New Level of Business Insight with Point of View Navigation." San Jose, Calif.: TopTier Software, Inc. (1999).

Walker, Joshua, Ted Schadler, Amanda J. Ciardelli, and Christine S. Overby. "Building an Intranet Portal." Cambridge, Mass.: Forrester Research, Inc. (1999).

White, Colin. "Using Information Portals in the Enterprise." *DM Direct* (December 1999).

Wilder, Ron. "The Future Is Now in Professional Publishing." *ZD Journals* (July 1999).

Williams, Edward E., Ph.D., James R. Thompson, Ph.D., and H. Albert Napier, Ph.D. *Business Planning: 25 Keys to a Sound Business Plan*. New York: Lebhar-Friedman Books, 1999.

Index